MASTERING C++

MASTERING C++

An Introduction to
C++ and
Object-oriented Programming
for C and
Pascal Programmers

CAY S. HORSTMANN
San Jose State University

JOHN WILEY & SONS

New York ▪ Chichester ▪ Brisbane ▪ Toronto ▪ Singapore

Library of Congress Cataloging-in-Publication Data:

Horstmann, Cay S., 1959–
    Mastering C+ + : an introduction to C+ + and object-oriented
programming for C and Pascal programmers / Cay S. Horstmann.
    Includes bibliographical references.
    ISBN 0-471-52257-0
    1. C+ + (Computer program language)   2. Object-oriented programming
(Computer science)   I. Title.
QA76.73.C153H67   1991
005.26′2−dc20   90-37691
                                                                      CIP

Printed in the United States of America

10 9 8 7 6 5 4 3

PREFACE

C++ is a superset of the hugely successful C programming language. (The + + in its name originates from the C increment operator + +.) C++ offers enhancements of C in four directions:

- Operator and function overloading
- Information hiding
- Inheritance
- Virtual functions (polymorphism)

This book contains a thorough introduction to C++, with particular emphasis on techniques used in real-life programs.

This book does not require knowledge of the C programming language. The reader familiar with Pascal or Modula-2 will find numerous "Pascal Notes" to aid in the transition to the C/C++ syntax. The reader who already knows C can skim through Chapters 2, 3, 4, and 6 and watch for "C Notes", which point out differences between C and C++.

In this book, I attempt to show C++ in the context of realistic programming situations. I purposely stay away from contrived examples. There are no data types for small appliances, furry animals, or edible objects. No objects are called `my_stack`, no data types `derived_1` when examples involving useful data structures can be easily given.

It is easy for students (as well as for some authors) to think they know a programming language when all they actually know is its syntax. I place little emphasis on syntax and mechanics; instead, I try to develop the ideas underlying the language concepts and show them in the context of realistic examples.

The policy of supplying realistic examples starts with Chapter 1, which gives a quick tour of two exciting capabilities of C++: operator overloading and virtual functions. (The introduction of classes is deferred until Chapter 5 because of the required syntactical overhead.) I didn't want to disappoint the reader with pointless toy examples; therefore some of the programs in Chapter 1 are quite long and, I hope, interesting. The reader should not be discouraged by their complexity. It is not necessary to grasp all details in Chapter 1. Later chapters provide in-depth coverage of all concepts.

I try to put the methodology of object-oriented programming in its proper perspective. Not all of C++ is concerned with object-oriented programming. And object orientation, while extremely useful for many applications, is not the appropriate paradigm for all programming tasks. The book shows the use of C++ in the context of both traditional and object-oriented programming.

Most differences between Pascal and C++ are cosmetic and easily mastered. However, C++ has a few irksome syntactical quirks that tend to confuse newcomers. I point this out when this is the case, so students can then place the blame for the confusion squarely where it belongs—on the language syntax, rather than themselves. C++ is an excellent language, but it is a human creation and as such not perfect or above criticism. I hope the reader does not construe such occasional comments as an indication that some other language is "better" just because it happens to employ a clearer syntax for some of its constructs.

There are many exercises. The exercises are part of the text, rather than at the end of the chapter. The reader is encouraged to skim through them as they appear. Some develop an interesting sideline, others simply give feedback on how much knowledge should have been acquired at that point.

Many chapters contain sections on "pitfalls," which illustrate common programming problems. These sections serve two purposes: (1) They can be read as textual material to illustrate complicated aspects of the language; and (2) they can be used as a reference to find a way out of problems arising during programming. The idea for these sections is stolen[1] from **[Koenig]**.

This book covers both versions 1 and 2 of C++. The main enhancement of version 2 is the implementation of multiple inheritance, but it also differs in numerous minor aspects from previous versions. These differences are pointed out throughout the book. At this time, version 2 has just become available, and it is expected that systems implementing version 1 will be in use for some time. Occasionally, versions before 2.0 are referred to as "older versions" of C++.

The reader should be familiar with standard data structures: arrays, stacks, queues, sets, linked lists, trees, hash tables, and their implementations. Some mild understanding of college mathematics is also assumed, but certainly no more than necessary for a computer graphics course. Lines, vectors, matrices, polynomials, and complex numbers are used in some of the examples.

My thanks go to Earl Tondreau of John Wiley & Sons for prodding me to write this book. I also thank my reviewer—John Vlissides of Stanford University, whose critical and insightful comments prodded me to rewrite the book and Michael Tripoli, who checked the code for correctness. Naturally, any remaining flaws are entirely their fault.

Cay S. Horstmann

---

[1] "Lesser artists borrow, great artists steal." (*Igor Stravinsky*)

CONTENTS

CHAPTER 1

A QUICK TOUR THROUGH C++

Let us start with some examples to illustrate the main features of C++. These examples are simple but complete—you can try them out on your computer. This is not a rigorous introduction to the language. Most details, rules, and exceptions are left for later chapters. No knowledge of C is assumed (although it would be helpful). You merely should know some modern programming language, such as Pascal or Modula 2. C programmers will notice that many program fragments could be improved by standard C tricks.

The **Pascal Notes** and **C Notes** compare C++ with those languages. If you know both Pascal and C, read them all. It is always helpful to see a new feature put into perspective by comparing it with something known. And you may well learn something about the "old" languages in the process.

I am consciously omitting several C++ features from this introduction, in particular the data-hiding and encapsulation mechanisms. Those mechanisms are extremely important for sound programming practice, so their relegation to later chapters should not prompt you to think otherwise. C++ makes it easy to perform data hiding, but it does require a certain amount of syntactic overhead that I believe obscures the discussion of more crucial language issues.

1.1. "HELLO, WORLD"

Here is our first C++ program:

```
#include <stream.h>

int main()
{    cout << "Hello, World\n";   // print a string
     return 0;
}
```

1

Let us look at its structure. `main` is a *function*. Every C++ program is a collection of functions, at least one of which must be called `main`. `int` means that `main` returns an integer (namely 0). The operating system may look at the value returned by `main`. Conventionally 0 denotes success—any nonzero value some error condition encountered during program execution. The braces `{}` denote the beginning and the end of the `main` function. Strings such as `"Hello, World\n"` are enclosed in double quotes. The `\n` denotes a *newline character*, which is a part of the string and causes a new line to be started after the string. The `<<` (put to) operator can take objects (such as strings or numbers) and send representations of them to an *output stream*. `cout` is the standard output stream; by default, anything sent to it will appear on the screen. The `//` start a *comment*, which extends until the end of the line. Finally, the `#include` is a directive to the *preprocessor* to include all lines from the file stream.h for inspection by the compiler. That file contains declarations of `cout` and the `<<` operator, as well as many others.

Pascal Note

In Pascal, a program is a single unit, called **program**, which contains variables, functions, and procedures nested within. In C++, no such nesting occurs, and the `main` function is the equivalent of the **program**. The type of the value returned by a function is written before the function name, and there is no special **function** keyword. The `(...)` signify a function declaration to the compiler. They are present even if the function has no arguments (like `main()`). C++ does not distinguish between functions and procedures. A procedure is simply a function returning `void`. The braces `{...}` are the equivalent of **begin** ... **end**. In C++, all statements are terminated with a semicolon, even the last statement of a block. But there is no semicolon following the closing brace. The operation `cout <<` is like the Pascal **write**. There is no special **writeln** analog. To obtain a blank line, simply send a string containing a newline `'\n'`.

Many Pascal compilers have an analog to the `#include` directive that opens another file and includes its contents for compilation. Sometimes this is implemented as a pseudocomment directive **(*$I** *filename***)**.

C Note

The `void` indicator has been present in C implementations for quite a while and is part of the ANSI standard. In C++, a function with an empty argument list (such as `main()`) has *no arguments*. In the rare case in which you must specify a function with some unknown number of arguments, use `(...)`. There are two valid styles of comment, C style `/* ... */` and the new C++ style `//`, which extends to the end of the current line. We will use the second style in this book. `cout` is the stream equivalent of `stdout`. The `<<` operator with a stream variable on the left side has nothing to do with left shift. It is like a super-`printf` that can tell the format from the type of the operand to be printed. We will see later how this is implemented by overloading the $\ll$ operator.

How do you get this program to run? First, use any file editor (such as vi or Brief) to create a text file containing the program lines. Depending on your compiler, you may have to choose the file name to end in .c, .cpp, or .cxx. (Some systems have header file names ending in .hpp or .hxx. Then change the names in the `#include` statements before compiling.) The command to invoke the compiler also depends on your system. Typical commands for compilation are

```
CC  hello.c
```

and

```
ccxx  hello.cxx
```

The name of the executable file also varies. Depending on your system, you might need to type

```
a.out
```

or

```
hello
```

to run your program. Of course, you should then expect to see the line

```
Hello, World
```

on your screen.

Exercise 1.1.1. Get the hello program to run on your system. What happens when you omit the \n? The n only? The line `#include < stream.h>`? Explain.

Exercise 1.1.2. Does your C++ translator produce intermediate C code? If so, find out how to save it and look at the C code of the hello program. Find the file stream.h on your system and look at it.

1.2. A CHEAP CALCULATOR

To illustrate the basic control structures in C++, let us write a program that can read in integers and operations from the keyboard such as

```
2 * 5 + 7 - 4 =
```

print the answer, and exit. Just like a cheap pocket calculator, addition and multiplication have the same precedence, and evaluation is strictly left-to-right. For example,

```
1 + 2 * 3 =
```

prints 9 because $1 + 2 = 3$ is computed before the multiplication.
Here is the program.

```
#include <stream.h>

int main()
{     int first, second;
      char ch;

      cin >> first >> ch;
      while( ch != '=' )
      {     cin >> second;
            switch( ch )
            {     case '+':
                        first = first + second; break;
                  case '-':
                        first = first - second; break;
                  case '*':
                        first = first * second; break;
                  case '/':
                        if( second != 0 )
                              first = first / second;
                        else
                              cout << "Division by zero.\n";
                        break;
                  default:
                        cout << "Input error.\n"; return 1;
            }
            cin >> ch;
      }
      cout << "Result: " << first << "\n";
      return 0;
}
```

The program consists of a single `main` function. The first two lines declare *variables*. `first` and `second` are declared to be of type `int`, and `ch`
is declared to be of type `char`. `int` is a data type denoting integers of the
size most conveniently handled by the processor. `char` is an integer type
just large enough to hold a single character. That is almost universally the
range $-128\ldots 127$ or $0\ldots 255$. All characters are represented by their integer code under the encoding scheme used by the system, such as ASCII
or EBCDIC. Character constants are enclosed in single quotes and denote
the *numerical* code of the character. For example, under the ASCII encoding
scheme, `'a'==95`. (To be precise, `'a'` is of type `char` and 95 of type `int`,
but they represent the same number.) The codes of nonprinting characters

are denoted by characters preceded by a \ . For example, '\n' is a new-line, '\t' is a tab. Note the difference between the character code '\n' (the number 10 if ASCII code is used) and the string "\n" containing the character '\n'.

The >> (get from) operator is used for reading from a stream. cin is the standard input stream; that is, the keyboard. Here we are reading an integer and a character from the keyboard and placing them into the variables first and ch. White space (the space character, tabs, and newline) is automatically discarded by >>. The != (not equal) operator tests for inequality. The while loop is executed while the condition inside the (...) remains true. The body of the while loop is enclosed in { ...} because it consists of more than one statement. The switch branches to one of the case labels, depending on the value of ch, or to the default label if none of the case labels match. Execution then resumes until a break or the end of the switch is reached.

In C++, assignment is denoted by =, as in first = first + second. To test for equality, == is used. The if statement tests the condition inside the (...). If it is true, the statement following it is executed. An else clause is optional.

The last line shows that the << operator can be chained to send more than one item to an output stream, just like the >> operator in the beginning of the program.

Pascal Note

Here we see variable declarations for the first time. Unlike Pascal, all declarations in C++ first list the type and then the variable name. This is consistent with the declaration of functions, which also has the return type before the function name. And it makes it easy to *initialize* variables when they are declared: int i = 0, n = 1;.

The differences between Pascal and C++ control structures are cosmetic. **while ... do begin ... end** becomes while(...) { ...} and **if ... then ...** becomes if(...) { ...}. The switch statement is like case, except for the curious break terminating each branch. The chained >> operator is just like **read**. Some operators are different, with :=, =, and <> becoming =, ==, and !=, respectively. That is unpleasant and can lead to nasty surprises. x = 0 does not test whether x is zero but stores a 0 into x!

C Note

The only unexpected constructs are >> and << and their chaining ability. The >> operator is a super-scanf that supplies both the format string and the &. For example, cin >> first >> ch is equivalent to scanf("%d %c", &first, &ch). We will see later that the amazing capabilities of these stream input/output operators, the chaining, automatic format recognition, and automatic address taking by >> are natural consequences of C++ features. No special knowledge of << and >> is hardwired into the C++ compiler.

In C (as well as old versions of C++) character constants (such as 'a') are *not* of type char but of type int.

Exercise 1.2.1. Enter the calculator program and run it.

Exercise 1.2.2. Extend the calculator to compute the remainder function. The C++ instruction **x % y** computes the remainder of the division **x/y**. In Pascal, this operator is called **mod**. Use the same **%** symbol for the remainder command. For example, the input 4 * 2 % 3 = should print 2.

1.3. A STACK-BASED CALCULATOR

In this example, arrays and the syntax of function definitions are introduced. We will program a reverse-polish calculator that places numbers on a stack. Operators act on the numbers most recently pushed. Some scientific calculators use reverse-polish notation, as does the PostScript printer control language. For example, when the user enters

    1 2 3 * + =

the calculator goes through the following sequence of events:

1	push 1
2	push 2
3	push 3
*	pop 2 and 3, multiply them and push the product 6
+	pop 1 and 6, add them and push the sum 7
=	pop 7 and print it

Parentheses are never required. To compute (1 + 2 * 4) / (1 + 2), the user enters

    1 2 4 * + 1 2 + / =

Here is the implementation of the stack.

```
const int STACKSIZE = 20;

int stack[ STACKSIZE ];
int stackPointer = 0; // points to the next free stack entry

void push( int n )
{   if( stackPointer <= STACKSIZE - 1 )
    {   stack[ stackPointer ] = n;
        stackPointer++;
    }
}
```

```
int pop()
{    if( stackPointer > 0 )
        stackPointer--;
    return stack[ stackPointer ];

}
```

The `const` declaration gives a symbolic name for the size of the stack. It is always a bad idea to use "magic numbers" such as 20 in a program. If the stack size changes, you would not want to search the program for 20s, 19s, etc. and modify them, except for all the 20s and 19s that have nothing to do with stack size. Compilers are smart enough to perform constant arithmetic such as `STACKSIZE - 1` at compile time.

The next declarations allocate an array of 20 `int` and a single `int` initialized with 0. The first array index is 0; that is, the array consists of `stack[0]`, `stack[1]`, ..., `stack[19]`.

Two function declarations follow. The first function takes an integer argument and returns nothing. It enters a number on the stack and increases the stack pointer. The second function has no argument and returns an `int`, namely the top of the stack. The ++ and -- operators increment or decrement the variable. `stackPointer++` is a convenient shortcut for `stackPointer = stackPointer + 1`. Error handling is poor. If the stack is full, further calls to `push` will simply do nothing. If it is empty, `pop` will return `stack[0]`.

Pascal Note

Array declarations require one number only, because all C++ arrays start at 0. An array with n elements has subscripts in the range $0...n - 1$. There are no keywords **function, var,** or **array**. The compiler deduces this information from the presence or absence of `()` or `[]`.

The mechanism for determining the return value of a function is very different in Pascal and C++. Rather than assigning a value to a variable with the same name as the function, the `return` statement is used. `return` sets the return value *and leaves the function immediately.*

C Note

The `const` declaration is new in C++. It is preferred over the use of `#define` to set manifest constants because it gives the compiler a chance to perform type checking. All C++ functions are in ANSI C format, with the function arguments inside the `()`. Old style declarations

```
push( n )
int n;
```

are not acceptable. Return types should be specified. Do not rely on `int` being the default. Use `void` if the function returns nothing. Contrary to ANSI C, the preferred syntax for functions with no arguments is an empty argument list ( ), not (void).

Here is the code for the main program.

```
int main()
{     char ch;
      int first, second, num;

      cin >> ch;
      while( ch != '=' )
      {
            if( '0' <= ch && ch <= '9' )
            {     cin.putback( ch );
                  cin >> num;
                  push( num );
            }
            else
                  switch( ch )
                  {     case '+':
                              push( pop() + pop() ); break;
                        case '*':
                              push( pop() * pop() ); break;
                        case '-':
                              second = pop(); push( pop() -
                                              second); break;
                        case '/':
                              second = pop(); first = pop();
                              if( second == 0 )
                              {     cout << "Divide by 0.\n";
                                    return 1; // error--return
                                               //   non-0 value
                              }
                              else
                                    push( first / second );
                              break;
                        default:
                              cout << "Input error.\n"; return 1;
                  }
            cin >> ch;
      }
      cout << pop() << "\n";
      return 0;
}
```

When reading a character, it may be an operator such as + or =, or it may be the first digit of a number. If it is a digit, we should not have used `cin >> ch` but `cin >> num`. Fortunately, we can push one character back onto the input stream, pretending that we had not read it, with the `cin.putback` function. (The appearance of the dot . in the function call will make sense later.) This effectively gives a one-character lookahead.

By the way, our calculator has a curious limitation. You cannot enter negative numbers. For example, -10 would be interpreted as the - operator followed by the integer 10. (For that reason, reverse-polish calculators have a special *change sign* key.) We will simply assume the user will not object to entering 0 10 - instead.

With noncommutative operators, one must be careful with the order of the popping. In an expression `pop() - pop()`, the compiler is free to evaluate subexpressions in any order, not necessarily left-to-right. The code above ensures correct results.

If a division by zero is attempted, a `return` statement is executed. This means an immediate exit from `main` and, as `main` is the top-level function, return to the operating system.

Pascal Note

In Pascal, the value of **input^** provides one character lookahead while keeping the character available for a subsequent **get**.

C Note

`cin.putback( ch )` is the stream equivalent of `ungetc( ch, stdin )`.

Exercise 1.3.1. Enter the reverse-polish calculator and test it.

Exercise 1.3.2. Improve the `push` and `pop` routines to give error messages at overflow and underflow.

Exercise 1.3.3. Implement a unary minus key _. For example, 3 _ 3 - = should print −6.

Exercise 1.3.4. Implement a debug feature. The input D (or d) should print the contents of the entire stack. Find out how to use the standard function `toupper` (which converts lowercase letters to uppercase) and write a separate function `printStack`.

Exercise 1.3.5. C++ does not have a built-in power function. Implement a power function by writing a function `int power( int, int )`. Enhance the calculator to call this function when a ^ command is entered. What is the correct `power` value for negative exponents?

1.4. A FRACTION CALCULATOR

Right now, the calculator handles integers only. Computing 4 3 / = will print
1 because division in C++ is integer division if both arguments are integers.
One could easily modify the calculator to handle floating-point numbers, but
we want to implement exact fractions instead. For example, we want to store
1/3 exactly rather than as 0.333333333. . . in such a way that

```
1 3 / 3 * =
```

computes 1 and not 0.99999999. . . . We will simply store numerator and
denominator separately:

```
struct Fraction
{    int num;
     int den;
} ;
```

We can now declare fractions

```
Fraction f;
```

and set values

```
f.num = 1;
f.den = 3;
```

Pascal Note

In Pascal, these aggregates are called **record**, not `struct`. To be able to
declare variables of a record type, one has to make a **type** declaration.

C Note

In C, one would have to declare `f` as a `struct Fraction` or have a
`typedef`. In C++, the structure name becomes a type name.

Naturally, we now want to add, subtract, multiply, and divide fractions.
We could supply functions `addFrac`, `subtractFrac`, . . . and, although this
would be entirely sufficient for our calculator, it would be very unpleasant
in other situations. Expressions such as

```
divideFractByInt( addFrac( multiplyFrac( a, b ), c ), 2 )
```

look terrible.

Pascal Note

In Pascal, one cannot even do that. A Pascal function cannot return a
record, so one would have to make do with

procedure addFrac(a: Fraction, b: Fraction, var result: Fraction)
. . .

and break up the computation into individual steps, saving intermediate results in temporary variables. The alternative would be to define a fraction as a pointer to a record because Pascal functions can return pointers. This, too, is a hassle because the memory for the fractions must then be allocated on the heap.

Fortunately, it is possible in C++ to define the standard arithmetic operators + - * / for fractions and write (a * b + c) / 2 where a b c are of the type Fraction. To do this, we define functions

```
Fraction operator+( Fraction a, Fraction b );
Fraction operator-( Fraction a, Fraction b );
Fraction operator*( Fraction a, Fraction b );
Fraction operator/( Fraction a, Fraction b );
```

This process is called *operator overloading*. When the compiler sees an expression

```
x + y
```

where x and y are Fractions, it will translate this into a call to operator+ (x, y). Of course, if x and y are of type int, they will just be added. This means extra work for the compiler. Whenever it sees a +, it has to consider the types of the operands and check whether to compile it into an addition or a call to operator+. In fact, operators may be overloaded more than once. It is possible to define another operator+ for strings (to concatenate them). Of course, that function has nothing in common with the fraction version of operator+, and the compiler has to make the correct choice depending on the types of the operands of +.

To program the operator functions for fractions, we observe that

$$\frac{r}{s} \pm \frac{t}{u} = \frac{ru \pm ts}{s \cdot u}, \qquad \frac{r}{s} \cdot \frac{t}{u} = \frac{r \cdot t}{s \cdot u} \quad \text{and} \quad \frac{r}{s} / \frac{t}{u} = \frac{r \cdot u}{s \cdot t}$$

and that it will be necessary to reduce to lowest terms afterward. For example, $\frac{2}{3} \cdot \frac{1}{2} = \frac{2 \cdot 1}{3 \cdot 2} = \frac{2}{6} = \frac{1}{3}$. Let us therefore first define

```
int gcd( int a, int b )  // compute the greatest common
                         // divisor
{    if( a < 0 ) return gcd( -a, b );
     if( a == 0 ) return b;
     if( b < a ) return gcd( b, a );
          // now 0 < a <= b
     return gcd( b % a, a );
          // b % a is the remainder of the division b/a
}
```

```
Fraction reduce( Fraction f ) // reduce to lowest terms
{    Fraction r;
     int g = gcd( f.num, f.den );

     if( g != 0 )
     {    r.num = f.num / g;
          r.den = f.den / g;
     }
     return r;
}
```

The gcd function recursively calls itself, with ever smaller values of a and b. It works for the following reason: Suppose $0 < a \le b$. Let q be the quotient of the division b/a, r the remainder. Then

$$b = a \cdot q + r \qquad \text{and} \qquad \gcd(a, b) = \gcd(a, a \cdot q + r) = \gcd(a, r)$$

because every number dividing a must also divide $a \cdot q$. The first and third line in the gcd function just arrange a and b to obtain the condition $0 < a \le b$, and the second line returns the final answer. ($\gcd(0, b) = b$ because every number divides 0.) Here is an example:

$$\gcd(\ 40, -15\ ) = \gcd(\ -15, 40\ ) = \gcd(\ 15, 40\ ) = \gcd(\ 10, 15\ )$$
$$= \gcd(\ 5, 10\ ) = \gcd(\ 0, 5\ ) = 5$$

Exercise 1.4.1. Rewrite the gcd function to be nonrecursive.

Pascal Note

The % operator is called **mod** in Pascal. It is important to realize that the return statement not only sets the return value, but exits the function immediately. For example, when computing gcd(0, 5), the second if is true, and the return statement returns the value 5 immediately. The third line is not executed. It is quite common to take care of exceptions or trivial cases at the beginning of a C++ function, with an immediate return exit. This is quite pleasant because it avoids confusing if ... else if ... else if ... else ... constructions and multiple indentations that crowd the really important code to the right margin of the screen.

C Note

In some pre-ANSI versions of C, functions could not receive or return struct values, only pointers to structures were permitted. In ANSI C, as well as in C++, struct values are permitted both as function arguments and as return types. Of course, this involves copying the members of the structure onto the stack.

We are ready to write the operator functions.

```
Fraction operator+( Fraction a, Fraction b )
{    Fraction r;

     r.num = a.num * b.den + b.num * a.den;
     r.den = a.den * b.den;
     return reduce( r );
}

Fraction operator-( Fraction a, Fraction b )
{    Fraction r;

     r.num = a.num * b.den - b.num * a.den;
     r.den = a.den * b.den;
     return reduce( r );
}

Fraction operator*( Fraction a, Fraction b )
{    Fraction r;

     r.num = a.num * b.num;
     r.den = a.den * b.den;
     return reduce( r );
}

Fraction operator/( Fraction a, Fraction b )
{    Fraction r;

     r.num = a.num * b.den;
     r.den = a.den * b.num;
     return reduce( r );
}
```

We would like to be able to perform computations such as $2 + 1/3$ without having to define

```
Fraction operator+( int n, Fraction b );
```

and the other seven corresponding operators (with + - * / and the int in the front or the back). This is achieved by supplying a type conversion int→ Fraction, with a so-called *constructor*. The constructor must be placed in the struct declaration. In fact, a second constructor (whose use will be explained shortly) is also required.

```
struct Fraction
{    int num;
     int den;
```

```
Fraction( int n, int d = 1 ) { num = n; den = d;}
   // for type conversion int-->Fraction
Fraction() { num = 0; den = 1;}
   // for array initialization
} ;
```

One can now declare and initialize fractions with

```
Fraction f(1,3);    // initialized as 1/3
Fraction t(2);      // initialized as 2/1
```

The = 1 in the constructor is a default argument, to be chosen if none is explicitly given. When the compiler sees 2 * f, it will use this constructor to make a new fraction 2/1, then call operator*.

Now we have all the tools together needed to enhance our calculator to handle fractions. The stack must be changed to an array of fractions: Fraction stack[STACKSIZE]. Care must be taken when declaring an array of any type that has one or more constructors. C++ wants to initialize such an array and requires that one of the constructors has *no* arguments. (Not even default arguments are allowed.) That is the second constructor in the struct Fraction declaration. It is used to initialize all array entries with 0/1. The push and pop functions are unchanged except for the argument and return type. The main function is almost unchanged, except that variables are now declared as fractions, integers are converted to fractions before being pushed onto the stack, and both numerator and denominator must be printed. It is quite remarkable that so much of the code can be reused without change.

```
const int STACKSIZE = 20;

Fraction stack[ STACKSIZE ];
int stackPointer = 0;

void push( Fraction n )
{    if( stackPointer < STACKSIZE )
     {    stack[ stackPointer ] = n;
          stackPointer++;
     }
}

Fraction pop()
{    if( stackPointer > 0 )
          stackPointer--;
     return stack[ stackPointer ];
}

int main()
{    char ch;
```

```
Fraction second, result;
int num;

cin >> ch;
while( ch != '=' )
{
    if( '0' <= ch && ch <= '9' )
    {   cin.putback( ch );
        cin >> num;
        push( Fraction( num ) ); // convert to
                                 // fraction

    }
    else
        switch( ch )
        {   case '+':
                push( pop() + pop() ); break;
            case '*':
                push( pop() * pop() ); break;
            case '-':
                second = pop(); push( pop() -
                                    second);  break;
            case '/':
                second = pop(); push( pop() /
                                    second);  break;
            default:
                cout << "Input error."; return 1;
        }
    cin >> ch;
}
result = pop(); // print as fraction
cout << result.num << " / " << result.den << "\n";
return 0;
}
```

Entering fractions into the calculator is not as pretty as it might be. One cannot enter 1/2 directly. This would be interpreted as pushing the 1, dividing the next element on the stack by 1, and pushing the 2. But entering 1 2 / will cause 1/2 to be deposited on the stack. This is similar to the problem of entering negative numbers discussed in the previous section.

Exercise 1.4.2. Implement and test the fraction calculator.

Exercise 1.4.3. Implement a power function operator^ for fractions. For example, Fraction(3,4)^3 should be 27/64. Add the ^ operation to the calculator. If the exponent is not an integer, you can generate an error message. But negative integers are okay: $(a/b)^{\wedge}(-n) = (b/a)^{\wedge}n$.

Exercise 1.4.4. Add a command ? that shows the top of the stack without popping it off. Do this by modifying the `push` function to return the value it pushed. Then use `cout << push( pop() )` to nondestructively print the top of the stack.

It is interesting to note that there is no "divide by 0" error in our fraction calculator. Why not? Use `operator/` to divide 1/2 by 0/1. The result is a `struct` with `num` containing 1 and `den` containing 0. There is nothing illegal about this. One might even call this value "infinity":

```
Fraction infinity( 1, 0 );
```

It behaves quite nicely like the mathematical ∞. Adding it to any number results in ∞. For example, 1/2 + ∞ yields `r.num` $= 1 \cdot 0 + 2 \cdot 1$, `r.den` $= 2 \cdot 0$ in `operator+`, and after the call to `reduce`, the result is again `num` $= 1$, `den` $= 0(\dots)$ (because gcd(2, 0) = 2).

However, the multiplication 0/1 · ∞ produces an even stranger number, with `num` and `den` both 0. Adding, subtracting, multiplying, or dividing this quantity with anything else replicates itself. There is no mathematical analog to this strange object. That is not a problem. Our pairs of integers are not fractions. They are merely a *model* of fractions, imitating them quite well under certain conditions and acting strangely under other, hopefully, less frequent circumstances. Providing reasonable *models* of objects and actions is an essential aspect of programming.

1.5. A FLOWCHART PLOTTER

In this section we will investigate a program that is a little off the beaten track, a *flowchart plotter*. This example will illustrate the concept of *object-oriented programming*. It is much longer than the previous programs. I want to present a nontrivial application that demonstrates the benefits, not just the mechanics, of object-oriented programming and hope that you will be patient and bear with me. Object-oriented techniques are particularly helpful for organizing large projects, typically far more complex than even the sample of this section.

Our objects are flowchart blocks, such as

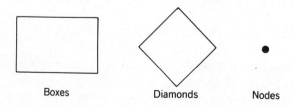

Boxes   Diamonds   Nodes

The program will read in boxes, specified by their type and the coordinates of their center; plot them; and place them on a stack. There will be a stack operation *join* that joins the top two objects on the stack

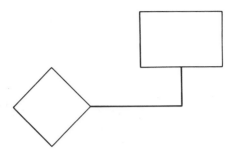

Together with two stack operations, *pop* and *exchange* (which exchanges the top two items on the stack), it will be possible to draw complex flow-charts.

1.5.1. Screen Display Routines

The flowcharts will be displayed on the screen. We therefore will use a coordinate system with 24 rows and 80 columns and represent lines by sequences of *'s in a 24 × 80 array of characters. Here is the code to manage the plotting of lines and the display of the accumulated drawing.

```
const int GRID_HSIZE = 80;
const int GRID_VSIZE = 24;

char grid[ GRID_VSIZE ][ GRID_HSIZE + 1 ];
        // + 1 to hold a '\0' at the end of each line

void gridClear()
// initialize the array with spaces
{    for( int i = 0; i < GRID_VSIZE; i++ )
     {    for( int j = 0; j < GRID_HSIZE; j++ )
              grid[i][j] = ' ';
          grid[i][GRID_HSIZE] = '\0';
     }
}

void gridLine(int rstart,int cstart,int dr,int dc,int n)
// plot a line, starting at (rstart, cstart), consisting of
// n * s and move by (dr, dc) after each *
```

```
// This is only good for horizontal, vertical and 45 degree
// lines
{   while( n > 0 )
    {   grid[ rstart ][ cstart ] = '*';
        rstart += dr;
        cstart += dc;
        n--;
    }
}

void gridShow()
// show the result on the standard output device
{   for( int i = 0; i < GRID_VSIZE; i++ )
        cout << grid[i] << "\n";
}
```

The local variables i and j are declared in the `for` loop, just when they are needed.

Pascal Note

Two-dimensional arrays are declared with the bounds in separate brackets: `char grid[24][81]`. Both bounds start at 0. Then of course the $(i, j)^{th}$ element is referred to as `grid[i][j]`. Omitting one of the brackets denotes a one-dimensional subarray, for example `grid[i]` is the ith row of the two-dimensional array. This is used in the `gridShow` function, which simply considers `grid` as an array of strings, strings themselves being one-dimensional arrays of characters. To print a string, its end must be known. It is a C++ convention that all strings end in a *zero byte*, that is, a byte with the numerical value 0 (*not* '0'.) The zero character is often denoted by '\0', although it really is no different from 0.

The += operator in `gridLine` stands for increment by. `rstart += dr` is the same as `rstart = rstart + dr`.

Exercise 1.5.1. Using the foregoing data structures, write a program that draws a stop-sign shape

and prints it.

1.5.2. Flowchart Objects

All flowchart objects (boxes, diamonds, nodes) have a center, and we will define

```
struct FlowObj
{   int centerRow;
    int centerCol;

    FlowObj( int r, int c ) { centerRow = r; centerCol = c;}
            // a constructor
    virtual int left() { return centerCol; }
    virtual int right() { return centerCol; }
    virtual int top() { return centerRow; }
    virtual int bottom() { return centerRow; }
    virtual void plot() {}
    virtual void list() { cout << centerRow << " " <<
                                        centerCol << "";
};
```

There are two notable aspects of this structure declaration. The structure contains functions, so-called *member functions*. And these functions are declared `virtual`. As we will see presently, this means that they can be replaced by other functions for certain `FlowObj`s. It is a coincidence that all member functions of `FlowObj` are virtual, and that all of them take no arguments. Member functions need not be virtual, and they can have arguments.

The syntax for a member function call is similar to selection of data members. For example, if `x` is a `FlowObj`, then `x.list()` lists its center coordinates. The particular `x` is an *implicit argument* [as if the call was `list(x)`], and its `centerRow` and `centerCol` values are printed. The member names used in member functions always refer to the implicit first argument that precedes the `.` in the call.

Here is the declaration of a box.

```
struct Box : FlowObj
{   int hsize;
    int vsize;

    Box( int r, int c, int h, int v ) : FlowObj( r, c )
            { hsize = h; vsize = v; }
            // a constructor, calling the base class
            // constructor
    int left() { return centerCol - (hsize + 1)/2 + 1; }
    int right() { return centerCol + hsize/2; }
    int top() { return centerRow - (vsize + 1)/2 + 1; }
    int bottom() { return centerRow + vsize/2; }
    void list() { cout << "Box "; FlowObj::list(); }
```

```
void plot()
{    gridLine( top(), left(), 0, 1, hsize );
     gridLine( top(), right(), 1, 0, vsize );
     gridLine( bottom(), right(), 0, -1, hsize );
     gridLine( bottom(), left(), -1, 0, vsize );
}
};
```

The : FlowObj denotes that a Box is *derived* from the *base class* FlowObj. That is, a box has all members of a FlowObj; in addition, it has other characteristics. For example, if b is a Box, b.centerRow is defined although the centerRow field is not explicitly mentioned in the structure definition. It is *inherited* from the FlowObj type. A box has special data fields, namely horizontal and vertical dimensions, and special ways of plotting and producing the left, right, top, and bottom margins.

The Box type refers to its base class in two instances: the Box constructor causes the base class constructor to be executed through the : FlowObj(r, c) clause, and when listing box data, the data listing function of the base class is invoked through the FlowObj::list() call. The FlowObj:: operator is called a *scope resolution operator*. It is often used in C++ to indicate to what a function or variable name belongs.

The next type, Node, relies much more heavily on the base class, because the default actions for finding the extent of a FlowObj with the left(), right(), top(), bottom() functions can be inherited. Only the plot and list actions need to be specified.

```
struct Node : FlowObj
{
     Node( int r, int c ) : FlowObj( r, c ) {}
     // a constructor, calling the base class constructor
     // and doing nothing else
     void plot() { grid[centerRow][centerCol] = '*'; }
     void list() { cout << "Point "; FlowObj::list(); }
};
```

Finally, we need to describe diamonds. One data element, radius, is required. It denotes the distance from the center to one of the four corners.

```
struct Diamond : FlowObj
{    int radius;

     Diamond( int r, int c, int h ) : FlowObj( r, c )
     { radius = h; }

     int left() { return centerCol - radius + 1; }
     int right() { return centerCol + radius - 1; }
     int top() { return centerRow - radius + 1; }
```

```
int bottom() { return centerRow + radius - 1; }
void list() { cout << "Diamond "; FlowObj::list(); }
void plot()
{    gridLine( top(), centerCol, 1, 1, radius );
     gridLine( centerRow, right(), 1, -1, radius );
     gridLine( bottom(), centerCol, -1, -1, radius );
     gridLine( centerRow, left(), -1, 1, radius );

}
};
```

Exercise 1.5.2. Write a program that prints a box and a diamond, both centered on the grid, and places a node at the center:

1.5.3. Joining Flowchart Objects

How are two objects joined? First draw a horizontal line from the left or right end of the first object to the center column of the second object, then draw a vertical line from the end point of the first line to the top or bottom of the next object. However, if the objects are centered in the same row or column, only one line is drawn. The details depend on how the first and second objects are located relative to each other. The following diagram shows various possibilities. The shapes of the objects are deliberately left vague because the same method should work for all shapes.

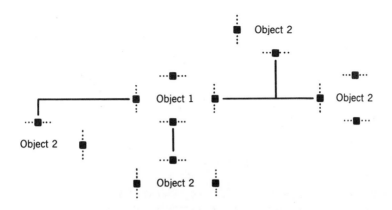

Joining is an asymmetric operation. The following diagram shows the difference between joining object 1 with object 2 (▬▬) versus joining object 2 with object 1 (▬▬)

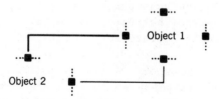

Here is the code for the join function. The function receives two pointers to FlowObjs. It does not matter whether they are boxes, diamonds, or nodes. Why pass the pointers rather than the real things? The various actual objects have different sizes! A box takes more storage than a node. Therefore, they cannot be simply passed to a function. At compile time, the size of each function argument must be known to generate the correct code to pass it to the function and locate it inside the functon. On the other hand, pointers (i.e., addresses) have uniform size no matter what object type they point to.

```
void join( FlowObj* from, FlowObj* to )
{       int r, c; // row, col of intermediate point

        if( from->centerCol == to->centerCol )
        {       if( from->centerRow < to->centerRow )
                        r = from->bottom();
                else
                        r = from->top();
        }
        else r = from->centerRow;

        if( from->centerRow == to->centerRow )
        {       if( from->centerCol < to->centerCol )
                        c = to->right();
                else
                        c = to->left();
        }
        else c = to->centerCol;

        if( from->centerCol < to->centerCol )
                gridLine( r,from->right(),0,1,c-from->right() );
        else if( from->centerCol > to->centerCol )
                gridLine( r,from->left(),0,-1,from->left()-c );
```

```
if( from->centerRow < to->centerRow )
    gridLine( r, c, 1, 0, to->top() - r );
else if( from->centerRow > to->centerRow )
    gridLine( r, c, -1, 0, r - to->bottom() );
}
```

Pascal Notes

At this time, it is necessary to master two syntactical quirks of C++. Pointer dereferencing is denoted by a *, not a ^, and the * is a prefix operator. Instead of p^, one writes *p. A pointer p to a type T is declared as T* p, for example FlowObj* from declares from as a pointer to a FlowObj. If one wants to find the centerRow field of the structure that from points to, one can write (*from).centerRow. The parentheses are necessary because . has a higher precedence than (). This is cumbersome, and as it appears so often, an operator ->, *dereference and access member*, exists that allows accessing the centerRow field as from->centerRow. In general, p->m is identical to (*p).m. In Pascal, no such syntactic problem exists because the dereferencing operator ^ is postfix, and one simply writes p^.m.

The Pascal style p^ is a better choice than the C style *p. This is not simply a matter of taste. Because the . [] ()operators are traditionally postfix, a postfix pointer dereferencing operator saves parentheses and makes complex expressions easier to read. The C style sometimes requires parentheses. It also forces the reader to scan complex expressions bidirectionally. But the overall greater flexibility of C pointers outweighs this syntactic annoyance.

To get a pointer that points to an existing object x, C has an *address* operator. &x is the address of x. (This will typically be the memory location of the first byte of x, although the language does not prescribe the relationship between pointer values and memory locations.) It can be assigned to a pointer variable (p = &x) or passed to a function with a pointer argument (join(&x,&y)). There is no analog to this operation in Pascal. All pointers in Pascal point to objects on the heap and are obtained through **new**.

The center coordinates of the objects are stored in the base class and hence accessible as from->centerRow, etc. The margins can be obtained through calls to from->bottom(), etc. (Recall that the syntax for calling a member function is identical to selection of member data, through the . or -> operator.)

However, there is one fundamental difference between the data member access from->centerRow and the function call from->bottom(). Locating the data members is independent of the actual type of the object. But, for example, computing the bottom margin is very different for a **Node** and a **Box**. The correct **bottom** function must be selected, and it must be selected at *run-time* because the `join` function may be called many times with pointers to different objects. This is precisely what is accomplished by the `virtual` attribute of the functions in the base class. A call to a virtual function is translated into code that at run-time selects the proper actual function, depending on which derived class the current object belongs to or the pointer points to.

Exercise 1.5.3. Write a program to test the `join` function. It should join a box and a diamond in two ways:

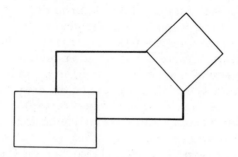

Construct the box and the diamond:

```
Box b(...);
Diamond d(...);
```

join them:

```
join( &b, &d );   // & takes the address. &b is a pointerto b
```

print the result, wait for a keyboard input:

```
char ch;
cout << "Hit [Return] to continue\n";
cin >> ch;
```

and join them in opposite order and print the result.

1.5.4. Putting It Together

Let us now settle on a command language for the flowchart plotter. For simplicity, assume that all boxes are 9 × 5 units and all diamonds have a radius of 4. The user can place a node, box or diamond by typing **N**, **B**, or **D** followed by the coordinates of the center. For example,

```
D  6  20
```

places a diamond with center at row 6, column 20. It also places a pointer to a Diamond on the stack. Typing J joins the two objects on the top of the stack, P pops the top of the stack, X exchanges the top two items on the stack, and L lists the stack. S shows the current contents of the grid buffer and Q quits. Here is the code for the stack routines.

```
const int STACKSIZE = 20;

FlowObj* stack[ STACKSIZE ];
int stackPointer = 0;

void push( FlowObj* n )
{   if( stackPointer <= STACKSIZE - 1 )
    {   stack[ stackPointer ] = n;
        stackPointer++;
    }
}

FlowObj* pop()
{   if( stackPointer > 0 )
        stackPointer--;
    return stack[ stackPointer ];
}

void xchg()
{   FlowObj* temp;
    if( stackPointer >= 2 )
    {   temp = stack[ stackPointer-1 ];
        stack[ stackPointer-1 ] = stack[ stackPointer-2 ];
        stack[ stackPointer-2 ] = temp;
    }
}

void joinTop2()
{   if( stackPointer >= 2 )
        join( stack[ stackPointer-2 ], stack
                                    [ stackPointer-1 ] );
}

void stackShow()
{   for( int i = 0; i < stackPointer; i++ )
        stack[ i ]->list();
}
```

Of course, the push and pop functions look precisely like the ones in previous examples, except that we are now stacking FlowObj*s. We cannot simply pack the various objects with types derived from `FlowObj`. They have varying sizes. But the pointers to them have uniform size and can be stacked.

Finally, here is the main function.

```
int main()
{    char ch; /* next input token */
     gridClear();
     cin >> ch;
     while( ch != 'Q' )
     {    int r,c;
          FlowObj* p;

          switch( ch )
          {    case 'B':
                    cin >> r >> c;
                    p = new Box( r, c, 9, 5 );
                    push( p ); p->plot(); break;
               case 'D':
                    cin >> r >> c;
                    p = new Diamond( r, c, 4 );
                    push( p ); p->plot(); break;
               case 'N':
                    cin >> r >> c;
                    p = new Node( r, c );
                    push( p ); p->plot(); break;
               case 'J':
                    joinTop2(); break;
               case 'P':
                    if( stackPointer > 0 ) { p = pop();
                                             delete p; }
                    break;
               case 'X':
                    xchg(); break;
               case 'S':
                    gridShow(); break;
               case 'L':
                    stackShow(); break;
          }
          cin >> ch;
     }
     return 0;
}
```

The `new` operator gets storage space from the *free store*. For example, `new Diamond( r, c, 4 )` allocates the appropriate number of bytes to hold a `Diamond` and causes the constructor to fill the newly obtained storage area with `r`, `c`, and `4`. It returns a pointer to the storage, which is then pushed onto the stack. When the stack is popped, the pointer is given to `delete`, which recycles the storage block and marks it as available for further allocation.

Pascal Note

`new` is similar to the Pascal `new`, except that in Pascal `new` takes the pointer as a `var` argument, as in `new( p )`, and manages to deduce the size of the object to be allocated from the type of the pointer. Of course, the Pascal `new` cannot thread in a constructor invocation. `delete` is the analog of `dispose`.

C Note

`new` and `delete` are super-versions of `malloc`, and `free`. `p = new Box` is equivalent to `p = malloc( sizeof Box )`. The major difference is that `new` and `delete` can invoke constructors and destructors. *They are not functions,* but built-in language constructs. As with `return` or `sizeof`, parentheses are not necessary.

The user input

`D 6 20`	make a diamond
`B 10 30`	make a box
`J`	join them
`N 14 20`	make a node
`X`	exchange the node and box
`J`	to join them in opposite order
`P`	pop the box
`J`	join the diamond and the node
`S`	show the flowchart

results in the following chart.

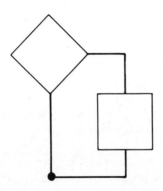

More complicated charts can be printed. For example,

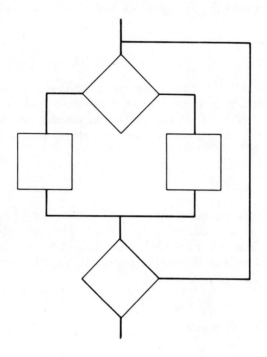

is the result of

```
N 1 20
N 2 20 J X P
D 6 20 J
B 10 10 J X
B 10 30 J X P
N 14 20 X J P
X J P
D 19 20 J X P
N 24 20 J P
N 10 40
J X P
J P P S Q
```

Because >> ignores any kind of white space, commands need not be typed on separate lines. If you try this out, issue an occasional S or L command to watch the intermediate results.

Exercise 1.5.4. Implement the flowchart plotter and test it. For testing, place the command lines in a file (maybe named infile) and redirect keyboard input to that file:

```
flow  <infile
```

We assume that you named the executable program flow. You can redirect output as well, capturing it in a file.

```
flow  <infile >outfile
```

That gives you a chance to edit the output before handing it to the grader.

Exercise 1.5.5. What input produces the mirror-image of the foregoing chart? A 90° clockwise rotation? Test your answers.

We are not proposing this as a serious aid to producing flowcharts. Clearly, it is difficult for a human user to come up with the correct command sequence to produce a desired chart. However, it is conceivable that the commands are generated by another computer program. Some printer control languages, notably PostScript, do use a stack for holding intermediate results during page composition. And PostScript code is usually generated by software and transmitted to the printer, untouched by human hands. Of course, PostScript is a lot more sophisticated than our command code, and we have resisted the temptation of calling it FlowScript.

The reader who has followed this far may well wonder what is so fundamentally different about the programming method employed in this example that it deserves to be called object-oriented. Let us outline a more traditional solution. To distinguish between the different objects, each one would carry a type field.

```
struct FlowObj
{     char type; // contains an 'N', 'D' or 'B'
      int centerRow;
      int centerCol;
      int hsize;  // 0 for points, radius for diamonds
      int vsize;  // 0 for points and diamonds
}
```

The join code would have to be rewritten. All calls r = from->bottom() must be replaced with code

```
switch( t->type )
{     case 'N': r = nodeBottom( t ); break;
      case 'D': r = diamondBottom( t ); break;
      case 'B': r = boxBottom( t ); break;
}
```

and similarly for all other calls to virtual functions. That is ugly, but of course the switch statements could be placed into separate functions. The real difference between the procedural and object-oriented style becomes apparent when the program is enhanced. Suppose we want to add circles to the flowchart. In the procedural model, the code needs to be searched for all occurrences of `switch( ...->type )`, and a `case 'C'` has to be provided each time. That is tedious and error-prone. In the object-oriented model, merely a new `Circle` type is derived from `FlowObj`, which specifies how to do the margin computations and plotting. *No further change* to the existing code is required.

Exercise 1.5.6. Implement the flowchart calculator without virtual functions.

Exercise 1.5.7. Add a "stop-sign" shape

to the flowchart plotter. Note that all changes are localized in the `StopSign` structure and its member functions. No existing code needs to be modified!

DATA

2.1. BASIC TYPES

Like every programming language, C++ has certain built-in types that are handled very efficiently by the underlying hardware. These types are

`int`	Integers of the size most conveniently handled by the machine
`char`	Integers in a range sufficient to hold a single character
`float`	Single-precision floating-point numbers
`double`	Double-precision floating-point numbers

The size of an integer depends on the underlying machine. On larger processors, integers are typically 4-byte quantities, but on smaller machines, for example, personal computers, they are 2-byte quantities. The `char` type just stands for a very short `int`, almost universally 1 byte. However, whether the range is −128 ... 127 or 0 ... 255 is system-dependent.

The most common type for floating-point operations is `double`, not `float`. The math library functions use `double`, and the limited precision of `float` (typically only 6 or 7 significant digits) make it unsuited for many computations. Of course, `float` only needs half the storage space, which can be a consideration when storing large amounts of data.

Pascal Note

In Pascal, there is a separate character type and you need the functions **ord** and **chr** to go between characters and integers. C treats characters as numbers that happen to fall into a small range. Characters coming from the keyboard or going to the screen are represented as small integers, namely the ASCII code (or other encoding used by the machine, such as EBCDIC), of the character.

Additional basic types can be produced with the modifiers

`unsigned`

```
long
short
```

An `unsigned int` is a type that occupies the same amount of space as an `int` does, but does not have a sign bit. For example, if the processor has 2-byte `int`s in the range −32768...32767, `unsigned int` has the range 0...65535. The range of `unsigned char` is 0...255. A `long int` is a type that is somewhat longer than a regular `int`. A `short int` is somewhat shorter. How much longer or shorter depends on the implementation. For example, if an `int` is a 4-byte quantity, a `long int` can be 8-byte (but often still is 4-byte) and a `short int` can be 2-byte. If `int` is 2-byte, `long int` can be 4-byte and `short int` still 2-byte.

As a shorthand, you can drop an `int` after these modifiers. For example, `short` is the same as `short int` and `unsigned long` is the same as `unsigned long int`. Finally, some implementations have a `long double`.

Constants ending in `L` are long, (e.g., `16777216L`) and constants ending in `U` are unsigned (e.g., `65535U`). Numbers starting with `0x` or `0X` are hexadecimal, numbers with `0` (zero) are octal. The latter is a truly bizarre convention. For example, `010` is 8!

There is a `sizeof` operator that gives the size of each type as multiples of the size of a character. That is, we always have

$$1 = \text{sizeof(char)} \leq \text{sizeof(short)} \leq \text{sizeof(int)} =$$
$$\text{sizeof(unsigned)} \leq \text{sizeof(long)}$$

and

$$\text{sizeof(float)} \leq \text{sizeof(double)} \leq \text{sizeof(long double)}$$

but it is unwise to assume anything further if one wants to write programs that can easily be moved between different processors.

In arithmetic operations with operands of mixed types, operands are converted to prevent information loss whenever possible. For example, consider the computation of `m + n` where `m` is an `int`. If `n` is a `long`, `m` is converted to a `long`. If `n` is `unsigned`, `m` is converted to `unsigned` as well. Actually, converting an integral type to a floating-point type can cause information loss as well (e.g., `long` to `float`). Nevertheless, in mixed expressions, the integral types are converted to floating point.

It is sometimes necessary or convenient to explicitly convert from one type to another. For example, if `n` is an `int`, then `double( n )` and `char( n )` denote the equivalent floating-point value or character value. This is called a *cast*. Casting an integer into a character can involve information loss; for example, `char( 288 )` is likely to be `32`.

C Note

The C style notation, such as `(char)n`, is also available in C++, but the functional notation `char( n )` seems clearer. Unfortunately, it does not work for pointers. (char*)p cannot be written as char*(p). But (char*)(p) is legal and reasonably consistent.

Exercise 2.1.1. Write a program that prints the sizes of all basic types on your computer. Use sizeof. Is char signed or unsigned on your machine?

Exercise 2.1.2. Write a program that determines the ranges of all basic types on your computer (e.g., int between −32767 and 32768). Your program should be portable (i.e., run without modifications on other computers) and show the correct values there. Do not use sizeof. This is hard for floating-point numbers.

Exercise 2.1.3. Write a program that prints an ASCII table:

|	4	5	6	7	10	11	12	13	14	15	16	17
0|		(	0	8	@	H	P	X	'	h	p	x
1|	!	)	1	9	A	I	Q	Y	a	i	q	y
2|	"	*	2	:	B	J	R	Z	b	j	r	z
3|	#	+	3	;	C	K	S	^	c	k	s	~
4|	$	,	4	<	D	L	T	[	d	l	t	{
5|	%	-	5	=	E	M	U	\	e	m	u	|
6|	&	.	6	>	F	N	V	]	f	n	v	}
7|	'	/	7	?	G	O	W	_	g	o	w	

In C++ version 1, you cannot use cout << ch to print a character ch. That would just print it as an integer. Use cout.put(ch) instead. Your program should consist of a loop traversing all printing characters between 040 and 0176 (octal).

2.2. VARIABLE AND CONSTANT DECLARATIONS

Here are a few declarations.

```
int m;
double x,y;
int daysPerMonth[12];    // an array of 12 integers
int calendar[12][31];    // a 2-dimensional array of int
```

Pascal Note

In C++, variables are declared "backward" —first the type, then the variable name. Arrays *always* start at 0, and the number in brackets gives the number of elements, *not* the highest permitted index. For example, daysPerMonth has 12 elements, daysPerMonth[0] ... daysPer-Month[11]. Two-dimensional arrays are written with a separate set of brackets for each dimension. The `calendar` elements range from `calendar[0][0]` to `calendar[11][30]`.

There is *no* run-time array bounds checking. Setting `daysPerMonth[100]` to 0 will not be flagged by the compiler nor cause a run-time exception—the 0 will simply be written 100 ints from the start of `daysPerMonth`, overwriting whatever happens to be there. Actually, as we will see later, it is possible to design a safe array type by overloading the `[]` operator to incorporate the out-of-bounds checking. (One can define a new data type in which the `[]` operator has a new meaning, just like we redefined the meanings of + -, etc... for fractions in the first chapter.)

Variables can be initialized when declared, for example,

```
int m = 2;
double x, y = 1;    // only y is set to 1
int daysPerMonth[12] =
      { 31, 28, 31, 30, 31, 30, 31, 31, 30, 31, 30, 31 };
char ch = '1';
char s[6] = "Hello";
```

In C++, strings are arrays of `char`, terminated by a zero byte. For example, the string *s* in the foregoing declaration contains the 6 bytes `'H'`, `'e'`, `'l'`, `'l'`, `'o'`, `'\0'`. The last byte is a zero code, *not* the character code `'0'`. The zero terminator allows functions to find the end of a string. This does mean that a string cannot contain a zero byte as information. Because zero is not a printable character in most encoding schemes, this is not a real limitation. Also note that strings are enclosed in double quotes (`"Hello"`), whereas individual character codes are enclosed in single quotes (`'H'`). Because there is no separate character type, those character constants are just a convenient notation for their integer codes. For example, `'1'` is identical to (and not just equivalent with) the number 49 under the ASCII encoding scheme. It is of type `int` in C++ version 1, `char` in version 2. Either way, it is not at all the same as `"1"`, a string of two bytes, a 49 followed by a 0, placed somewhere in memory. Nonprinting characters are coded with a back-slash control sequence—for example, a newline is `'\n'` and a zero byte is `'\0'`. These are still single characters, not strings.

Exercise 2.2.1. Write a function that reads in a string from standard input:

```
char s[20];
cin >> s;
```

and prints all values of the string in decimal (`cout << int( s[i] )`), up to and including the terminating 0. What happens if you enter a string with 20 characters or more? Write another program that prints all 20 characters in s.

The *sizeof operator* can be applied to variables. For example, `sizeof( x )` = `sizeof( double )` and `sizeof( daysPerMonth )` = `12 * sizeof( int )`.

Constants can be declared with the prefix `const`.

```
const int DAYSPERYEAR = 365;        // different on Mars
const double PI = 3.1415926535897932385;
const int daysPerMonth[12] =
    { 31, 28, 31, 30, 31, 30, 31, 31, 30, 31, 30, 31 };
const unsigned char MASK = OxFO; // numbers starting with
                                 // Ox are hex
```

C Note

The C++ `const` differs slightly from its ANSI C counterpart. When applied to a basic type, it is inline replaced with the constant, and no storage is allocated. We prefer it to using `#define` because it is type-safe.

Enumerated types can be defined with an `enum` declaration.

```
enum Bool { FALSE, TRUE };
enum Color { RED = 4, GREEN = 2, BLUE = 1 };
```

This defines `Bool` and `Color` as enumerations and constants `FALSE` = 0, `TRUE` = 1, `RED`, `GREEN`, and `BLUE`. Specific values for the constants can be provided. They need not be distinct, increasing, or positive. If not provided, the enumeration constants are assigned 0, 1, 2, ... Variables of enumerated types are defined in the usual way.

```
Bool more;
Bool done = FALSE;
```

C Note

In C, as well as C++ version 1, there is *no* type checking for enumerations. `Bool` is not a type distinct from `int`; it is merely a synonym. A `Bool` variable can hold any integer value, such as −1, 2, or `RED`. Values of type `int` and `Bool` (as well as `Color`) can be freely interchanged. In C++ version 2, explicit casts must be used to convert between `enum` and from `int` to `enum`. The conversion from `enum` to `int` is still automatic.

2.3. ARITHMETIC

C++ has the usual complement of arithmetic operators, +, -, *, /, %. The / operator is integer division if both arguments are integers, floating-point division if at least one of them is floating-point. For example, 14 / 4 is 3, 14.0 / 4 is 3.5. The % operator is the remainder of an integer division; for example, 14 % 4 is 2. It is undefined for floating-point arguments. There is no exponentiation operator, but there is a function `pow` in the math library.

Pascal Note

For integer arguments, / and % correspond to the Pascal `div` and `mod` operators. Do not use ^ for computing powers—it denotes "bitwise XOR."

There are bitwise operators that operate on the binary representation of integers.

x & y	bitwise AND
x | y	bitwise OR
x ^ y	bitwise XOR
x ≪ n	left shift by n
x ≫ n	right shift by n
~x	bitwise complement

Exercise 2.3.1. Write a function `binPrint` that prints a number in binary. To convert a number into binary, repeatedly divide by 2 and store the remainders in an array. Then print that array in reverse order. Assume the number has `8*sizeof(int)` binary digits.

Exercise 2.3.2. Modify the cheap calculator from Section 1.2 to a cheap bitwise calculator that implements AND, OR, XOR, shift, and complement. Use the < and > keys for shift. If you solved the preceding exercise, print the answers in binary.

Finally, there are the famous increment and decrement operators that give C++ its name. The statement

```
n++;
```

adds 1 to the value of n, and, of course, n-- subtracts 1. These operators have two aspects: the side effect of incrementing or decrementing, and a value that can be used in expressions. The value depends on the placement of the ++ before or after its argument. For example,

```
2 * n++
```

evaluates to twice the value of n *before it was incremented*, whereas

```
2 * ++n
```

is twice the new value of n after increment. It is easy to remember which does which. In the expression n++, the n comes before the ++ and hence its value is used before it is incremented. Conversely, in ++n the ++ comes first and n is incremented, then used.

(It can therefore be argued that C++, the incremental improvement to C, should really be called ++C, after all, we want to use it after it is improved.)

It is very common to step through an array with code like

```
const int ASIZE = 10;
int i = 0;
```

```
int a[ASIZE];
while( i < ASIZE )
    cin >> a[ i++ ]; // read in the next array element
```

and the placement of the ++ is crucial for the functioning of the loop. For example,

```
while( i++ < ASIZE )
    cin >> a[ i ]; // read in the next array element
```

would never read in a[0] but would read the out-of-range a[ASIZE]!

The original motivation for the introduction of the ++ and -- operators may have been to have the compiler generate efficient machine instructions. Many processors have an INC instruction that is much faster than fetching an operand, loading 1 in a register, performing an addition, and storing the result. Furthermore, a[i++] could take advantage of the fact that i is still in a register when a[i] is computed. Some processors even have a single machine instruction for a[i++]. With modern optimizing compilers, these considerations should *not* overly affect one's coding style. Modern compilers are devilishly clever about optimizing operations (e.g., replacing a*8 with the faster a<<3) and keeping frequently used variables in registers. Always code in the clearest possible fashion. Short code is clearer than long code because the reader has to digest less information. The rich collection of C++ operators is a great help in this respect. However, stay away from convoluted code. Use good taste with nested assignments and increment/decrement operations, or the next person maintaining your code must waste time playing "C++ puzzles." C++ has the undeserved reputation of being a "write-only" language, whereas a skilled coder with good judgment can write programs that are easier to read than the best equivalent versions in wordier languages such as Pascal or Modula 2.

2.4. ASSIGNMENT

Assignment is written using =, as in a = 2 * b. The assignment is an *operator*, that is, an assignment a = 2 * b has a *value* (namely the value placed into a). This allows for multiple assignments: a = b = 1 places the value of b = 1 into a. The = operator binds right to left to make this work. The value of an assignment can be used in other subexpressions as well. For example,

```
while( !isupper( ch = s[i++] ) && ch != '\0' )
    ;
```

sets ch to the first uppercase letter in the string s.

Pascal Note

For Pascal programmers, the choice of the = symbol rather than := for assignment takes getting used to. Being able to nest assignments inside arithmetic expressions is quite useful, though. One can casually store an intermediate result in a variable without breaking up an expression.

Arithmetic operators can be combined with the assignment operator, for example

```
x += 2;      // same as x = x + 2
x <<= 2;     // shift x to the left twice, i.e. multiplyby 4
```

The operators += -= *= /= %= &= |= ^= <<= >>= can be similarly used. This corresponds rather nicely to the way one often thinks. It is more natural to say "increment *x* by 2" than "take *x*, add 2 to it, and place the value back into *x*". This is especially true for complicated expressions like

```
yyval[ yypv[ p3 + p4] + yypv[ p1 - p2 ] ] += 2;
```

The reader does not have to check that two lengthy expressions on the left and right side of an = are identical, or, if they are not, wonder whether that is a bug.

The assignment operator cannot copy arrays:

```
int a[10];
int b[10] = { 1, 1, 2, 3, 5, 8, 13, 21, 34, 55 };

a = b; // ERROR
```

Arrays should be copied with an explicit loop.

There are important differences between the assignment operator = and the role of = in variable initialization. For example,

```
char s[] = "Hello";
```

allocates 6 characters (including a '\0') of contiguous storage and gives this storage area the name s. No copying of characters takes place. This is not an assignment, but an initialization. A subsequent statement

```
s = "Henry"; // ERROR
```

is illegal.

2.5. RELATIONAL AND BOOLEAN OPERATIONS

There is no Boolean type in C, and all Boolean operations and flow-control structures operate on integers, under the convention that 0 is false and any nonzero value is true. The comparison operators

```
<    <=    >    >=    ==    !=
```

yield 0 if the comparison is false, 1 it is true. For example, 3 < 4 has the value 1, and it is possible to use these operations in arithmetic expressions:

```
sign = ( x > 0 ) - ( x < 0 )    // 1 if x > 0, 0 if x == 0,
                                // -1 if x < 0
```

Pascal Note

This completes the confusion for the Pascal programmer. Pascal : = = <> correspond to C++ = == !=. Using = when == is intended can have disastrous effects.

```
if( x = y )    // assigns y to x
{     // always gets here unless the value of y is 0
   ...
}
```

This is a legal construct, and most compilers issue no warning. (Some compilers *do* warn, which is annoying whenever you actually do want to assign and test whether the assigned value is 0.)

Just as arrays (and in particular strings) cannot be copied with =, the comparison operators cannot be used for comparison testing. For example,

```
char s[] = "Harry", t[] = "Hong";

if( s > t ) // NOT a lexicographic comparison!
```

does not test whether s comes lexicographically after t. As we will see later, the code is nevertheless legal and it tests whether the *starting address* of s is larger than the one of t, a much less useful comparison in most circumstances. The `strcmp` function in the string library performs lexicographic comparison of strings.

Exercise 2.5.1. Write a program that reads in two strings:

```
char s[20],t[20];
cout << "Enter string followed by [Return]: ";
cin >> s;
// ...
```

and prints out the result of the comparison s < t (this should be 0 or 1), strcmp(s, t), and the integer values of s and t. (Use int(...) to convert.) You must #include <string.h>.

Boolean conditions can be joined with

&&   Boolean AND
|| Boolean OR
!   Boolean NOT

These operators interpret 0 as false, any non−0 quantity as true and return a 0 or 1. For example, ∃ || ☐ is ⅃. Arguments are evaluated only until the truth value of the expression is determined. When the first true expression in an || or the first false expression in an && is encountered, the remaining arguments are not evaluated. It is therefore safe to write

```
if( x != 0 && y/x < eps )      // y/x only evaluated if x != 0
    // ...
```

Pascal Note

&& || ! are equivalent to the Pascal **and, or, not** operators. However, the Pascal operators do not have the *short-circuit* feature. Writing **if x<>0 and y/x < eps then** ... will cause an error whenever x is zero because Pascal first computes the values of all subexpressions before applying the **and** operator. Ada has **and then** and **or else** operators for short-circuit evaluation.

Do not confuse the Boolean and logical operators. & operates on the bit patterns of its arguments, whereas && only looks whether they are zero or not.

Exercise 2.5.2. Write a program that reads in a date in the form ᑲ ⅃ᑲ ⅃Գ5Գ and computes how many days it is away from January 1 of the same year. Recall that a year is a leap year if it is divisible by 4 but not by 100, or if it is divisible by 400.

Finally, there is a ternary selection operator. *expr1 ? expr2 : expr3* evaluates to *expr2* or *expr3*, depending on whether *expr1* is true (non-0) or not. For example,

```
x = a > b ? a : b;          // set x to the maximum of a and b
```

Conditional expressions are indeed expressions and can be nested inside other expressions, for example, `sqrt( a > 0 ? a : -a )`. This distinguishes them from `if ... else` statements.

Exercise 2.5.3. Write `toupper` and `tolower` functions converting lowercase letters to uppercase and conversely and leaving all other characters unchanged. Use ?:.

2.6. OPERATOR PRECEDENCE AND ORDER OF EVALUATION

The following table summarizes the precedence of all C++ operators, including the ones we have not yet discussed. Operators are listed in decreasing strength. Operators on the same line have the same strength and are evaluated in the order indicated in the right-hand column.

Operators	Associativity
: :	
[ ] ( ) -> .	left to right
! ~ ++ -- unary+ - * &	right to left
(*type*) sizeof new delete	
* / %	left to right
+ -	left to right
<< >>	left to right
< <= > >=	left to right
== !=	left to right
&	left to right
^	left to right
|	left to right
&&	left to right
||	left to right
?=	left to right
= += -= *= |= %= &= ^= <<= >>=	right to left
,	left to right

The *scope resolution* operator : : will be introduced in Chapter 5. The [ ] and ( ) operators stand for array access and function call. The unary * and & will be discussed in Chapter 4, and the . and -> in Chapter 5. The , operator is a curious *sequencing* operator that executes its subexpressions one at a time and returns the value of the last one. For example, the value of n=5,a[n] is a[5]. It is most commonly used in loop headers,

```
while( n = k, a[ n + 1 ] > 0 )
    // ...
```

to shoehorn multiple actions into a single expression. It is also common in code generated from C++ to C translators. Note that its precedence is below that of =. The commas in a function call are *not* comma operators (after all, you would not want all but the last value discarded).

This table says *nothing* about the order of evaluation. Like most programming languages, C does not guarantee in which order the operands are computed before an operation is applied. For example, in

```
n = 2;
x = a[n++] - 2 * n++;
```

the precedence rules guarantee that parentheses are set like

```
x = ( a[n++] - ( 2 * n++ ) );
```

leaving no doubt that the 2 is multiplied with n++ (rather than subtracted from a[n++]), but it is not clear when it happens. Will the operation be evaluated left to right, with a[n++] computed and parked somewhere, followed by the computation of 2 * n++ and finally the subtraction? Or will the subexpression 2 * n++ be computed first and subtracted from a[n++]? It is up to the discretion of the compiler. The results are, of course, very different:

```
x = a[2] - ( 2 * 3 ) ;
```

or

```
x = a[3] - ( 2 * 2 ) ;
```

It is the responsibility of the programmer to organize the code in an unambiguous manner by breaking up the computation into two steps. Even if your current compiler performs an ambiguous computation in the desired order, break it up. Another compiler, or even another release of your compiler, might act differently. In practice, such situations are rare and easily handled.

The difference between operator precedence and order of evaluation is subtle. Operator precedence determines *how* the components are combined. Order of evaluation specifies *when* this happens. Only four operators have a guaranteed order of evaluation:

```
&&   ||  ?:   ,
```

We have discussed the short-circuit evaluation of && and || earlier. The first argument of ?: is guaranteed to be evaluated first to enable the choice between the second and the third. The arguments of the , operator are guaranteed to be executed left to right. Note again that the , in function calls is not the , operator. In a function call

```
pow( a[n], n++ );
```

there is *no guarantee* whether a[n] or n++ is evaluated first.

Exercise 2.6.1. Write a program that tests in which order your compiler evaluates expressions such as a[n++] - (a[n++] - (a[n++] - a[n++]))). Also test in which order function arguments such as pow(a[n], n++) are evaluated.

2.7. PITFALLS

Welcome to the first "pitfalls" section of this book. In C++, almost every properly formatted expression has *some* meaning, but not necessarily the one you have in mind. It is easy to write code that is legal and accepted by the compiler but that does not quite do what you think it does. Read through these "horror stories" even if you do not intend to program right away. Seeing how uncommon expressions are evaluated by the compiler can be very illuminating.

Most of these pitfalls are not indications of "design flaws" in C++. They are just consequences of a rich set of operators and a concise set of rules that occasionally clash with intuition. The language designers are to be applauded for sticking to general and elegant concepts rather than cluttering the language with exceptions. The appearance of some pitfalls, which are easily mastered with some practice, is a small price to pay.

2.7.1. = vs. ==

```
if( n = 10 )
      k = 0;
else
      a[n] = k;
```

always sets k to 0 and n to 10. The expression n = 10 has the value 10, because the value of an assignment is the value being assigned. The if statement considers 10 as true because it is non-0.

Of course, once you are used to typing ==, you might make the opposite mistake:

```
n == 10;
a[k]= n;
```

This does not put a 10 into a[k]. The value of n == 10, is computed (it is 1) and quietly ignored because you did not provide code to do anything with it. It is legal to write statements that do nothing with their value. For example,

```
n + 2;
```

is correct (but useless).

2.7.2. Operator Precedence

Stashing away a value inside an expression is very useful, but it is important to observe that = has very low precedence. For example,

```
while( ch = a[i++] != '\0' ) ...
```

does not place a[i++] into ch but a 1 or 0, depending on whether a[i++] was the terminating '\0' or not. The correct syntax is

```
while( ( ch = a[i++] ) != '\0' ) ...
```

Most operators have reasonable precedence, but the bitwise operators do not. To test for presence of a bit, you cannot write

```
int mask = 0x1000;
if( n & mask != 0 ) ...
```

because & has lower priority than !=, and you do not want to compute n & (mask != 0), which is n & 1. And n<<3 + 1 does not multiply n by 8 before adding 1, instead it adds 3 and 1 first and hence multiplies by 16.

2.7.3. Overrunning Array Boundaries

Unlike Pascal, C++ does not check indices before array access. If an array index is out of range, the access is performed anyway, fetching or modifying the memory location that happens to be at the specified distance from the start of the array. The most dangerous location is the one right after the end of the array. When declaring an array of 10 `int`s,

```
int a[10];
```

legal values are a[0], a[1], ... a[9]. a[10] would be the eleventh element and is therefore out of range. Consider the following code to fill an array with zeros.

```
int a[10];
int i = 0;

while( i <= 10 ) { a[i] = 0; i++; }
```

On many machines, this code will run into an infinite loop because `i` is located right after the array `a`, and the assignment `a[10] = 0` actually stores a 0 in `i`. Of course, there is no guarantee how the compiler allocates the variables, and the same code might create some other damage.

2.7.4. Order of Evaluation

The order in which subexpressions are evaluated is largely left to the discretion of the compiler. This can lead to problems when using ++, --, or assignments inside expressions. For example,

```
n = 2;
x = pow( a[n], n++ )
```

will most likely not compute $a[2]^2$ but $a[3]^2$ because most compilers push function arguments onto the stack from right to left.

2.7.5. char Can Be signed

Here is just one example that can occur in practice. Many ASCII code extensions use the characters above 127 for international characters. For example, an IBM extension uses 129 for ü.

```
char ch = 129;
if( ch == 129 )
        cout << "u\b\""; // \b: backspace, \": " inside string
```

This will not work with many machines because `char` is often signed. The 129 is changed into the 2's complement equivalent -127 and the comparison fails: $-127 \neq 129$.

2.7.6. `int` Is Promoted to `unsigned`

`unsigned`s are often useful for quantities that cannot be negative, for example, memory block sizes. But computations may involve subtractions, so great care must be taken.

```
int n = -1;
unsigned baseSize = 40000;
const unsigned adjust = 100;

baseSize += n*adjust; // WRONG
```

The `int` value n is "promoted" to an unsigned number (e.g., 65535 if integers occupy 2 bytes) and that number is multiplied with 100. The result is truncated to fit into `sizeof( unsigned )` bytes and added to 40000.

If you need `unsigned`, you must explicitly avoid negative numbers in subexpressions:

```
if( n < 0 )
    baseSize -= (-n)*adjust;
else
    baseSize += n*adjust;
```

FUNCTIONS

3.1. FUNCTION DECLARATIONS

A function declaration typically has the format

type funcname (type argname, type argname, ...)

For example,

```
double power( double x, int n )
```

The declaration lists the return type, the function name, and the types and names of all arguments. It is followed by the function body, describing the function's action. For example, a complete definition of `power` is

```
double power( double x, int n )
{    double r = 1;

     if( n == 0 ) return 1;
     if( n < 0 )
     {    if( x == 0 ) return 0; // not mathematically
                               // correct

          x = 1/x;
          n = -n;
     }
     while( n-- > 0 ) r *= x;
     return( r );
}
```

Pascal Note

From the point of view of the Pascal programmer, C++ declarations are "backward," so it should come as no surprise that the return type comes before the function name.

An important difference is the way the function value is assigned. In Pascal, the return value is assigned to a dummy variable with the same name as the function, and execution continues even after this assignment until the function body is exited. In C++, the return value is assigned via the `return` statement, and the function exits *immediately* whenever a `return` statement is encountered. This is very convenient for treating abnormal cases, such as the case of a 0 exponent just illustrated, without yet another `else` and another indentation level.

There are no procedures in C++. A procedure is a function returning `void`.

C Note

Are you still using pre-ANSI C style function declarations?

```
double power( x, n )
double x;
int n;
```

You will have to change your habits. These declarations are not acceptable in C++. The new style is a major convenience, catching argument mismatch bugs during compilation. It is also essential for overloading of functions.

If a function does not take any arguments, you must still supply the parentheses. For example,

```
x = rand(); // get a random number
```

It is legal (but uncommon) to omit the parentheses. A function name without the parentheses denotes the *starting address* of the function, which can be passed to other functions, for example,

```
x = integral( -1, 1, exp );
    // pass address of exp
```

This will be discussed later in Chapter 6.

C Note

The ANSI standard requires that a function with no argument have an argument list `f( void )` to distinguish it from an old-style `f()`. Because in C++, explicit argument lists are required, `f()` denotes a function without arguments.

Unless specifed otherwise, function arguments are passed by *value*. The function allocates local variables on the stack for each argument. They are *initialized* with the values passed to the function in the call. Once they are initialized, they behave the same way as any other local variables of the function. The values of argument variables can be modified (like `n--` in the **power** function in the foregoing example). The contents are forgotten when the function exits. They are *not* copied back in any way to the caller. For example, if power is called as

```
y = power( 2.0, n );
```

the n in the scope of the call is unaffected, although the local n inside the function is counted down to zero.

Exercise 3.1.1. Rewrite the power function to compute the result faster. When n is even, multiply r by itself and divide n by 2. If n is odd, multiply r by x and decrement n. Write down and verify a *loop invariant* for your code. Discuss the improvement in execution time.

Arguments passed by value can never be modified by a function. However, array arguments *can* be modified. For example, this function clears an array:

```
void clear( char a[], int n )
{     int i = 0;
      while( i < n )
           a[i++] = 0;
}
```

Note the omission of the array limit in a[ ]. The function can clear arrays of any length. The number of elements to clear is explicitly passed as a second argument.

Pascal Note

This is patently impossible in Pascal. The array limits are part of the array type. One cannot write a single Pascal function that can clear arrays of different lengths.

In contrast, a function cannot clear a single integer. It appears inconsistent that nonarray arguments are passed by value and cannot be changed, whereas array arguments can be modified. But actually there is a logical explanation. The array is not copied in and out of the function, but the function allocates a local pointer variable that gets initialized with the starting address of the array. Because the location, and not merely the contents, of the array is communicated to the function, the array values can be modified. This will be explained in detail in Chapter 4.

Pascal Note

Think of array arguments as automatic **var**, all others as value arguments.

If one wishes to protect an array argument from modification, it must be explicitly declared const:

```
int max( const int a[], int n );
```

Certain functions cannot be implemented using value arguments. For example, the following function does not swap two integers:

```
void swap( int x, int y )      // WRONG
{       int temp;

        temp = x; x = y; y = temp;
}
```

When called with swap(a, b), the local variables x and y are created, and initialized with the current values of a and b. The values of the local x and y are swapped and forgotten upon function exit. The values of a and b are unaffected. To change the contents of a variable, use a *reference* argument. The C++ syntax is as follows:

```
void swap( int& x, int& y )      // OK
{       int temp;

        temp = x; x = y; y = temp;
}
```

Now when swap(a, b) is executed, the addresses of a and b (and not their values) are passed to the function, and the function swaps the contents of the memory location referenced by those addresses. What happens behind the scenes is similar to array parameters. x and y are actually pointers, initialized with the addresses of a and b. We will discuss the relationship between pointers, arrays, and references in the next chapter.

Pascal Note

For Pascal programmers, this offers no surprise (except for the odd placement of the & operator). It is simply the **var** argument passing mechanism. However, because array arguments are automatic **var**, do not use f(int& a[]).

C Note

In C, one has to use pointers to achieve this effect.

```
void swap( int* x, int* y )
{       int temp;

        temp = *x; *x = *y; *y = temp;
}
```

and call it with swap(&a, &b). The C++ reference mechanism merely takes care of placement of the * and & operators for you.

The following table summarizes the behavior of function arguments.

Function	Behavior
f(int n)	modification of n affects local copy only
f(int& n)	modification of n affects variable from call
f(int a[])	modification of a[i] affects array from call
f(const int a[])	no modification of a[i] is possible

Exercise 3.1.2. Write a function that sorts an integer array of arbitrary length. Use quicksort.

Exercise 3.1.3. Write a function s3 that arranges three integers in ascending order. For example,

```
x = 3; y = 1; z = 2;
s3( x, y, z );
// now x == 1, y == 2, z == 3
```

Exercise 3.1.4. Write a function int median(const int a[], int n) that computes the median of an array (of course, without modifying it).

Often it is convenient to specify *default values* for function arguments. Let us rewrite the clear function to fill an array with zeros if no other value was requested, or with a specified value if desired.

```
void clear( char a[], int n, char value =0 )
{    int i = 0;
    while( i < n )
        a[i++] = value;
}
```

The call clear(a, sizeof(a)) fills a with zeros, whereas

```
clear( a, sizeof( a ), ' ' )
```

fills the array with spaces. A function can have any number of default arguments, but they must all be grouped at the end of the argument list. Whenever there are fewer arguments in a call, the remaining ones are set to the default.

Exercise 3.1.5. Write a function print that prints an integer in a given base between 2 and 36, with a default of base 10. For example, print(10) prints 10 and print(10, 3) prints 31. If the base is > 10, use 0..9A..Z for digits. Be sure to handle negative numbers.

Sometimes functions are very short, and a function call may take more space and time than direct coding. For example, to compute the larger of two integers, one can write

```
int max( int m, int n )
{      return m > n ? m : n;
}

c = max( a, b );
```

or simply

```
c = a > b ? a : b;
```

The first method is definitely slower, but the second one is harder to read. The compiler can be instructed not to generate code for a function call but to replace the function invocation with the actual code by declaring the function `inline`.

```
inline int max( int m, int n )
{      return m > n ? m : n;
}
```

This is fine for functions with very small bodies, but should be avoided otherwise. For all but the shortest functions, it takes more code to do the computation "on the spot" each time a function is invoked rather than having the code occur only once in a true function. This is simply a run-time versus code-size trade-off.

The `inline` attribute is merely a recommendation to the compiler that may be ignored at the compiler's convenience. Many compilers cannot or will not make functions containing loops inline.

C Note

Default arguments and inline expansion are new features of C++. Inline expansion is much safer than preprocessor macros. For example, using the inline function call `max( a[n++], b )` truly computes the maximum of `a[n]` and `b` and increments `n` once. In contrast, the macro

```
#define max( x, y ) ( (x) > (y) ? (x) : (y) )
```

causes computation of the expression `a[n++] > b ? a[n++] : b`, which can increment `n` twice.

The preprocessor simply performs lexical replacement without any knowledge of the language, whereas inline functions are clever enough to replace `c = max(a,b)` with `c = a > b ? a : b` and `c = max( a[n++],b )` with

```
int templ = a[n++]; c = templ > b ? templ : b;
```

On the other hand, the macro is typeless and can compute the maximum of `doubles` as well, whereas the inline function can only handle `ints`.

Exercise 3.1.6. Write an inline version of `toupper`, a function converting lower-case characters to uppercase. Write a program containing 100 calls to `toupper` and a loop that executes them 100 times. Measure how removing the `inline` attribute affects its space and time behavior.

Exercise 3.1.7. If you have a C++ → C translator, look at the code that is generated by an inline `max`. How are tricky situations like `max( a[n++], b )` handled?

3.2. CONTROL FLOW

In C++, each simple statement ends in a `;`. Statements can be grouped together by `{ ... }`. It is our style to have matching braces either on the same line or lined up vertically, as in

```
{       ...;
        ...;
}
```

Other authors follow different conventions. If you are free to choose a style for yourself, observe others and select the method that appeals to you the most.

Pascal Note

The `{ ...}` correspond to Pascal **begin** and **end**. In Pascal, the `;` is a statement separator, not a terminator. That is, the last statement before an **end** does not carry a `;` in Pascal whereas in C++ all statements, including the one just before the `}`, end in a `;`.

The `if` statement has the form

```
if( expression )
    statement
else
    statement
```

The statements can be simple or a sequence of simple statements enclosed in braces. The `else` part can be missing. The *expression* is evaluated, and, if it is non-0, the first statement is executed, otherwise the second. In a situation such as

```
if( ... ) if( ... ) ... else ...
```

the `else` groups with the closest `if`. If the other grouping is desired, braces must be used. However, it seems wise not to rely on readers of your code to remember this and to use braces either way. A common situation is a multiple decision structure like

```
if( ... )
    ...
else if( ... )
    ...
else if( ... )
    ...
else
    ...
```

which performs as expected without requiring braces.

There are two loop formats, one with condition testing at the top

```
while( expression )
    statement
```

and one with testing at the bottom

```
do
    statement
while( expression );
```

You will often encounter loops with empty body. For example,

```
i = j = 0;
while( ( b[j++] = a[i++] ) != '\0' )    // copy the string
                                        // a to b
    ;
```

has no loop body—all the work (copying characters and incrementing indices) is already performed in the termination condition as a side effect of testing for the end of the string. This is quite normal, and it is customary to place the ; on a line by itself to amplify the intent. That way, a ; on the same line as the `while` is sure to arouse suspicion. For example, the code segment

```
while( a[i] != '\0' ) ;        // TYPO
    n = 10 * n + a[i++] - '0';
```

does not do what the indentation level suggests. The ; behind the `while` is the sole body of the `while` loop. Because ; are so frequent in C++, such an error is easily made.

Pascal Note

The `do ... while` loop is very similar to the Pascal `repeat ... until` loop, except that the termination condition is reversed.

C++ has a very general `for` loop facility. The most common form looks like

```
for( i = 0; i < n; i++ )
    a[i] = 0;
```

There are three parts—an initialization, a termination condition, and a reinitialization. The `for` loop

```
for( expression1 ; expression2 ; expression3  )
    statement
```

is completely identical to

```
expression1
while( expression2  )
{      statement
       expression3
}
```

There is no limit to what these expressions are, and it is easy to write inscrutable code like

```
for( r = i = 0; s[i] != '\0'; r += s[ i++ ] - '0' ) r *= 10;
```

This should be discouraged because the sequence in which the instructions are executed is not intuitive. A `while` loop is much clearer:

```
i = r = 0;
while( s[i] != '\0' )
{      r *= 10;
       r += s[ i++ ] - '0';
}
```

I recommend you use "for" loops only when a variable runs from somewhere to somewhere with some constant increment/decrement.

```
for( i = 0; i < N; i += 4 )
     // ...
```

Occasionally, a "for" loop traversing a linked list can be neat and intuitive:

```
for( l = head; l != 0; l = tail( l ) )
     // ...;
```

That is fine—use your judgment and good taste.

Some of the expressions in the `for` header can be missing. If the second expression is missing, it is construed to be always true. In particular, an infinite loop, presumably to be broken by a `return`, can be written as

```
for(;;)
     // loop never terminates
```

Think of it as "forever." If you need to squeeze two unrelated actions into a `for` header expression, you can use the sequencing operator.

```
for( i = j = 0; ( b[i] = a[j] ) != '\0'; i++, j++ )
     ;
```

This could be a signal that a `for` loop may not be the adequate control structure. In that case, rewrite it as a `while`.

Pascal Note

Pascal programmers will particularly welcome the possibility of controlling the step size of a `for` loop. The Pascal **to** and **downto** can be easily realized with `i++` and `i--` in the third slot of `for`, and the more general `for( i = 0; i < N; i += 2 )` has no convenient Pascal counterpart.

Exercise 3.2.1. There are an endless number of C++ puzzles of the form: "What does this `for` loop do?" Describe what the following loops do:

```
for( i = 0, r = a[0]; r = r > a[++i] ? r : a[i]; )
    ;


for( i = c = 0; i < n; c += a[i++] != 0 )
    ;
```

These are fun, but before putting these into your programs, ask yourself whether you want your colleagues to remember you for your clever puzzles or for your well-crafted, readable code.

Finally, there is a multiple branching statement of the form

```
switch( expression )
{   case constant :
        statements
    case constant : case constant :
        statements
    default:
        statements
}
```

If the expression matches the value of one of the constants, execution starts there. If none of the constants match and there is a `default`, execution starts there. If there is no `default`, no action is taken at all. Once started, execution continues, possibly *falling through* one or more `case` labels, until explicitly stopped with a `break` statement or the closing `}` . Here is an example:

```
switch( ch )
{   case '0': case '1':
        x = 2*x + ch - '0';
        break;
    case '\n'
        linecount++;
        // fall through to next case
    case ' ':
```

```
        return( x ); // exit current function
    default:
        cout << "Error"; // print error message
        break;
}
```

A break statement exits the switch; a return statement exits the enclosing function. Each branch of a switch should end in either a break, a return, or an explicit comment // fall through. Strict adherence to this rule makes it easy to flag a forgotten break, a common error.

Pascal Note

It takes some effort to switch from the Pascal case to the C++ switch construct. There are few opportunities for the "fall through" behavior, certainly not enough to compensate for the grief caused by the common error of omitting a break. There is no way of specifying a subrange like case 'A'..'Z', making the switch useless for such a test because the alternative of writing 26 case labels is ridiculous. On the other hand, a default clause is supported. It is obviously useful, but missing from standard Pascal. It is present in many actual Pascal implementations as **else** or **otherwise**.

Exercise 3.2.2. Write a function that uses a switch with fall-through in a useful and realistic way.

C++ also has three forms of nonlinear flow control. break can be used inside while, do, and for loops to exit the innermost enclosing loop. This is completely analogous to the break action inside a switch statement. A continue statement causes the next iteration of the innermost enclosing while, do, or for. Finally, goto label jumps to label:which must be in the same function. We recommend against using these constructs. It is just too difficult to understand code behavior if one cannot easily answer the question "How did the program get to this spot?" The goto statement is not completely useless—it sometimes occurs in programs written by other programs.

3.3. VARIABLES

Variables can be declared *anywhere* inside a function. Their *scope* ranges from the point of declaration to the end of the enclosing block. It is good programming practice to declare variables at the time they are first needed and initialize them at the same time. This minimizes problems with forgotten initializations. It is even possible to declare a variable in the header of a for loop, such as

```
for( int i = 0; i < 10; i++ ) ...
```

This is completely equivalent to

```
int i = 0;
for( ; i < 10; i++ ) ...
```

and i is known until the end of the block enclosing the `for`.

Normally, variables are allocated on a run-time stack. Whenever a block is left, all variables that are local to that block are forgotten and the space they occupied on the stack will soon be reused by other variables. Such variables are called *automatic*. They get created and reinitialized every time their scope is entered and forgotten whenever their scope is left. For example, the variable j in

```
for( int i = 0; i < 10; i++ )
{    int j = i;
     ...
}
```

is created and initialized 10 times, once at each loop entry, and forgotten at each loop end.

The function arguments are automatic variables as well, initialized by the values passed to the function in the call. In fact, the only difference between them and other variables is initialization. In all other aspects, they are ordinary variables whose scope extends until the end of the function. They can be modified in any way. On function exit, their values are forgotten.

Sometimes it is not desirable to have the value of a variable forgotten at function exit. Declaring a variable as `static` makes it persistent. When the function is reentered, the old value is still there. For example,

```
void getword( char buffer[], int buflen )
{    static int linecount = 0;
     int ch;

     cin.get( ch );
     if( ch == '\n' ) linecount++
     ...
}
```

The `linecount` variable is initialized only *once*, at the beginning of the program (before main starts). Thereafter, it is incremented inside `getword`, and its value is retained whenever `getword` exits. Of course, the scope of the variable is still the `getword` function. It is inaccessible from outside. Applying the `static` attribute to a local variable changes its lifetime but not its scope.

In recursively called functions, there can be multiple copies of the same automatic variable in existence, one for each invocation. But there is only one copy of each static variable, shared by all invocations.

Variables declared outside functions are accessible to all functions from the declaration on until the end of the file. Such variables are called *global*.

They can be initialized as well, and initialization takes place before `main` starts. It is good programming practice to minimize the number of global variables. Global variables are error-prone because they can be modified by many functions and it can be difficult to find the culprit if a global variable has been set to an improper value.

Static variables (all globals and `static` locals) that are not explicitly initialized are guaranteed to be filled with 0. Automatic variables without explicit initialization are guaranteed to be filled with garbage (whichever value happened to be on the stack when their space is allocated there).

To summarize, variables have two distinct attributes, their *scope* and their *lifetime*. Automatic variables get created whenever their scope is entered, forgotten when it is left. They always have local scope. Static variables get created once before the start of `main`. They can have local or file scope. Any variable can be initialized at its time of creation.

Exercise 3.3.1. `static` local variables are uncommon because it is not possible to reset their value from outside. Here is an example of the problem, a recursive program for counting the number of nodes of a binary tree.

```
int countNodes( Tree t )
{   static int count = 0; // shared by all recursive
                          // invocations

    if( t != 0 ) // not the null pointer
    {   count++; // found a node
        countNodes( t->left ); // do the same with both
                               // subtrees
        countNodes( t->right );
    }
    return count;
}
```

Explain why this function is not useful.

Exercise 3.3.2. Give a useful example of a function with a `static` local variable.

Exercise 3.3.3. Explain the difference between

```
void main()
{   int a[100];
    // ...
}
```

and

```
void main()
{   static int a[100];
```

```
        // ...
}
```

3.4. PITFALLS

3.4.1. `return` Returns Immediately

Pascal programmers often make the mistake of equating *functionName := value* and `return( value )`. For example, suppose your job is to write a function

```
int reverse( char s[] )
```

that reverses a string and returns the number of characters in the string.

```
{       int n = 0;
        while( s[n] != 0 ) n++; // find end of string
        // now n = #characters in s
        return( n ); // WRONG--returns immediately
        for( int i = 0, int j = n - 1; i < j; i++, j-- )
        {       char temp = s[i]; // swap s[i] and s[j]
                s[i] = s[j];
                s[j] = temp;
        }
}
```

The `return(n)` statement should be moved to the end of the function.

3.4.2. Functions Cannot Modify Arguments

The arguments of a function are local variables, initialized with the values used in the call. Any modifications affect the local copies only and do not propagate back to the caller.

```
int vscan( char s[], int v ) // WRONG
// return length of string, compute #vowels in v
{       int i = 0;
        v = 0;
        while( s[i] != 0 )
        {       char ch = tolower( s[i] );
                if( ch == 'a' || ch == 'e' || ch == 'i' ||
                    ch == 'o' || ch == 'u' ) v++;
                i++;
        }
        return i;
}

nchars = vscan( "Hello", nvowels ); // nvowels not set to 2
```

To have a function modify a value, use pointers (see Chapter 4) or references. References are easier.

```
int vscan( char s[], int& v ) // OK
```

3.4.3. Omitting ( )

Some functions take no arguments, for example, the random number generator `rand`. Contrary to Pascal, the `()` must nevertheless be supplied in the call.

```
n = rand(); // OK
```

Unfortunately,

```
n = rand; // WRONG
```

will be flagged by some compilers as a warning, not an error, because it has a legal meaning. `rand` without the `()` denotes the starting address of the `rand` function, which is a number (although not an integer). The compiler may generate code to force that number into an integer. Always pay attention to compiler warnings and treat them just as seriously as errors.

3.4.4. Missing `return` Values

It is easy to forget a `return` at the end of a function.

```
int pow( int a, int n )
{       r = 1;
        if( n >= 0 )
        {       for( int i = 1; i <= n; i++ )
                        r *= a;
                return( r );
        }
        // no return value for n < 0;
}
```

A random value will be returned for n < 0.

Exercise 3.4.1. What value should be returned? Note that a and the return value are `int`.

3.4.5. Mismatched Arguments

Be extremely careful when using a function that is only known to the compiler as `f( ... )`, for example,

```
char* form( char*, ... ); // section 8.3
```

The compiler cannot check the arguments at compile-time, or perform conversions, and you are responsible for *exactly* matching the types. For example,

```
int n = 2;
cout << form( "%8.2f", n ); // WRONG--won't print     2.00
```

It will print something, because the function has no way of checking the type of a bit pattern on the stack at run-time. It will just take what it finds and print it as a **double**.

3.4.6. Misplacing **;**

There are so many semicolons in C++ code that it is easy to add one accidentally at the end of an **if**, **for**, or **while** statement:

```
for( i = 0, j = n - 1; i < j; i++, j-- ) ; // WRONG
{    char temp = a[i]; // swap a[i] and a[j]
     a[i] = a[j];
     a[j] = temp;
}
```

The **for** loop has an empty body and will be executed until i $\geq$ j. Then the code inside the { } block is executed only once.

These are mean bugs that can be very hard to detect. We recommend *never* to place a **;** in the same line as a **for** or **while**, even if the loop body is empty on purpose

```
while( ( ch = s[i++] ) != 0 && ( s += ch == ' ' ) < 10 )
     ; // place on separate line
```

3.4.7. Omitting **break** in a **switch**

It is easy to omit a **break** in a **switch** statement accidentally.

```
switch( ch )
{    case '+': sign = 1;       // WRONG--no break
     case '-': sign = -1;
     default: cin.putback( ch );
}
```

If ch is '+', execution starts at sign = 1 and continues until the next **break** or the end of the **switch** block. The lines sign = -1 and cin.putback(ch) are executed!

Always end each branch of a switch with a **break**, **return**, or an explicit **// FALL** comment, even the last one! One day, someone will add another branch beyond it.

POINTERS, ARRAYS, AND REFERENCES

4.1. POINTERS ARE ADDRESSES

Pointers are a central and rather technical concept of C++. The declaration

```
int* p;
```

declares a variable p that can contain the address of an integer. Then *p is the integer whose address is stored in p. For example:

```
int n = 5;
p = &n;      // store the address of n in p
*p += 2;     // increment n by 2
```

Here & is the address operator that yields the memory location of a variable. It is not too common to have a pointer to a single integer. More often, a pointer points to a variable in an array, for example,

```
int a[10];   // an array of 10 integers;

p = &a[0];   // store the address of the 0 location of a in p
*p = 5;      // and store a 5 into the 0 location
p++;         // now p points to the next location in the
             // array
```

If a pointer points into an array, one can move it to other memory locations in that array by adding or subtracting integer values. This *pointer arithmetic* takes into account the sizes of objects pointed at. Adding 1 to an `int*` actually adds `sizeof( int )` to the address, adding 1 to a `double*` increments it by `sizeof( double )` instead. In general, if p,q are pointers to a type X (i.e., p,q are of type X*), it is legal to add or subtract an integer and to compute the pointer difference: $p + n$ is the address of the nth X away from *p, and $q - p$ is an integer denoting how many Xs are between *p and *q . (This makes sense only if p and q point to the same array.) The arithmetic is simply address computation, scaled by `sizeof( X )`.

By the way, note that `sizeof( int* )` is the same as `sizeof( double* )` because both an `int*` and a `double*` hold a memory address. Generally, all pointer variables have the same size. (Actually, this is not always true. Depending on the processor and the selected memory model, some classes of pointer variables might be larger than others.) No assumption should be made whether `sizeof(X*)` equals the size of some basic type.

In pointer declarations, we like to group the `*` with the type name: `int* p`. This appears to declare an object `p` to be of type `int*`. However, this does not accurately reflect the compiler's point of view. The compiler groups the `*` with the variable name: `int *p`. This declares "p is an object whose `*` is an `int`". (White space is completely ignored by the compiler, except when necessary to separate tokens—`int*p` and `int * p` would be legal, too.)

If you decide to follow my convention for placement of the `*`, be careful not to declare two pointers in the same line! The declaration

```
int* p,q;
```

does *not* declare two pointers `p` and `q`, but one pointer `p` and one *integer* `q`. The `*` really groups with the `p`, not with the `int`. It is correct to declare

```
int *p, *q;
```

But we prefer to use two lines and declare the pointers separately:

```
int* p;
int* q;
```

The keyword `const` also interacts strangely with pointer declarations:

```
const int* p;
```

declares a pointer to a `const int`, not a constant `int*`. That means it is okay to look at `*p` but not to modify it. `*p = 0` is an error. Because `p` is not a constant, `p++` is legal and makes `p` point to the next `const int`. To declare a pointer that is itself constant, place the `const` next to the pointer name:

```
char* const q = "Version 12.3d";
```

This means that `q` may not be modified in any way, but the character it points to may be. Of course, both may be held unchangeable:

```
const char* const r = "Version 12.3d";
```

means that neither `r` nor `*r` may be changed. The most frequent case is the first one. For example, the function

```
int max( const int* p, int n )
```

receives a pointer to an integer (and more integers following that one, `n` in all). The function may not touch the integers, only look at them. But `p` may change; for example, repeated execution of `p++` makes `p` traverse the array.

Pascal Note

Pointers do occur in Pascal, and they are dereferenced with the ^ operator rather than *. In Pascal, there is no concept of pointer arithmetic. The only legal operation on a Pascal pointer is to dereference it. Pascal does not have an address operator either. The only way of obtaining a memory address is from the heap via **new**.

Pascal pointer variable declarations cleanly separate the type name from the variable name.

Exercise 4.1.1. Find out what `sizeof( X* )` is on your system. Does your compiler have different "memory models"? If so, find the size of a pointer in each one of them.

Exercise 4.1.2. Pointers are addresses, that is, numbers. You can print out the value of a pointer, simply as `cin << int( p )` (or `long( p )`). Write a program to compare p,p+1 and q,q+1, where p is an `int*` and q a `double*`.

4.2. ARRAYS AND POINTERS

There is an intimate connection between arrays and pointers in C++. When declaring an array, for example,

```
int a[10];
```

the name of the array a denotes a pointer (constant), namely the address of the 0 element of the array. Similarly, a+1 is the address of the next array element. *(a+1) is the integer stored at that location, a value customarily referred to as a[1]. In fact, the C++ compiler always translates all array references a[n] into the pointer computation *(a+n). Conversely, if p is a pointer variable, for example,

```
int* p = a+3; // p points to the 3 location in a
```

p[4] is legal, and it means simply *(p+4), that is, the contents of 4 integers away from p, or a[7] . Under all circumstances it is true that for all pointers p and all integers n,

$$\boxed{\text{p[n] equals *(p + n)}}$$

This is the *universal array-pointer law*.

To summarize, if we declare an array of objects of type **X**,

```
X a[ N ];
```

then `sizeof( a ) = N · sizeof( X )`. From the declaration, it is apparent that the type of a is `int[N]`, but if it is used in any expression except `sizeof` (which is computed at compile-time), a is converted to type `X*` (or more precisely, `X* const`). All uses of a, such as computing `a[n]`, are simply pointer arithmetic, via the universal array-pointer law. By the way, all C++ arrays start at zero to make the pointer arithmetic work.

Pascal Note

In C++, all array expressions become pointer expressions. In particular, the size of the array is ignored. Contrast this with Pascal, which suffers from the problem of having *too many* array types. When you declare an array, you must specify the lower and upper bounds, and these are inextricably tied to the type. You can write a sort routine that sorts arrays of type **array [1..20] of int,** but that routine cannot sort an array with 21 elements, or even an array with 20 elements numbered from 0 through 19.

Let us write a function that finds the largest number in an array of integers. The call

```
max( a, 10 );      // find the max of an array with
                   // 10 elements
```

computes the maximum of

```
int a[10].
```

The function should expect to receive an `int*` and an `int`:

```
int max( const int* p, int n )
```

This declares two local variables: p, which is initialized with the starting address of the array; and n, which is initialized with the number of elements. Note that the array is not copied into the function; merely its starting address is passed to the pointer variable p. To refer to the ith element of the array, we can nevertheless use the notation `p[i]`, as if there was an actual array passed to `max`. Recall that `p[i]` is `*(p+i)`, the contents of the memory location obtained by adding the size of i integers to the address stored in p.

In fact, there is another style of declaring a pointer argument that is permissible only in a function declaration:

```
int max( const int p[], int n )
```

This gives the illusion that p is an (open-ended) array. In fact, the array has not been copied, no large amount of space has been allocated, p is still an `int*`, and `sizeof(p) = sizeof( int* )`. There is no difference between an argument `int p[]` and `int* p`, just as there is no difference between `p[n]` and `*(p+n)`.

This empty-bracket notation has *no* relationship with an earlier use of empty brackets. At that time, we saw array declarations with an initializer that enables the compiler to count the elements.

```
int a[] = { 1, 1, 2, 3, 5 };
```

which is a convenient shorthand for

```
int a[5] = { 1, 1, 2, 3, 5 };
```

and really allocates 5 `sizeof( int )`'s worth of storage. Similarly,

```
char s[] = "Harry";
```

declares an array of 6 characters, not a pointer variable. However,

```
char* p = "Harry";
```

does declare a pointer variable and allocates 6 characters somewhere else, initializing p with the starting location of these characters.

Let us have a look at two distinct ways of writing the `max` function:

```
int max( const int p[], int n )
{    int m = p[0];
     int i = 0;

     while( ++i < n )
          if( m < p[i] ) m = p[i];
     return( m );
}
```

This is an obvious and easily understood solution. The `p[i]` are actually pointer computations, but the convenient `[ ]` notation hides that. Another possible solution makes use of the fact that p is a local pointer variable, and we can modify it.

```
int max( const int* p, int n )
{    int m = *p;

     while( --n > 0 )
     {    p++;
          if( m < *p ) m = *p;
     }
     return( m );
}
```

The pointer p steps through the array one by one.

In these solutions we have chosen the `int [ ]` notation in the declaration of the version using `p[i]` in the body and the `int*` notation in the declaration of the version with `*p` in the body. This was dictated merely by good taste, not by any requirement of the language. It is permissible to switch freely between the [ ] and the * notation at any time. The programmer should choose the notation that makes the code most readable.

Exercise 4.2.1. Write a function that computes the average value of an array of integers.

```
double average( double* a, int n )
```

Use pointers, with the pointer variable a traversing the array.

Exercise 4.2.2. Write a program that prints sizeof(a) in the following two situations:

```
int f( int a[], int n );
int a[] = { 1, 1, 2, 3, 5 };
```

4.3. STRING FUNCTIONS

To illustrate some pointer techniques, we will consider strings. (This section can be skipped if you are familiar with C-style string-handling functions.) *Strings* are arrays of characters, terminated by a zero byte. Here is a string and a buffer capable of holding a string:

```
char s[] = "Harry";      // same as s[6] = ...
char buffer[10];
```

Let us start with an easy function. strlen computes the string length, the number of nonzero characters in a string.

```
int strlen( const char* p )
{     int n = 0;
      while( *p++ != '\0' )
            n++;
      return n;
}
```

For example, strlen(s) is 5. The pointer p gets initialized with the starting address of the string. Inside the loop header, the curious expression *p++ is executed. Looking at the operator precedence table, we find that * and ++ have the same precedence and are executed right to left. p++ is executed first, incrementing p. But the *value* of p++ is the old value of p, before the increment. And to this value the * operator is applied, resulting in the contents of the old p location. As long as that contents is not zero, we are not yet at the end of the string and n is incremented. Once the terminating zero is encountered, we leave the function.

Note how the argument p was treated like an ordinary variable that happened to be initialized with the starting address of the string in the function call.

To copy s into `buffer`, one cannot simply write

```
buffer = s; // WRONG
```

and a moment's reflection on the material of the previous section will show why. `buffer` and `s`, written without the [ ], are pointers, pointing to the starting addresses of the array. In particular, `buffer` is a constant (because the array is at some fixed location) and cannot be modified. The foregoing statement is the pointer equivalent of attempting an assignment 10 = 6. It simply is not possible to modify the value of the pointer constant `buffer`.

Of course, what we really want to do is to copy the contents. Another function must be provided for this purpose.

```
char* strcpy( char* to, const char* from )
{      char* r = to;
       while( ( *to++ = *from++ ) != '\0' )
            ;
       return r;
}
```

Calling `strcpy( buffer, s )` performs the string copy. In this function, both the pointers `from` and `to` traverse the character arrays. The `*to++ = *from++` assignment increments `to` and `from`, but the `*` is applied to the values of those increment operators, that is, to the pointer values before increment. And the contents of the old `from` address gets copied to the old `to` address. As long as the value of the assignment is not zero, this process is repeated.

All the work is being performed simultaneously with the test for completion in the loop header, and the loop body is empty. Because any nonzero value is considered true, it is even possible to write

```
while( *to++ = *from++ )
     ;
```

Of course, the = really is assignment, not test for equality, and the loop continues until a zero is assigned.

The function returns the original address of `to`. That seems unnecessary; after all, the caller of `strcpy` supplied that value and will not need it back. But it is convenient for nesting calls, such as

```
n = strlen( strcpy( buffer, s ) );
```

To concatenate two strings, the + operator cannot be used. Again, we need a function. The `strcat` function appends t to s.

```
char* strcat( char* s, const char* t )
{      char* r = s;

       while( *s ) s++;   // go to the end of the first string
       while( *s++ = *t++ )
            ;              // copy
```

```
        return r;
    }
```

Why not simply while(*s++) ; to go to the end of s? The ++ is executed regardless of whether the loop test is true or false. When s points to the terminating zero of the first string, *s++ will be zero, but s now points one character beyond the zero. Because we want the zero to be overwritten with the first character in t, we would then have to move s back with an additional s--.

Both for strcpy and strcat, there is no check whatsoever for overrunning the space in the first array. The functions merely receive pointers to the character arrays to be filled, which give no indication of their size. Only the size of an already existing string can be determined by the location of the zero terminator. If a long string is copied into a buffer with not enough space, adjacent memory locations will be overwritten.

```
char buffer[10];
char s[] = " Harry";
char t[] = " Hacker";
strcpy( buffer, s );   // OK
strcat( buffer, t );   // WRONG--buffer can only hold
                       // 10 chars
```

The following is worse:

```
char* p;
strcpy( p, s );        // WRONG--memory will be overwritten
```

This causes placement of a copy of s into whatever area in memory p happens to point to, simply overwriting the previous contents of those memory cells. How could it do anything else? p itself is quite small, only 2 or 4 bytes, and cannot itself hold all the characters from the string s. And memory does not come for free. However, this is fine:

```
char* p;
p = buffer;            // p points to buffer
strcpy( p, s );        // places a copy of s in buffer
```

When writing down a string such as "Harry", that too has a value (like most things in C++). The value is the starting address of the string that has been placed somewhere in memory. For example, the call

```
strcpy( buffer, "Harry" )
```

causes the string "Harry" to be allocated somewhere in memory, and its starting address is given to strcpy. Note the difference between

```
char s[] = "Harry";
```

and

```
char* p = "Harry";
```

The first declares s to be an array with six characters. The second declares p to be a pointer variable; in addition, it allocates six characters somewhere and places the location into p. s will always denote the address of the same block. p can be changed simply by assigning it another address.

Exercise 4.3.1. Write a function char* strchr(const char* s, char c) that returns a pointer to the first occurrence of c in s, 0 if none is found. Use pointers, not arrays.

Note: In conformance with the standard C string library, the function receives a const char* (because one might be passed to it) and returns a char* (because it might be used to modify the string). You will need to cast the return value. Ideally there should be two functions

```
const char* strchr( const char* s, char c )
```

and

```
char* strchr( char* s, char c ).
```

Exercise 4.3.2. Write a function char* strstr(const char* s, const char* t)that returns a pointer to the first occurrence of the string t in s, 0 if none is found. Use pointers, not arrays.

Exercise 4.3.3. Write a function unsigned strspn(const char* s, const char* t) that returns the length of the prefix of s consisting of characters in t. Use pointers, not arrays.

Exercise 4.3.4. Write a function void reverse(char* s) that reverses a character string (e.g., "Harry" becomes "yrraH").

Strings cannot be compared lexicographically with the standard relational operators.

```
if( s == "Harry" ) ...
```

tests whether the *starting address* of s is the same as the starting address of a freshly allocated string "Harry". It certainly is not. The function strcmp compares two strings. It returns some negative number if the first string comes before the second, zero if they are identical, and some positive number otherwise.

```
int strcmp( const char* s, const char* t )
{    while( *s && *s == *t ) { s++; t++; }
     return int(*s) - int(*t);
}
```

The cast to int is necessary because char is unsigned in some implementations. For example, strcmp("Harry", "Hong") returns int('a')-

int('o'), a negative number, because the strings differ at that position for the first time.

Exercise 4.3.5. Write a function strncmp(const char*, const char*, int n) that compares two strings but only looks at the first n characters.

Exercise 4.3.6. Write a function strncpy(char*, const char*, int n) that copies the second string into the first but copies at most n characters. If the second string is longer than that, there will not be a terminating 0.

Suppose you need to convert a string containing digits only (such as "159") into its numerical equivalent (the integer 159). The following does not work:

```
char a[4] = "159";
int n = int( a ); // WRONG
```

This code takes the starting address of the array a, interprets that number as an int, and places it in n. Instead, the library function atoi ("ASCII to integer") can be used:

```
int n = atoi( a ); // OK
```

atoi takes any string and computes the decimal equivalent. Conversion stops when the first nondigit (not necessarily the zero terminator) is encountered.

```
int atoi( char* s )
{       int r = 0;
        while( '0' <= *s && *s <= '9' )
            r = 10*r + *s++ - '0';
        return r;
}
```

The functions introduced in this section are part of the standard string library. To use them in your program, you need not retype them. Just place the line

```
#include <string.h>
```

in the top of your program file. atoi is declared in stdlib.h.

4.4. REFERENCES

References were briefly introduced in Chapter 3 as a way of implementing reference (Pascal **var**) parameters. If a function modifies regular arguments, the modification extends to the local copy only and is not communicated back to the variables in the function call. If modification of a variable in the function call is desired, reference arguments should be used. This situation frequently arises when a function computes two values simultaneously. Consider a function computing the mean

$$\bar{x} = \frac{1}{n} \sum x_i$$

and standard deviation

$$\sigma = \sqrt{\frac{\sum x_i^2 - \frac{1}{n}(\sum x_i)^2}{n}}$$

of a set of data $x_1 \ldots x_n$.

```
void parameters( double x[], int n, double& mean,
                                          double& std )
{    double sum = 0, squaresum = 0;

    for( int i = 0; i < n; i++ )
    {   sum += x[i];
        squaresum += x[i]*x[i];
    }
    if( n > 0 )
    {   mean = sum/n;
        std = sqrt( ( squaresum - sum*sum/n ) / n );
    }
}
```

When called with

```
const int NSTUDENT = 35;
double classgrades[ NSTUDENT ], m, s;

// ...

parameters( classgrades, NSTUDENT, m, s );
```

the mean and standard deviation are deposited into m and s.

Behind the scenes, all references are translated to pointers, according to the following two rules:

- Whenever a reference variable p is used, replace p by *p.
- Whenever a reference variable is initialized with a, replace a by &a.

Initialization can occur directly through a reference declaration

```
double& p = m;        // really means double* p = &m;
```

Much more frequently, though, function arguments are initialized through call values. For example, the function `parameters` is translated to

```
void parameters( double x[], int n, double* mean,
                                     double* std )
{    //...

    if( n > 0 )
    {    *mean = sum/n;
         *std = sqrt( ( squaresum - sum*sum/n ) / n );
    }

}
```

and *each* call to `parameters` is modified by adding & operators:

```
parameters( classgrades, NSTUDENT, &m, &s );
```

The function actually receives the addresses of m, s and places the values directly into those addresses (*mean = sum/n . . .).

References are a convenience. It is easier to use a reference argument than a pointer argument because the compiler automatically supplies the necessary & and *. You do not even have to be conscious of this process when using references simply to implement Pascal-style `var` parameters. On the other hand, many C++ programs use references in other ways for which it is helpful to understand the precise mechanism.

Not only can functions take reference arguments, they can *return* a reference! To give a realistic example, consider the problem of efficiently storing the values of a sparse matrix, a matrix whose entries are mostly zero. In particular, we will consider square matrices of the form

with zero entries except for the main diagonal and the diagonal above (e.g., Jordan canonical forms). To store a 10×10 matrix of this shape, it would be wasteful to allocate 100 `doubles`, most of them 0. It suffices to store the 19 values on the diagonals. A simple function `elem` can be written to access the $(i,j)^{th}$ element:

```
double diag[10];
double above[9];

double elem( int i, int j )
{    if( i == j ) return( diag[i] );
     else if( i+1 == j ) return( above [i] );
     else return 0;
}
```

Although `elem( i, j )` reports the matrix entry at that location, a different function must be written to change an entry. However, modifying `elem` to return a reference makes it possible to write:

```
elem( 2, 3 ) = 3.14;
```

The `elem` function needs to be rewritten:

```
double& elem( int i, int j )
{    if( i == j ) return( diag[i] );
     else if( i+1 == j ) return( above [i] );
     else // ...
}
```

Because the function returns a `double&` , it actually returns the address of `above[2]` (and not the value stored there). In each function call, a `*` is supplied.

> `* (returned pointer)` = `3.14`;

The `*` is also supplied when the function value occurs on the right side of an =. Consider

```
x = elem( 2, 3 );
```

Again, `elem( 2, 3 )` returns a pointer, and the assignment sets

> `x` = `*` *(returned pointer)*

In the `elem` function, we have left open the case of accessing a 0 element ($j \neq i, i + 1$). What is wrong with returning 0?

```
double& elem( int i, int j )
{    // ..
     else return 0;
}
```

Recall that the function actually returns an address. It must therefore create a `double`, place 0 in it, and return the address of that `double`. However, the storage for the 0 will be allocated on the stack of `elem`. Being a local variable of that function, it no longer exists after `elem` returns. Using that value—or, worse, writing to it,—can cause disaster. Instead, we will explicitly allocate a variable `zero` and return a reference to it:

```
double zero = 0;

double& elem( int i, int j )
{    // ..
     else
     {    if( zero != 0 )
          { warn( "Illegal access occurred previously" );
```

```
            zero = 0;
        }
        return zero;
    }
}
```

We check whether `zero` is 0 every time because it might have been changed by an (illegal) call such as `elem(4,1) = 3.14`. Unfortunately, `elem` does not know whether it is called on the left or right side of an =, and it cannot report an error when a 0 element is being modified.

Exercise 4.4.1. Model a triangular matrix containing elements a_{ij} for $i \geq j$ only. Store them in a linear array, in a sequence $a_{00}\ a_{10}\ a_{11}\ a_{20}\ a_{21}\ a_{22}\ldots$ and write an `elem` access function. Test your code by computing the Pascal triangle:

```
for( i = 0; i < n; i++ )
for( j = 0; j <= i; j++ )
    elem(i,j) = j == 0 || j == i ? 1 :
    elem(i-1,j-1) + elem (i-1,j);
```

Exercise 4.4.2 Implement an *associative array* that can store pairs of floating-point numbers, for example,

Key	Value
4.0	1
3.7	2
3.3	2
3.0	5
. . .	

such that `assoc( 3.3 )` returns 2, and `assoc( 3.3 )++` increments the entry to 3. Store the keys and values in parallel arrays of `double` and have `assoc` return the appropriate reference in the value array. If a new entry is referenced (e.g., `assoc( 3.8 )`), append it to the key list and set its corresponding value to 0.

Exercise 4.4.3. The most common use for references is the implementation of "var" parameters. We know that all array parameters are "var" anyway. Explain what happens if such a parameter is declared as a reference argument, such as

```
void reverse( char*& s )
```

Explain the meaning of

```
void reverse( char& s[] )
```

4.5. PITFALLS

4.5.1. Copying Without Allocating Storage

This is the most common beginner's bug:

```
char* p;
strcpy( p, "Harry" );
```

There is no syntax error. `strcpy` expects two `char*`. However, where is the string copied to? The declaration `char* p` allocates a variable `p`. It can hold an address and is not initialized. It points to a random location in memory. The string `"Harry"` is copied to that random location, overwriting whatever was there before.

There is an easy method to avoid this bug. Whenever declaring anything, ask yourself: What is `sizeof(...)`? `sizeof( p )` is 2 or 4 bytes on most systems. There is *no way* that a 6-byte string can be placed into it. In C++, storage is never allocated automatically. (This does not mean that a very short string of 2 or 4 bytes might be profitably stored in a pointer variable. The point is that a pointer variable has a fixed small size, and that string storage is variable and potentially large.)

Exercise 4.5.1. Find out the sizes of the most common types (`char`, `int`, `char*`, `double`, etc.) on your system. Just write a program containing commands `cout` ≪ `sizeof( char* )`.

4.5.2. Different Levels of Indirection

Unfortunately, some compilers flag mixing pointers and integers as a warning, not as an error.

```
int* p;
int n = 10;

p = n; // WRONG--should have been p = &n
```

Take these warnings very seriously!

The same applies for mixing pointers of different types. If you did indeed intend to perform the conversion, use a cast.

```
int e;

char* p = &e; // BAD
char* p = (char*)(&e); // MAYBE
```

4.5.3. Pointing to Data that No Longer Exists

Never have a function return a pointer or reference to a local object!

```
char* num2str( int n ) // number to string conversion
{    char buffer[ 10 ];

    // compute answer in buffer

    return buffer; // WRONG
}
```

The storage space for `buffer` is forgotten and overwritten with other information when `itoa` exits. The same holds for references.

```
double& elem( int i, int j )
{    double r = 0;

    // compute answer in r

    return r; // WRONG
}
```

If the function were to return a `double` instead of a `double&`, there would be no problem.

There are three remedies for this problem:

- Return a pointer to a static object (Section 3.3).
- Return a pointer to an object on the free store (Section 10.1).
- Have the caller pass a pointer or reference to storage for the result (`num2str( int, char* )`).

4.5.4. Forgetting a String Terminator

All C++ string-handling functions expect a string to be terminated with a zero byte. If it is not, the functions will continue searching through memory until a byte that happens to be zero is encountered.

```
char buffer[80];
for( int i = 0; i < 80; i++ ) buffer[i] = '-';
cout << buffer;
    // WRONG--prints 80 dashes + random characters
```

4.5.5. Using Omniscient `sizeof`

If a is an array, declared as

```
int a[5];
```

or

```
int a[] = { 0, 1, 4, 9, 16 };
    // size determined by counting initializers
```

then `sizeof( a )` measures the number of bytes in a: 5 · `sizeof( int )`.
One might well wonder why a function operating on arrays cannot use the
`sizeof` operator to determine the size of the array passed to it:

```
int max( const int p[] )
{     int m = p[0];
      int i = 0;

      while( ++i < sizeof( p ) ) // WRONG
            if( m < p[i] ) m = p[i];
            return( m );
}
```

Here, `sizeof( p )` does *not* obtain the size of the array passed to the function (which after all is neither a constant value, known at compile time, nor
available at run time, as it is not stored with the array). It obtains the size
of the pointer variable p (which is initialized with the starting address of the
array passed to the function).

It is necessary to supply a second parameter `size` to the `max` function.
The function can be called with

```
max( a, sizeof( a )/sizeof( int ) )
```

because the compiler can compute `sizeof( a )` at compile time.

CHAPTER 5

STRUCTURED TYPES

5.1. STRUCTURES

An array collects objects of the same type, whereas a structure collects objects of different types. Here is the classic example:

```
struct Employee
{    char name[30];
     int age;
     double salary;
     char ssNum[12];
};
```

This structure defines a new type Employee, with *members* name, age, salary, and ssNum. Individual employees can be obtained by

```
Employee harry = { "Harry Hacker", 20, 34500,
                                    "000-00-0123" } ;
```

and members can be accessed with the . operator:

```
if( harry.age < 21 ) ...;
```

Structures can be assigned.

```
Employee staff[100];
staff[ i ] = harry;
```

This makes a copy of all members of the structure. We call such a copy a *memberwise copy*.

Structures can be passed to functions as arguments, and they can be returned as function values. For example, if a Date structure is defined as

```
struct Date
{    int day, month, year;
};
```

we can (with sufficient patience and observance of the variable number of days per month and leap years) write functions

```
int daysBetween( Date d1, Date d2 );
     // returns the number of days between d1, d2.

Date daysFrom( int n, Date d );
     // returns the date n days from d.
```

Pascal Note

Structures are called records in Pascal. Returning a record from a function is not possible in Pascal.

C Note

In C++, the `struct` keyword may be dropped when using the structure name as a type. In C, a new employee must be declared as `struct Employee harry;` or a new type must be produced with `typedef`. Structure assignment, passing structures to functions, and returning structure values is defined in the ANSI standard but is missing from some pre-ANSI compilers.

When passing a structure into a function, the argument is a local variable of that function that gets initialized with a memberwise copy of the calling value. When returning a structure with a `return( r )` statement (where r is a structure variable in the scope of the function), a memberwise copy of r is placed into a temporary location. These memberwise copies take time, especially for large structures. Therefore, it can be preferable to pass a (constant) reference:

```
void addDays( const Date& d, int n )
{     // ...
      if( isleap( d.year ) )  // access member via . operator
      // ...
}
```

Because of the `const`, the function cannot modify the date. But the function receives a pointer to the argument, not the argument itself. (As explained in Section 4.4, the compiler generates code to supply a & in each call and *s in the body of the function.) The time-consuming copying of all members into a local variable is avoided.

Or, the function can be defined to receive the address of the structure explicitly:

```
void addDays( Date* d, int n )
{     // ...
      if( isleap( d->year ) )  // access member via ->
                               // operator
      // ...
}
```

Then it must be called as

```
addDays( &d, n );
```

The expression d->year is merely an abbreviation for (*d).year. (The ()
around *d are necessary because . binds stronger than *.) The -> operator
was introduced because the construct "take the member of a pointer to a
structure" is so common, and the parentheses are awkward.

Pascal Note

In Pascal, there is no special -> operator. The pointer dereferencing operator comes *behind* the pointer, and one simply writes *d*^.**days**.

Different structures can have members with the same name. For example, another structure can have a year member, and there can even be a
global year variable. The compiler can tell the difference simply by looking
left of the . or -> operator.

Exercise 5.1.1. Implement the addDays and daysBetween functions. Pass the
Date arguments as const Date &.

Exercise 5.1.2. Write a function readEmployee that reads an employee record
from a text file in the format.

```
Harry Hacker    20   34500   000-00-0123
Joe M. Conrad   49   84000   363-30-6330
...
```

Hint: Read one line of input with the command

```
char line[200],ch;
//...
cin.get( line, sizeof( line ) );
cin.get( ch ); // read off terminating '\n'
```

where line is an array of char. The last three items (separated by spaces)
are age, salary, and social security number. Everything before that must
be the name. Transfer the information into a variable of type Employee
(using atoi and atof to convert the digit strings to numbers) and return
it.

Exercise 5.1.3. Write a program that reads in a list of employees, as in the
previous exercise, places them into an Employee[] array, and prints out the
information of the employees with the highest, lowest, and median ages and
salaries.

5.2. MEMBER FUNCTIONS

In addition to data members, structures can have function members.

```
struct Date
{    int day, month, year;
     void print();
     void advance( int );
     Date add( int );
     long diff( Date );
};

void Date::print()
{    cout << month << "/" << day << "/" year;
}

Date bday = { 16, 6, 1959 };

bday.print();
```

The `Date::` in the function definition indicates that the member `print` of the `Date` structure is being defined. Other structures could also have a `print` function. Within the definition of `print`, the data member names are used without a variable and without . or -> preceding them. The member names refer to the variable in front of the . in the function call `bday.print()`. This is called the *implicit argument* of the function. Each member function has at least one argument, the implicit argument. It may have explicit arguments as well, like the `advance` function in the foregoing structure definition. To add a number of days to a date `d`, the function call is

```
d.advance( 30 );
```

The implicit argument `d` comes before the ., the explicit argument `n` within parentheses. Here is the function.

```
int daysPerMonth( month, year )
{    static int dpm [] = { 0, 31, 28, ... };
     if( month != 2 ) return dpm[ month ];
     return 28 + (year % 4 == 0) - (year % 100 == 0) +
                                   (year % 400 == 0);
          // recall that the result of the == is 0 or 1
}
void Date::advance( int n )
{    int d;

     day += n;
     while( day > ( d = daysPerMonth( month, year) ) )
     {    day -= d;
          if( ++month > 12 ) { month = 1; year++; }
     }
```

```
    while( day < 1 ) // if n was negative
    {   if( --month < 1 ) { month = 12; year--; }
        day += daysPerMonth( month, year );
    }
}
```

Again, the members of the implicit argument are used without prefixing them with a **..** This function modifies its implicit argument.

Exercise 5.2.1. Add member functions `print` and `raise` to the `Employee` class. If `e` is of type `Employee`, `e.print()` prints it and `e.raise( x )` raises the salary by `x` percent.

Exercise 5.2.2. Make the `readEmployee` function of Exercise 5.1.2 into a member function. Write a program that reads in an array of employees, raises each one's salary by 4 percent, and prints them.

Sometimes it is necessary or desirable to refer to the implicit argument in its entirety, or to pass its address to another function. Each member function gets a pointer `this` to its implicit argument. You can think of the use of `day` in a member function as a shortcut for `this->day`. A member function can use `this` to refer to the address of the structure that appeared to the left side of the **.** in the call, or `*this` to refer to the actual structure. Here is a function that returns a date + n days without modifying the original:

```
Date Date::add( int n )
{   Date r = *this; // make a copy of the implicit argument
    r.advance( n );
    return r;
}


Date e = d.add( 30 );   // d is unchanged
```

It is curious that the implicit argument appears like a reference argument in the call (no **&** is taken) and like a pointer argument `add( Date* this, ... )` in the function.

If a pointer to a structure is given, member functions are called with the `->` operator. (This is entirely consistent with data-member access.)

```
struct Employee
{   //...
    void print();
}


Employee* staff[ 100 ]; // pointers only, actual info
                        // stored elsewhere
```

```
for( int i = 0; i < 100; i++ )
    staff[i]->print();
```

The fact that a function does not modify an (explicit) argument can be expressed with the const indicator, for example,

```
int Date::diff( const Date& );
```

But how does one indicate that a function does not modify the implicit argument? The const must be placed behind (!) the argument list, as in

```
Date Date::add( int n ) const;
int Date::diff( const Date& ) const;
```

This usage is new to version 2 of C++.

Why use member functions? Any member function can be rewritten as a regular function by explicitly passing the implicit argument. There are several reasons:

- Member functions of different structures can have the same name. You can have print() members of Employee and Date. When calling x.print(), the compiler can tell which one to use by looking at the type of x. Actually, member functions are not strictly necessary for this purpose because, as we will see later, regular functions can behave in this way too.

- It is often convenient to package all functions allowing access to the data members of a data type together, giving the user of the data type a consistent user interface that remains stable even if the internal data representation changes. Member functions are not necessary for achieving this, but they come neatly packaged inside the structure declaration.

- It is sometimes intuitive to single out the implicit argument as something special. One can think of a function call car.accelerate(5) as sending a *message* to the object car. This terminology is used in some object-oriented programming languages. Structure variables are called objects, member functions are called methods, and member function calls messages. Whether it is more intuitive to send an "add 30 days" message to a date than making a function call add(d, 30) is probably a matter of taste.

- It is somewhat convenient to refer to the members of this just by their name because the prefix this-> is implicit. (This is similar to the Pascal **with** construct.)

- Some functions necessary for memory management (so-called constructors and destructors) as well as operator =, operator->, operator[ ], and operator() *must* be member functions.

- Functions dynamically selected at run-time (so-called virtual functions) *must* be member functions.

Short member functions can be defined inside the structure definition.

```
struct Date
{    int day, month, year;
```

```
    void print() const
    { cout << month << "/" << day << "/" year; }
    // ...
};
```

This has the same effect as declaring `Date::print` to be `inline`. A call to `bday.print()` is literally replaced with

```
cout << bday.month << "/" << bday.day << "/" bday.year;
```

rather than the code for a function call. Be aware that inline replacement can significantly increase code size, especially if one inline function calls another, and that inline replacement is a recommendation to the compiler that it can ignore. It is actually not terribly good practice to use this notation for inlines. If you later change your mind about the inline status, you have to move the function body outside the structure declaration. Because inline functions are not recognized by many debuggers, it is common to remove the inline attribute during debugging and restore it later. This is more easily achieved with a separately defined function.

In new versions of C++, enumeration constants defined inside structures are considered members. When used by non-member functions, they must be preceded by *class name*+`::`. For example, the following enumeration constants

```
struct Date
{    // ...
    enum { MONDAY = 1, TUESDAY, WEDNESDAY, THURSDAY,
                       FRIDAY, SATURDAY, SUNDAY };
};
```

can be used as `MONDAY` inside a member function of `Date`, as `Date::MONDAY` elsewhere.

Exercise 5.2.3. Write a `Point` structure storing the x- and y-coordinates of a point. Write a `Line` structure with two data members of type `Point`, that is, two points on that line. Write a member function `Point::read()` that reads in a point in the format `(10.5,2)` and `Line::read` that reads in the line coordinates in the format `[(10.5,2),(-2.3,0)]`. Use `Point::read` in `Line::read`.

Exercise 5.2.4. Write a member function `Line::isVert` returning 1 if the line is vertical and 0 otherwise, a function `Line::slope` returning the slope of a nonvertical line, and a function `Line::equation` that prints the equation of a line in the format `y = 6.4x + 3.7` (or `x = 2` for a vertical line). Write a member function `Line::isEqual( Line )` that tests whether two lines are actually the same (just defined by different pairs of points). Be careful about equality testing of floating-point numbers.

Exercise 5.2.5. Write a member function int Line::onLine(Point) returning 1 if the point is somewhere on the line, 0 if not.

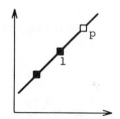

Exercise 5.2.6. Write a function Point Line::intersect(Line) that computes the point of intersection between the lines. If the lines do not intersect
(because they have the same slope), return (0,0).

5.3. CLASSES

Data representation can change. A major goal of object-oriented programming is to keep the code that uses the data completely unchanged when the
internal representation is modified.

Even as simple a structure as Date is not immune from change. If a
program performs a lot of date arithmetic, the repeated adjusting of month
lengths can be time consuming. Instead, it may be preferable to store dates
as single integers, the number of days from 1/1/1900. Many spreadsheets use
this format internally, sometimes called *Julian date*. Now computing "date
+ integer" and "date − date" become trivial, but printing is more difficult.
That trade-off will be beneficial if date arithmetic is much more frequent than
printing.

Now consider a program *P* that uses Date a lot. How can we, the designers of the Date type, present to our client, the programmer of *P*, the
Date type in such a way that we can switch between the two representations
without changing a line of code in *P*? We can suggest to the client never
to access the day, month, year member data (which might be replaced by
int julian), supplying member functions day(), month(), and year() (in
addition to add(), diff(), print(),...) instead. Unfortunately, programmers do not always have a good track record in following such suggestions.
For this reason, C++ enables the supplier of structures to enforce privacy of
structure members. Such structures become *abstract data types*. In an abstract
data type, the details of the implementation are hidden from the type user.
The user accesses the data through an interface that is stable even if the
internal representation changes.

This is achieved by separating member data and functions into a private
and a public section. The private section is the representation, the public
section the abstract data type. C++ uses the class construct for this purpose. A class is the same as a struct, except that all its members are hidden

unless they are explicitly declared public. (It works the other way around, too. A `struct` is a `class` with all its members public unless explicitly declared `private`.) For a `Date` type, it looks like this:

```
class Date
{   int d, m, y;
public:
    int day() const;
    int month() const;
    int year() const;
    void print() const;
    void advance( int );
    Date add( int ) const;
    long diff( const Date& ) const;
    // ...
}
```

If the private section is changed into

```
long julian;
```

the public section is completely unchanged. Any attempt to access the private portion

```
Date bday;
bday.d = 16; // WRONG
```

will be flagged by the compiler as an error.

It is a coincidence that this class has all member data private and all member functions public. Functions can be private and data can be public.

The private member data of a class can be accessed by the member functions of the class only (as well as friend functions—see Section 5.5). Similarly, private member functions can be called only inside other member function of the same class. For example, `Date::print()` can immediately access the data members. Other functions need to call *access functions* such as `Date::year()`.

Exercise 5.3.1. Present a `class Employee` with member functions for reading, printing, and data access, and for raising the salary by a percentage.

The next example, which will be used in later programs, abstracts a terminal display grid, as used in Section 1.5. We hide the representation (a double array of `char`) and only allow access via certain functions.

```
class Grid
{   char g[GRID_HSIZE][GRID_VSIZE+1];
                        // might change in a later
                        // implementation
public:
    void clear();       // fill with ' '
```

```
        void show() const; // display current picture
        void set( int r, int c, char ch ='*' ) { g[r][c] = ch; }
        void line( int rstart, int cstart, int dr, int dc,
                                                      int n );
                      // for horizontal, vertical and 45
                      // degree lines only
};
```

Exercise 5.3.2. Implement the member functions of the Grid class. Be sure to write safe set and line functions that check for proper array indices. If you entered the code for the flowchart plotter program (Section 1.5), modify it by allocating a global Grid display and replacing calls to gridLine to display.line, etc., then test it.

It is possible to define a data member that is shared by all instances of a class by declaring it static. For execution profiling purposes, one might want to keep track of how many (time-consuming) calls to the date print function have been performed. Add a static field printCount to the Date structure:

```
class Date
{    long julian;
public:
     static int printCount;
     void print() const;
     // ...
}
```

There is only a single storage location printCount in the entire program, not one for each instance of Date. It can be accessed in any member function.

```
void Date::print()
{    printCount++;
     // ...
}
```

If printCount has been declared in the public section, it can be accessed from anywhere as Date::printCount. In old versions of C++, static class members cannot be initialized explicitly, but like all static objects, they are initialized with 0. In new versions, explicit initialization is possible but must be outside the class, even if the static member is private.

```
class Shape
{    static double trans[2][2]; // a transformation matrix
     // ...
};
```

```
double Shape::trans[2][2] = { 72, 0, 0, 72 };
```

Compare the use of the `static` keyword with the declaration of a `static` local variable. Such a variable also occurs only once, even if the function in which it is defined is recursive and has multiple invocations pending, each with its own set of automatic variables.

Finally, member functions can be declared as `static`. Such functions have no implicit `this` argument and can only operate on the static data members. For example,

```
class Shape
{    static double trans[2][2]; // a transformation matrix
     // ...
public:
     static void scale( double s ); // multiplies trans
                                    // with s
} ;
```

Static member functions are accessed like static member data, as

```
scale( .5 )
```

inside other member functions of `Shape` and with the scope resolution operator

```
Shape::scale( .5 )
```

elsewhere.

Exercise 5.3.3. Design a `String` class

```
class String
{    char s[ MAXSIZE ];
public:
     void read(); // reads a string from cin, delimited by
                  // white space
     int length() const;
     void print() const;
     String substring( int, int ) const;
              // extract a substring
     int find( const String& ) const;
              // find first occurrence of substring,
              // return -1 if none found
     String concat( const String& b ) const;
              // returns concatenation of *this and b.
} ;
```

implementing strings with an upper bound on their size. For example, the following code adds the reverse of a string to its end:

```
String s;
s.read();
```

```
String r = s;
for( int i = s.length()-1; i >= 0, i-- )
{    String t = s.substring( i, i );
     r = r.concat( t );
}
r.print();
// e.g. Harry becomes HarryyrraH
```

The following two exercises show that global variables can often be replaced by static members in C++. Static members have two advantages over global variables: the class mechanism protects them from uncontrolled modification, and the *names* used by them are not blocked. For example, users of the Date class in the foregoing example are free to use the name printCount elsewhere in their programs. This consideration is particularly important when designing class libraries for use by others.

Exercise 5.3.4. Short strings waste a lot of storage, because they only occupy a fraction of the char[MAXSIZE] array. Implement a more efficient scheme: Use a large character array buffer to store the actual strings. The read function, as well as the functions concat and substring with a String result, should append strings at the end of the buffer. Each string contains the starting index in the buffer, a single int.

```
class String
{    int start;    // start of string in buffer

     static const int STRINGBUFSIZE;
     static char buffer[ STRINGBUFSIZE ];
     static int bufend;
public:
     // ...
};
```

Rewrite the member functions using this implementation.

Exercise 5.3.5. Consider the bidiagonal matrices of Section 4.4. Design a class Bmat10 for 10×10 bidiagonal matrices. Define a member function elem returning a double&, as described in that section. Use a static member to implement the zero location.

5.4. CONSTRUCTORS

There is a problem with the Date class of the previous section: How can one set a date? The statement d.day = 16 is illegal and, if the Julian representation is chosen internally, nonsensical. The access function d.day() can report a day, but does not set it. One could provide a member function

```
void Date::set( int m, int d, int y )
```

and use it to set dates:

```
Date d;
d.set(b,1b,59);
```

C++ provides a better way: The class can define a *constructor* that sets the values as the variable is declared:

```
Date d(b,1b,59);
```

A *constructor* is a special member function whose name is the same as the name of the structure or class.

```
class Date
{    int day, month, year;
public:
     Date( int, int, int );
     // ...
};

Date::Date( int m, int d, int y )
{    day = d;
     month = m;
     year = y;
}
```

Constructors are not real functions. They are only called when an object is created. Once an object exists, its value cannot be changed with a constructor. Constructors do not have a return type. *You cannot call a constructor, you can only cause it to be called.*

One can supply more than one constructor, and it is often convenient to do so.

```
struct Date
{    // ...
     Date( int, int, int );
     Date( char* );
     Date(); // initializes to today's date
     // ...
};

Date d("June 1b, 1959");
Date t; // initialized to today's date
```

The correct constructor is called, depending on the type of the initializer. Constructors often have default arguments.

```
Date::Date( int m, int d, int y =0 )
{    month = m;
     day = d;
```

```
    if( y == 0 )
        // set year to current year
    else
        year = y;
}
```

```
Date d(6,16); // sets year to current year
```

Constructors can create temporary objects.

```
Date today;
// ...
age = today.diff( Date(6,16,1959) ) / 365;
```

This code causes creation of an unnamed temporary variable that is initialized and passed to `Date::diff`. It is equivalent to:

```
Date temp(6,16,1959);
age = today.diff( temp ) / 365;
```

Afterward, the temporary variable is forgotten.

Exercise 5.4.1. Write the `Date( int, int, int = 0 )`, `Date( char* )`, and `Date()` constructors, using the `day month year` representation.

Exercise 5.4.2. Write the constructors of the previous exercise using the Julian representation.

Exercise 5.4.3. Write constructors for the `String` class of Exercise 5.3.3.

```
String::String( char* )
String::String( char )
```

that enable construction of

```
String s("Harry"), t('a');
```

Exercise 5.4.4. Write a constructor for the `Point` class of Exercise 5.2.3. making a `Point` from a pair of `doubles`. Write constructors `Line( Point, Point)`, `Line( double slope, double yIntercept)`, and `Line( double xIntercept )`, the last-named for vertical lines. For the last two constructors, you have some freedom in choosing the points. Pick some with convenient values.

5.5. FRIENDS

The level of protection given by the `class` mechanism can be too restrictive. Suppose a type for vectors in 3-space has been defined as

```
class Vec3
{    double vcoord[3];
```

```
public:
     Vec3();
     double elem( int );
     double sprod( const Vec3& ) const; // scalar product
     Vec3 xprod( const Vec3& ) const; // cross product
};

Vec3::Vec3()
{    vcoord[0] = vcoord[1] = vcoord[2] = 0;
}

double Vec3::elem( int i )
{    if( 0 <= i && i < 3 )
          return vcoord[i];
     else error();
}

double Vec3::sprod( const Vec3& v ) const
{    double r = 0;
     for( int i = 0; i < 3; i++ )
          r += vcoord[i]*v.vcoord[i];
     return i;
}
```

and a matrix type similarly

```
class Mat3
{    double mcoord[3][3];
public:
     Mat3();
     double elem( int i, int j );
     // ...
}
```

The `elem` access functions provide safe access to the entries, for example

```
Vec3 v;
double a = v.elem( 3 ); // ERROR
```

causes the `error()` function to be called because the vectors only have three coordinates indexed as 0, 1, 2. Of course, this access checking takes time. The member function `Vec3::sprod` dispenses with it and it can do so because it has access to the private part.

Consider the problem of writing a function that multiplies a matrix and a (column) vector, resulting in a vector. The function must be a member function of `Vec3` because it needs to build the result and the public `elem` function can only look up, not change a value.

```
Vec3 Vec3::multiply( const Mat3& a ) const
                                    //  mulitplies a and *this
{    Vec3 r;
     for( int i = 0; i < 3; i++ )
     {    double sum = 0;
          for( int j = 0; j < 3; j++ )
               sum += a.elem(i,j) * vcoord[j];
                                    // i.e. this->vcoord[j]
          r[i] = sum;
     }
     return r;
}
```

But this is inefficient. Each call to `a.elem` checks the bounds before handing out the value. If `multiply` was a member function of `Mat3`, it could bypass `elem` and directly access `a.mcoord[i][j]` and `v.vcoord[j]`. But a function cannot be a member function of two classes. This problem can be overcome by having `Mat3` declare the function a `friend`:

```
class Mat3
{    // ...
     friend Vec3 Vec3::multiply( const Mat3& ) const;
};
```

Or, the function could be rewritten as a nonmember

```
Vec3 multiply( const Mat3& a, const Vec3& b )
                                    // multiplies a and b
{    Vec3 r;
     for( int i = 0; i < 3; i++ )
     {    double sum = 0;
          for( int j = 0; j < 3; j++ )
               sum += a.mcoord[i][j] * b.vcoord[j];
          r.vcoord[i] = sum;
     }
     return r;
}
```

and declared a `friend` by both classes:

```
class Vec3
{    // ...
     friend Vec3 multiply( const Mat3&, const Vec3& );
};

class Mat3
{    // ...
     friend Vec3 multiply( const Mat3&, const Vec3& );
};
```

Actually, our example is a bit contrived because it relies on hiding the implementation details of 3×3 matrices, something one might not bother with in practice. But for large vectors and matrices, different representations are indeed appropriate. Sparse matrices (with many zero entries) can be represented in special ways, and changing yet efficient implementations are very important.

Exercise 5.5.1. Consider the bidiagonal matrix class of Exercise 5.3.5. Make a class **Vec10** for vectors with 10 components. Code a fast function for computing the product of a **Bmat10** and a **Vec10**. It should be a friend of both classes.

Sometimes, friend functions are preferred for their syntax. For example, the **String** class of Exercise 5.3.3 has a **concat** member function: **s.concat (t)** returns the concatenation of **s** and **t**. It seems more natural to make **concat** a friend instead, to be called as **concat(s, t)**.

Class definitions are not supposed to be edited by class users (and are best stored in a read-only file). Friend declarations are part of the class definition. A class user therefore cannot gain access to private parts of a class by declaring a function a friend. The initiative must come from the class designer.

A member function of one class can be a friend of another (like the **Vec3::multiply** function already seen). It is not uncommon that all member functions of one class are friends of another. There is a shorthand for this.

```
class Mat3
{       // ...
        friend class Vec3;
};
```

5.6. CLASS INTERFACES

By now, an important dichotomy has presented itself several times. On one side of the fence is the class designer who has to worry about supplying enough functions (or *methods*, in the terminology of some object-oriented languages) to satisfy the legitimate needs of the class user, yet hide all details that might change when the data representation is modified. On the other side is the class user who, depending on temperament, may be grateful not to be bothered with the details of the representation or infuriated by the inability to obtain access. Designing classes that are easy and efficient to use can be surprisingly hard.

What makes a good class?

- Something that you might need more than once (in the same or different projects).
- Something that you might want to have more than one of.

In this section, we look at some classes that are desirable from the point of view of the class user, ignoring the complexities of the implementation.

A safe integer array type, with bounds checking and arbitrary starting index can be designed with the following interface:

```
class IntArray
{    // ...
public:
     IntArray( int lo, int hi );
     int& operator[]( int );
};
```

Once someone has taken the trouble to implement the class, it is easy to declare an array:

```
IntArray a(10,20); // like Pascal a:Array[10..20] of integer
```

Thanks to the overloading of the [ ] operator, it is used exactly like an ordinary array

```
a[12] = 5;
cout << a[5]; // calls error function--index out of range
```

Operator overloading is discussed in Chapter 7.

Vector and matrix classes with arbitrary sizes can be defined and used with the standard mathematical operators, almost as if they were built-in types.

```
class Vector
{  // ...
public:
   Vector( int dim );
   friend Vector operator+( const Vector&, const Vector& );
   friend Vector operator-( const Vector&, const Vector& );
   friend double operator*( const Vector&, const Vector& );
      // dot product
   friend Vector operator*( double, const Vector& );
      // scalar multiplication
   friend Vector operator*( const Vector&, double );
      // scalar multiplication
   friend Vector operator*( const Matrix&, const Vector& );
      // matrix multiplication
   friend Vector operator*( const Vector&, const Matrix& );
   double length() const; // distance from origin
   double& operator[]; // access coordinates
   friend ostream& operator<<( ostream&, const Vector& );
      // print
   friend istream& operator>>( istream&, Vector& ); // read
};
```

```
class Matrix
{   // ...
public:
    Matrix( int rows, int cols );
    friend Matrix operator+( const Matrix&, const Matrix& );
    friend Matrix operator-( const Matrix&, const Matrix& );
    friend double operator*( const Matrix&, const Matrix& );
        // dot product
    friend Matrix operator*( double, const Matrix& );
        // scalar multiplication
    friend Matrix operator*( const Matrix&, double );
        // scalar multiplication
    friend Vector operator*( const Matrix&, const Vector& );
        // matrix multiplication
    friend Vector operator*( const Vector&, const Matrix& );
    friend Matrix identity( int n );
        // computes n x n identity matrix
    Matrix& inv(); // invert and return *this
    double det() const; // determinant from origin
    Vector& operator[]( int ); // access row vector
    Matrix operator^( int ) const;
        // powers a^0 = id, a^2 = a*a, a^-1 = inv
    friend ostream& operator<<( ostream&, const Matrix& );
        // print
    friend istream& operator>>( istream&, Matrix& ); // read
};
```

Here is how you use them:

```
Vector v(4); // a vector with four components
v[0] = 1; v[2] = -1;
Vector w(4) = 2*v; // w = (2,0,-2,0);
Matrix a(4,4); // a 4 x 4 matrix
cin >> a;
cout << a*v + w;
a[1][1] = 0; // a[1] is a row vector,
             // so second [] makes sense
Matrix b(4,4) = a.inv();
cout << b.det();
Vector u(4) = w*(A-identity(4));
```

Where does all the memory come from? The class did not know that we were going to do linear algebra in 4-space only. We could have asked for 10×8 matrices. Well, it isn't our problem, is it? Right now, we are just users of the class and can be blissfully ignorant about the details.

I hope that I have whetted your appetite in this section. Wouldn't you enjoy using some of these classes, especially if you knew that someone else was to implement them?

Exercise 5.6.1. Design the class interface for a `Set` class implementing finite sets of integers. What operations are desirable on sets? Adding an element, taking the union or intersection of two sets. Computing the set difference (all elements in *A* but not in *B*). Finding out whether a number is an element of a set. Whether one set is equal to another, or a subset of another.

Write the `class` definition only. Do not worry where the memory for potentially large sets comes from or how any of the operations might be implemented.

Exercise 5.6.2. Full-fledged sets require dynamically allocated storage, which we have not covered yet. Let us consider sets containing numbers between 0 and 255 only. These can be easily implemented through bit vectors, sequences of 256 bits with the ith bit 1 if *i* is an element of the set. Such vectors can be represented as arrays of 8 bytes. Union and intersection become bitwise | and &. Implement the class interface of Exercise 5.6.1 with bit vectors.

5.7. UNIONS

Unions are a space-saving device to use the same storage space for different items when there is no possibility that more than one of them applies for any given instance. Such situations are rare and inherently dangerous. In C++, many problems can be solved better with derived classes (Chapter 10) than with unions. After these words of warning, let us proceed to the classic example. A compiler symbol table stores names, types, and values of constants.

```
union Value
{    int ival;
     double dval;
     char* sval;
};

struct Constant
{    char* name;
     char type; // 'i' for integer, 'd' for double,
               // 's' for string
     Value val;
};

Constant c;

switch( c.type )
{    case 'i': cout << c.val.ival; break;
     case 'd': cout << c.val.dval; break;
     case 's': cout << c.val.sval; break;
}
```

It is entirely the programmer's responsibility to ensure that the type field and the branch of the union correspond. The compiler has no conception of the rules that dictate what value is currently stored in the union. There is no field to remember what, if anything, has been stored previously in a union. The following code is legal but almost certainly meaningless:

```
Value v;
v.ival = 10;
double x = v.dval; // unpredictable
```

It is very easy to write buggy code with unions. Yet the alternative, to have three fields `ival`, `dval`, `sval` in the `struct`, of which all but one are always zero, is also unattractive.

The notation `c.val.dval` is cumbersome, with `val` selecting the union and `dval` the item inside it. The union declaration can be placed inside the structure, with the union name omitted,

```
struct Constant
{       char *name;
        char type;
        union
        {       int ival;
                double dval;
                char* sval;
        }
} ;
```

and the items inside the union can be accessed like `c.dval`. These constructs are called *anonymous unions*.

Unions can have member functions, constructors, and destructors. However, unions are rare and unions with such full-fledged support even rarer. Currently, most systems cannot initialize unions like structures:

```
Value v = { 12 }; // may not be implemented
```

However, if all its members have different type, a set of type-sensitive constructors can be used for initialization.

```
union Value
{       int ival;
        double dval;
        char* sval;
        Value( int i ) { ival = i; }
        Value( double d ) { dval = d; }
        Value( char* s ) { sval = s; }
} ;
```

```
Value v(12); // OK. Calls Value( int ) constructor
```

Pascal Note

Unions in Pascal are called *variant records,* and they are safer because they contain a built-in variant selector.

C Note

As with enumerations and structures, the union name becomes a type name. Anonymous unions are new to C++.

Exercise 5.7.1. Write a safe union type

```
class SafeValue
{    char type;
     union
     {    int ival;
          double dval;
          char* sval;
     };
     //...
};
```

with constructors and access functions `ivalue()`, `dvalue()`, `svalue()` that generate an error message if a different item (or no item) was stored in the union.

Exercise 5.7.2. The implementation of the `Line` class in Exercise 5.2.3 was wasteful. You do not *need* two points (4 `doubles`) to specify a line. Reimplement the `Line` class by storing line segments in the form `struct{ double slope,yIntercept;}` , except that vertical lines are stored as `double xIntercept`. The `struct Line` should contain a `union` of those types and a field `int vertical` to describe the two situations. Write constructors

```
Line( double, double ) // not vertical
Line( double ) // vertical
Line( Point, Point )
```

and a function `equation` that prints the equation of the line. Do use classes, not structures, for points and lines, hiding the coordinate representation. (It will change in Exercise 5.7.5.)

Exercise 5.7.3. Implement the `intersect` function of Exercise 5.2.6 using the data structure of Exercise 5.7.2. Make `intersect` a friend of both `Point` and `Line`. You may make it a member of `Line` or just an ordinary function—the choice is yours.

The remaining three exercises have nothing to do with unions, but they show that in the case of lines just a little mathematical sophistication can lead to a much more useful data representation.

Exercise 5.7.4. The trouble with lines is that vertical lines are treated differently. Reimplement the **Line** class by storing $[a, b, c]$ if its equation can be written as $ax + by + c = 0$. Write a constructor **Line(double, double, double)** and **isEqual** and **intersect** member functions. Two lines $a_1x + b_1y + c_1 = 0$ and $a_2x + b_2y + c_2 = 0$ are equal if the coordinates $[a_1, b_1, c_1]$ and $[a_2, b_2, c_2]$ differ by a constant factor. For example, $[1.5, -2, 4.2]$ and $[3, -4, 8.4]$ denote the same line.

Exercise 5.7.5. The trouble with the **intersect** function is that parallel lines do not intersect. Represent points by projective coordinates $[x, y, z]$. The point (x, y) on the plane has projective coordinates $[x, y, 1]$. Two projective coordinates denote the same point if they differ by a constant factor, just as with line coordinates.

For example, $[5, -1.5, 2]$ and $[2.5, -0.75, 1]$ denote the same point. The point $[x, y, z]$ lies on the line $[a, b, c]$ if $ax + by + cz = 0$. This makes the **onLine** function of Exercise 5.2.5 quite simple.

z is nonzero if the point is a "real point." In that case, one can divide by the z-coordinate and get the regular x- and y-coordinates. For example, $[5, -1.5, 2]$ corresponds to the point $(2.5, -0.75)$ on the plane. Points with $z = 0$ are brand-new points, called "points at infinity."

Two parallel lines meet in such a point. For example, $2x - y - z = 0$ and $2x - y - 2z = 0$ meet in $[1, 2, 0]$. Therefore, *all lines have a common point of intersection.*

Using projective coordinates, write an **intersect** function. If the lines are identical, return an arbitrary point thereon.

Exercise 5.7.6. Using projective coordinates, write a **join** function that computes the line joining two points. (If the two points are identical, return an arbitrary line passing through.) *Hint:* You are using representations for points and lines that are identical (three **doubles**, considered the same if they differ by a common factor). Joining two points is *very* closely related to intersecting two lines.

5.8. PITFALLS

5.8.1. Forgetting the ;

The most common error when using **struct** (and **enum**, **union** as well as **class**—see Section 6.1) is to forget the ; behind the closing brace. Some compilers produce *strange* error messages when this happens. It is, of course, a common error since functions do not have a terminating ;.

Here is a particularly unsettling example:

```
struct Date
{    int month, day, year;
```

```
}     // WRONG--no semicolon

main()
{    // ...
}
```

In conformance with classic C, this is interpreted as defining `main` to be a function with return type `Date`!

5.8.2. Confusing . and ->

Beginners are often unsure when to use . and ->. It is actually very simple. . is used with actual `struct` values, -> with pointers to `struct`. For example,

```
void f( Date* pd )
{    Date d;

     d.year = pd->year; // d is a Date, pd a Date*
     // ...
}
```

A `Date&` reference behaves just like a `Date` and the . is used (although internally it is represented as a `Date*`).

The same applies to `union` and `class` types.

ADVANCED POINTER TOPICS

6.1. TWO-DIMENSIONAL ARRAYS

We have already seen that two-dimensional arrays are declared and accessed with two separate [ ]s.

```
char month[12][10] = { "January", "February", "March",
     "April", "May", "June", "July", "August", "September",
     "October", "November", "December" } ;
```

This allocates an array of 120 consecutive characters. The second array bound is chosen to be 10 because the longest month name, September, has nine characters and one additional character is required for the zero terminator. The empty space after all other names is uninitialized.

D e c e m b e r \0
N o v e m b e r \0
O c t o b e r \0
S e p t e m b e r \0
A u g u s t \0
J u l y \0
J u n e \0
M a y \0
A p r i l \0
M a r c h \0
F e b r u a r y \0
J a n u a r y \0

month, the array name without any brackets, points to the bottom of the array. month[2] is also a pointer. It points to the third string (because the index starts at 0). month[2][3] is 'c'.

What is the type of `month`? Of `month[2]`? Of `month+2`? There are unambiguous answers that are consequences of the universal array/pointer law. `month[2]` is a `char[10]`. It gets converted to a `char*` when used in any expression. For example, applying `[3]` to `month[2]` computes `*(month[2]+3)`. The expression `month[2]+3` has type `char*` and applying the `*` yields a character. Of course, `month` has type `char[12][10]`. To see the type of `month+2`, imagine adding 1 to it. This moves it by 10 characters, which shows that `month+2` is a pointer to `char[10]`.

Although `month+2` and `month[2]` have the same value (both are 20 characters away from `month`), their types are very different. Adding 1 to `month+2` moves it by 10 characters. Adding 1 to `month[2]` moves it by one character. Note that `month[2]` is `*(month+2)`. In this situation, the `*` operator does not actually perform a memory lookup but changes the type of the pointer expression.

We have seen that `month+2` is a pointer to blocks of 10 characters. One might call it a `char[10]*`. Unfortunately, the C++ syntax requires a much more cumbersome description because the `*` operator must come before the `[]`. `month+2` is a constant pointer, always pointing to the same place. Imagine declaring a pointer variable `m` of the same type as `month+2`. It is either

```
char *m[10];
```

or

```
char (*m)[10];
```

The operator precedence table tells us that `[]` has a higher precedence than `*`. That makes the first declaration an array of 10 `char*`. The second declaration is what we want, a pointer to `char[10]`s. The type of `m`, and of `month`, is obtained by removing the variable name from the declaration. They are `char (*)[10]`.

Nothing charitable can be said about expressions like this. They are a consequence of declaring variables by placing type names and `*`s before variable names, `[]` behind. Languages like Pascal do not suffer from that problem because array, pointer, and type specifiers all follow the variable name in a declaration.

You might find the following table helpful. Note the repeated application of the array-pointer law.

Expression	Type	Offset
`month`	`char [12][10]`	0
`month+2`	`char (*) [10]`	20
`*(month+2) = month[2]`	`char[10]`	20
`month[2]+3`	`char*`	23
`*(month[2]+3) = month[2][3]`	`char`	

Note again that the first *, changing month+2 to month[2], did not perform a memory lookup. It did affect the type, changing the pointer from a char (*)[10] to a char[10].

Exercise 6.1.1. Write a program that declares the month array and prints the integer values of the pointers month, month+2, month[2], etc. from the table and verify the offsets.

If a two-dimensional array is passed to a function, the first bound can be left open, but the second one must be specified.

```
dateprint( Date d, const char mnames[][10] )
{    cout << mnames[ d.month-1 ] << " " << d.day << ", "
                                              << d.year;
}
```

This is not surprising. For the address computation, it is necessary to know by how many chars to move up to reach mnames + d.month-1. This is also consistent with the discussion of Section 4.2. The empty [] behind an argument is identical to a * in front; that is, we could have equally well declared

```
dateprint( Date d, const char (*mnames)[10] )
```

This is as it should be. When calling

```
dateprint( hiredate, month )
```

the value of the expression month is the array's starting address and of type char (*)[10]. It is copied into the local variable mnames. Again, mnames is not an array but merely a pointer variable. sizeof(mnames) is the same as the size of any pointer, certainly much smaller than sizeof(month) = 120. Only the array address has been transferred to dateprint.

In general, when a function receives a multidimensional array, all bounds but the first one must be specified.

```
void rubik( int cube[][3][3] );
```

Exercise 6.1.2. Write a function

```
matmul(double a[3][3], double b[3][3], double result[3][3])
```

that multiplies two 3 ×3 matrices.

Exercise 6.1.3. Explain why the first 3 in the matmul declaration from the previous exercise can be omitted:

```
matmul( double a[][3], double b[][3], double result[][3] )
// OK
```

but the second cannot.

```
matmul( double a[][], double b[][], double result[][] )
// WRONG
```

Exercise 6.1.4. Because only the first array bound can be omitted, it is difficult to write a program that multiplies two square matrices of arbitrary size **n**. To do this, the function must receive **double***s and do the address computation itself: a[i][j] becomes a[i*n+j]. Write a function

```
matmul( double* a, double* b, double* result, int n )
```

that performs this multiplication. To use the function, you must cast the argument types:

```
double a[4][4], b[4][4], c[4][4];
// ...
matmul( (double*)(a), (double*)(b), (double*)(c), 4 );
```

Exercise 6.1.5. What is wrong with this code?

```
double a[4][4], b[4][4];
// ...
double* result;
matmul( (double*)(a), (double*)(b), result, 4 );
```

Exercise 6.1.6. Improve the **matmul** function to multiply two matrices of size **m** × **n** and **n** × **k**. The result is a **m** × **k** matrix.

6.2. ARRAYS OF POINTERS

Storing strings in a two-dimensional array is wasteful. The shorter strings do not need all the space allotted for them. It is better to store the characters somewhere and remember their locations in an array of pointers. The declaration is quite similar to a two-dimensional array

```
char* pmonth[12] = { "January", "February", "March",
     "April", "May", "June", "July", "August", "September",
     "October", "November", "December" };
```

but the memory layout is completely different.

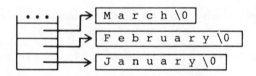

There is no guarantee that the month names are stored consecutively.

`pmonth` is an array of `char*`, containing the addresses of the individual strings. `pmonth[i]` is the ith address. Because `pmonth` points to an array of `char*`, its type is `char**`. Let us follow up on the computation of `pmonth[2][3]`.

Expression	Type	Offset
`pmonth`	`char*[12]`	0
`pmonth+2`	`char**`	$2 \cdot$ `sizeof( char* )`
`*(pmonth+2) = pmonth[2]`	`char*`	(outside `pmonth`)
`pmonth[2]+3`	`char*`	(outside `pmonth`)
`*(pmonth[2]+3) = pmonth[2][3]`	`char`	

Although `pmonth` is an array of pointers, the magic of the array-pointer law makes it possible to access the jth element of the ith string as `pmonth[i][j]`, giving the illusion of a two-dimensional array. Of course, it is not. There is no `pmonth[2][9]`.

Exercise 6.2.1. Write a program that declares the `pmonth` array and prints the integer values of the pointers `pmonth`, `pmonth+2`, `pmonth[2]`, etc. from the table. Explain the output.

Exercise 6.2.2. Write a function that can print a date in the format `June 16, 1959`. The prototype should be `dateprint( Date d );` use a static local array `pmonth` of pointers.

Exercise 6.2.3. Given a type `enum Language{ ENGLISH, GERMAN, FRENCH}` and three arrays of pointers to month names `emonth, gmonth, fmonth`, write a function

```
dateprint( Date d, Language l )
```

Inside the function, declare a

```
static char** monthName[] = { emonth, gmonth, fmonth };
```

Exercise 6.2.4. In Exercise 6.2.3, what is the type of `monthName`? `sizeof (monthName )`?

6.3. THE COMMAND LINE

Many operating systems interact with the user through a command line. Programs are executed when the program name is typed at a command prompt. The operating system locates the executable file and starts it. The program name can be followed by other items: options and redirection information. The operating system handles the redirection, connecting standard input and output to the specified files. The other command line arguments are passed to the program.

Consider a program called `count` that counts how often a word occurs in the input. The word to be searched for is specified on the command line. If desired, a `-i` option can be specified to make the comparison case-insensitive. A -n option counts all words except the one specified. It is a common convention that program options start with a -. Some programs require that the options appear in a certain order, but we will write `count` to accept the options and the word to match in any order. For example,

```
count dracula <input.txt -i
```

counts how often the word "dracula" occurs in the input text, ignoring the distinction between upper- and lowercase letters. The input could come from the keyboard, but in the call here it is redirected from a file. In fact, without redirection this program is next to useless. When was the last time you felt inclined to type a bunch of words on the keyboard, just to be told how often you entered one of them?

We need to know how our program can gain access to the command line. The strings on the command line are passed to `main`. The correct declaration for `main` is actually

```
int main( int argc, char *argv[] )
```

When `main` starts, it receives an argument count (including the program name but excluding redirection information—in the foregoing example, `argc` is 3) and an array of string pointers.

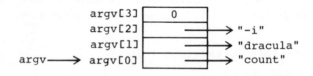

`argv[2]` is a pointer to the string "-i", and `argv[2][0]` is the '-' character. `argv` is a pointer to an array of pointers. Note that the redirection information (`<input.txt`) is stripped off by the operating system and not included in `argv`.

Exercise 6.3.1. What is `sizeof( argv )` ? The type of `argv` ?

Here is the program. Pay particular attention to the characteristic loop analyzing `argv`.

```
#include <stream.h>
#include <string.h>
#include <ctype.h>
```

```
void usage( char* progname )
{    cerr << "USAGE: " << progname << " word [-n] [-i]\n";
}

int stricmp( const char* s, const char* t )
// case-insensitive string compare.
{    int d;
     while( *s && ( d = toupper(*s)-toupper(*t) ) == 0 )
     { s++; t++; }
     return d;
}

int main( int argc, char* argv[] )
{    int countMatch = 1;
     int caseSens = 1;
     char* mw = 0;              // the word to match
     int count = 0;

     for( int i = 1; i < argc; i++ )
         if( argv[i][0] == '-' )
             switch( argv[i][1] )
             {    case 'n': countMatch = 0; break;
                  case 'i': caseSens = 0; break;
                  // more options can be added later
                  default: usage( argv[0] ); return 1;
             }
         else
         {    if( mw )
             {    cerr << argv[0] <<
                          ": Can count only one word.  \n";
                  return 1;
             }
             else mw = argv[i]; // doesn't copy the word,
                                // just the address
         }

     char word[ 100 ];
     while( cin >> word ) // fails at end of file
     {    int match = ( caseSens ? strcmp(word,mw) :
                                   stricmp (word,mw) ) == 0;
          count += countMatch ^ !match;
     }
     if( !countMatch ) cout << "Not ";
     cout << mw << ": " << count << "\n"
     return 0;
}
```

Note that the program name (count) in argv[0] is passed to the usage function–after all, someone might have renamed the program file to ct, and the program might have been launched as ct dracula -i <input.txt). We programmed main to return an integer value, 1 for a command line error and 0 for successful completion. This return value can be tested by the operating system (through $? in Unix, IF ERRORLEVEL in DOS.) The convention is that a zero return value from main indicates success, a nonzero value failure. You can indicate what kind of failure by exiting with different error codes. Return values are optional. You could return a random value (by having no return statement in main), but the polite thing is to return 0.

The argv variable is an argument of main. Like all other array arguments, it is a pointer variable, initialized to point to the actual array. The strings are stored elsewhere. One can take advantage of that and rewrite the for loop:

```
for( char* progname = *argv; --argc; )
    if( **++argv == '-' )
        switch( *(*argv+1) )
        {   case 'n': countMatch = 0; break;
            case 'i': caseSens = 0; break;
            default: usage( progname ); return 1;
        }
    else mw = *argv;
```

Exercise 6.3.2. Explain the meaning of **++argv.

You will find code like this in some programs. I cannot find a convincing reason to advocate it. Sure, the pointer access and increment are marginally more efficient. And you can show off your mastery of pointers. But this is hardly a time-critical code. The run-time saved over the lifetime of the program may well be dwarfed by the time spent by future maintainers who have to decipher the code.

Exercise 6.3.3. Enhance the count program to print the counts for a number of words, for example,

```
count  transsylvania  station  <input.txt
```

Exercise 6.3.4. Write a program that takes a string argument on the command line, reads in lines from standard input, and prints the lines containing that string to standard output. Call the program find. A sample call is

```
find  object  <chapter1.txt
```

Exercise 6.3.5. Write a program that takes a number of strings on the command line, reads in lines from standard input, and prints the lines containing *all* those strings. For example,

```
find object oriented <chapter1.txt
```

Exercise 6.3.6. Modify the program in Exercise 6.3.5 to support a − *n* option. If it is present (as any one of the strings, not necessarily the first or last one), all lines containing at least *n* of the keywords are printed. If not, all keywords must be present for the line to be printed. For example,

```
find object oriented programming -2 <chapter1.txt.
```

You will need to convert the string "2 " into a number. Use

```
if( argv[i][0] == '-' ) n = atoi( argv[i]+1 ).
```

6.4. POINTERS TO FUNCTIONS

Consider the task of plotting the graph of a function f for x-values in an interval $[x_{min}, x_{max}]$. We will make use of the Grid class of Section 5.3 that encapsulates a screen grid of 24 × 80 characters. To fit the graph, we will scale the x-values so that x_{min} corresponds to column 0, x_{max} to column 79. Similarly, we will scale the y-values. Here is an outline of the program:

```
double f( double x ) // the function to be plotted
{     return( 2 - x + x*x*x );
}


void plot( double xmin =-10, double xmax =10 )
                                 // default values -10,10

{     Grid disp;
      disp.clear();

      double y[ GRID_HSIZE ];
      double ymin, ymax;
      for( int i = 0; i < GRID_HSIZE; i++ )
      {    double x = xmin + ( xmax - xmin ) * i
                                   / (GRID _HSIZE-1);

           y[i] = f( x );
           if( i == 0 ) ymin = ymax = y[0];
           else
           {    if( y[i] < ymin ) ymin = y[i];
                if( y[i] > ymax ) ymax = y[i];
           }
      }

      for( i = 0; i < GRID_HSIZE; i++ )
           disp.set( i,
               int( (GRID_VSIZE-1) * (ymax - y[i]) / (ymax
                                            - ymin)));
      disp.line( int((GRID_VSIZE-1) * ymax/(ymax-ymin)),
           0, 0, 1, GRID_HSIZE ); // x-axis
      disp.line( 0, int((GRID_HSIZE-1) * xmin/(xmin-xmax)),
```

```
            1, 0, GRID_VSIZE ); // y-axis
       disp.show();
   }
```

Note how inflexible the `plot` function is. While the *x*-bounds are passed as parameters, the function `f` is hard-wired into the code. It would be desirable to supply the function as another parameter. For example,

```
   plot( sin, 0, 3.15 );
```

In C++ this can be achieved by giving `plot` a *pointer* to a function, that is, the starting address of its code. The starting address of a function can be obtained by simply omitting the `()` from the function name, for example, `sin`. (This is entirely analogous with arrays where the starting address is obtained by removing the `[]`.)

We will modify `plot` to receive a pointer `pf` to a function. For example, in the given call `pf` will be initialized with `sin`, the starting address of the sine function. To see how `pf` must be declared, observe that `pf` is a pointer to a function, hence `*pf` is a function, and the declaration is

```
   double (*pf)(double)
```

The parentheses around `*pf` are necessary because the operator precedence table tells us that the function call `()` operator is stronger than `*`. Without the parentheses,

```
   double *pf(double)
```

would declare a function (and not a variable) that eats a `double` and returns a `double*`. (The placement of spaces before or after a `*` is immaterial.) The function pointer is used inside `plot` as

```
   y[i] = (*pf)(x);
```

because `(*pf)` is a function and capable of consuming `x`.

Exercise 6.4.1. What is the size of a pointer to a function on your system? Probably the shortest program to determine this is: `cout << sizeof( main )`. Of course, this tells only the size of the pointer to the starting address of the function, not the number of bytes in the function code.

Exercise 6.4.2. Write a function that computes a numerical value for an integral $\int_a^b f(x)\,dx$. a, b, and f are passed as function arguments:

```
   double integrate( double a, double b, double (*f)(double) );
```

To compute the integral, split the interval $[a, b]$ into n pieces (starting with $n = 16$) and add up the sizes of the rectangles with base $= (b-a)/n$ and height $= (*f)$ (midpoint of ith interval). This sum of rectangles approximates the integral. Then double the number of intervals n. Compute the sum again. Compare it to the previous sum. Keep on going until two consecutive results differ by less than, say, 10^{-6}, or n becomes too large.

Try not to recompute all function values in each iteration, but reuse values from the previous one.

Test your function with the following integrals:

```
#include <math.h>

double f( double x ) { return ( x*x*x-x+1 );}

cout << integrate( 0, 3.14159, sin );
cout << integrate( 0, 1, exp );
cout << integrate( -1, 1, f );
```

A common application for pointers to functions is sorting. Algorithms to sort an array a typically consist of some way of selecting elements a[i], a[j] to compare them and then swapping them if they are out of order. Merely by modifying what it means to be "out of order," one can implement different sorting behaviors. For example, strings can be sorted lexicographically, or without regard to case, or taking into account sort orders of European alphabets (such as aäbc . . . in German), or by length first, or in a number of other ways.

Here is such a flexible string sort function. To keep the code at a minimum, we are merely using the inefficient bubblesort algorithm.

```
void sort( char* a[], int n, int (*comp)(char*, char*)
                                                  =strcmp )
{     // bubblesort
    for( int i = n-1; i > 0; i-- )
        for( int j = 0; j < i; j++ )
            if( (*comp)( a[j], a[j+1] ) > 0 )
            {     // lines not in order--swap them
                char* temp = a[j];
                a[j] = a[j+1];
                a[j+1] = temp;
            }
}
```

The argument `comp` is a pointer to a function returning a positive number if the strings are out of order. The default comparison is to use the standard `strcmp`. By calling

```
sort( a, sizeof( a )/sizeof( *a ), stricmp )
```

the strings are sorted without regard to case. (See Section 4.3 for the `stricmp` function.)

Exercise 6.4.3. Improve the `sort` function by implementing the quicksort algorithm.

Exercise 6.4.4. Write a comparison function that can be used to sort strings by increasing length, with strings of the same length sorted lexicographically.

Pointers to functions are extremely useful. Whenever you need to communicate to a function some behavior that is too complicated to put into a number, consider writing a small function and passing a pointer to it. If you have a bunch of those, it can be handy to pack them into an array. Consider, for example, a stack-based calculator program receiving commands

+	pop two numbers off the stack, add them and push the result
−	same, but subtract
*	same, but multiply
/	same, but divide
xchg	exchange the top two stack elements
print	pop and print the top of stack
dup	duplicate the top of stack (e.g., dup print is a nondestructive print)
pop	pop off the top of the stack

For example, 4 dup dup * xchg 2 / − computes $4^2 - 4/2$.

To execute a command, we can keep an array of commands and a parallel array of function pointers:

```
char* name[8]
    = { "+", "-", "*", "/", "xchg", "print", "dup", "pop" };
void (*action[8])()
    = { add, sub, mul, div, xchg, print, dup, pop };
```

This says "action is an array of eight things whose * are functions eating void and returning void." In the next section, we will see how to clarify declarations like this. Each of the elements of action is the address of an actual function that must be supplied, for example,

```
void sub() { double b = pop(); push( pop() - b ); }
```

The following function finds and executes a command:

```
void exec( char* cmd )
{    for( int i = 0; i < sizeof( name ) / sizeof( char* );
                                                    i++ )
        if( strcmp( cmd, name[i] ) == 0 )
        {   (*action[i])();
            return;
        }
}
```

Exercise 6.4.5. Implement the stack calculator, using this technique. Read in the commands from the command line:

```
for( int i = 1; i < argc; i++ )
    if( argv[i]   is a number  )
push( atof( argv[i] );
```

```
else
  exec( argv[i] );
```

The commands can then be entered like

```
calc 4 dup dup * xchg 2 / - print.
```

For easier maintenance, replace the two parallel arrays with an array of

```
struct Command
{    name[8];
     void (*action)();
};
```

Exercise 6.4.6. Enhance the calculator with commands for sqrt, sin, cos, exp, and log.

Exercise 6.4.7. Combine the plot function and the calculator to plot an arbitrary function that can be specified on the command line. For example,

```
plot  dup 2 xchg - xchg dup dup * * +
```

pushes numbers x between -10 and 10 onto the stack, applies the commands "dup 2 xchg - xchg dup dup * * +" (which compute $2 - x + x^3$), pops the result, and plots it. *Hint*: Write a function double execcmds(double x) that pushes x on the stack, executes all commands in argv, and returns pop(). Pass its address to plot.

Exercise 6.4.8. Add a constructor Set(int (*f)(int)) to the Set class of Exercise 5.6.1 that constructs the set of all $x, 0 \le x < 256$ for which the function returns a true (nonzero) value. For example, if int isprime(int n) tests whether n is a prime number, then Set(isprime) returns the set of primes < 256.

6.5. TYPE DEFINITIONS

To clear up complicated type declarations such as arrays of function pointers, the typedef construct can be used. typedef introduces new names for types. The general rule for its use is:

- Pick a name for the desired type.
- Write a declaration defining the name as a variable of the desired type.
- Precede the declaration by typedef.

For example, to make String a synonym for char*, first think how you would declare a single String as a char* variable:

```
char* String;
```

Now prepend typedef :

```
typedef char* String;
```

The type `String` can be used like any other type:

```
String s,t;
```

```
int main( int argc, String argv[] );
```

These type synonyms are smart. In the foregoing example, both s and t are `char*`, whereas in the declaration

```
char* s, t; // MAYBE WRONG
```

only s is a `char*`, t is a char, because the * really binds with the s.

To untangle the declaration of function pointers, it is quite common to declare types

```
typedef int (*Stringfun)( String, String );
```

making `Stringfun` a pointer to an integer function eating two strings. Thereafter, such function pointers can be declared as

```
Stringfun comp;
```

and arrays of them as

```
Stringfun sortfuns[3] = { strcmp, stricmp, numcmp; };
```

This is a big improvement over `int (*sortfuns[3])(char*,char*)`.

Pascal Note

`typedef` is not quite the same as the Pascal **type**. It merely introduces synonyms for the same type. For example, `String` and `char*` variables can be freely assigned to each other. The Pascal **type** introduces new types, incompatible with the defining **type**.

Exercise 6.5.1. Write a type definition `Mat3` for a 3 × 3 matrix. For example,

```
Mat3 a,b;
```

should declare two such matrices, and the `matmul` function of Exercise 6.1.2 could have the prototype

```
matmul( Mat3 a, Mat3 b, Mat3 result )
```

Exercise 6.5.2. Using the `Mat3` type of the previous exercise, why can't one write a function

```
Mat3 matmul( Mat3 a, Mat3 b )
{       Mat3 r;
        // compute r as the matrix product of a and b
        return r;
}
```

```
c = matmul( a, b );
```

Exercise 6.5.3. Declare a function **f** receiving an **int** and returning a pointer to a procedure without arguments. Do this without, then with, **typedef**.

Exercise 6.5.4. As we have seen, the C++ style pointer syntax can lead to declarations that some might find hard to read. In this exercise, we consider a logical alternative. We choose ^ as pointer dereferencing operator and make it postfix. We separate type and variable names. The following examples should speak for themselves.

`int x;`	`x: int;`	
`char* c;`	`c: ^char;`	pointer to char
`double a[10];`	`a: [10]double;`	10 doubles
`char *p, *q`	`p,q: ^char;`	
`char (*a)[10];`	`a: ^[10]char;`	pointer to 10 char
`c = (*a)[k];`	`c = a^[k];`	
`char *b[10];`	`b: [10]^char;`	10 pointers to char
`c = *b[k];`	`c= b[k]^;`	
`char **c;`	`c: ^^char;`	pointer to pointer to char
`int (*f)(int);`	`f: ^(int)int;`	pointer to int -> int function
`n = (*f)(x);`	`n = f^(x);`	
`int (*g[10])(int);`	`g: [10]^(int)int;`	10 pointers to int -> int function
`n = (*g[k])(x);`	`n = g[k]^(x);`	
`char *p="Hi";`	`p: ^char="Hi";`	Cannot initialize two variables
`Employee* e[100]`	`e: [100]^Employee;`	
`e[i] -> age`	`e[i]^.age`	

Look, ma, no parentheses! Let us refer to this as the D-style syntax. Write a program **encrypt** that reads a D-style declaration such as ^ [10]int p; and translates it into the C++ equivalent int (*p)[10].

Exercise 6.5.5. Write a program **explain** that translates C++ style into D-style. (*Hint*: Use recursive-descent parsing.)

6.6. ERROR HANDLING

Consider a stack class

```
class Stack
{     int stack[ STACKSIZE ];
      int sptr;
public:
      void push( int );
```

```
            int pop();
            // ...
      };
```

How should errors (underflow, overflow) be handled? In general, there are four different possibilities:

- Return an error code
- Set a global variable
- Call an error function
- Call a user-supplied error function

None of these are ideal. If a function already returns a value (such as `pop`), it is not feasible to return an error code because there is no way of distinguishing it from an integer return value. Functions returning a pointer are luckier; they can send a 0 pointer as an error code.

Setting a global variable is ugly and error-prone. (Someone else might reset it.) It also requires constant monitoring of the variable. Calling an error function is not ideal either. What should the error function do? Print a message on the screen and call `exit`? (`void exit( int )` is a system function that terminates the current program and passes an exit code to the operating system—see Section 6.3.) That works fine for debugging, but is hardly a good solution for a commercial program.

The most flexible and least distasteful method is to use a user-modifiable error function. (This then leaves the class user the choice between the first three unpleasant options.) We demonstrate this method with the stack class.

```
int error( char* s ) // default error handler
{     cout << "Stack error: " << s << ".\n" );
      exit( 1 ); // exit with an error code
      return 0;  // never gets here, but it keeps the
                 // compiler happy
}


typedef int (*ErrorFun)( char* );
      // a function eating a char* and returning int
ErrorFun stackError = error;

int Stack::push( int n )
{     if( sptr < STACKSIZE ) return s[sptr++] = n;
      else return (*stackError)( "Overflow" );
}


int Stack::pop()
{     if( sptr > 0 )return( s[--sptr] );
      else return (*stackError)( "Underflow" );
}
```

Once the code has been fully debugged and is ready to ship, the error function could be replaced with

```
int zerror( char* s ) { return 0; }
```

This replacement can be performed with a function providing access to the `stackError` variable.

```
ErrorFun setStackError( ErrorFun f )
{     ErrorFun r = stackError;
      stackError = f;
      return r;

}
```

To install the new error handler, call `setStackError( zerror )`. The function returns the old error handler, making it possible to install `zerror` temporarily and later restore the old handler.

It would be desirable to package the error-handler variable more closely into the stack class. The function pointer could be a data member, giving each instance of the stack class its own personal error handler. For stacks, this might be quite reasonable because any program will only have few of them. On the other hand, in a matrix class it makes no sense to store an individual function pointer with each matrix. If a thousand matrices are allocated, there would be that many copies of an identical pointer. Or worse, if different matrices have different error handlers, which one should be chosen in an operation involving two matrices? The answer is to make `ErrorFun error` a `static` data member inside the stack class, shared by all instances (see Section 5.3).

```
class Stack
{     int s[ STACKSIZE ];
      int sptr;
      static ErrorFun error;
public:
      Stack();
      static ErrorFun setError( ErrorFun );
      // ...
};

int defaultStackError( char* s )
{     cout << "Stack error: " << s << ".\n" )
      exit( 1 ); // exit with an error code
      return 0;   // never gets here, but it keeps the
                  // compiler happy
}

Stack::error = defaultStackError;
```

```
Stack::Stack()
{    sptr = 0;
}


static ErrorFun Stack::setError( ErrorFun f )
{    ErrorFun r = error;
     error = f;
     return r;
}


int Stack::push( int n )
{    if( sptr < STACKSIZE )
         return s[sptr++] = n;
     else
         return (*error)( "Overflow" );
}
```

To set the error function, the client calls the `static` member function

```
Stack::setError( zerror );
```

This changes the error function for all stacks. (Recall that a `static` member function has no implicit `this` argument and can act on the static data members only.)

In old versions of C++, it is not possible to initialize a static data member. In that case, you should modify the stack constructor to test whether `error` has been assigned previously. If it is still 0, set it to the default value. You will also need to make `setError` non-static because static member functions are new to version 2.

Exercise 6.6.1. Alternatively, the constructor could have an error function as a second argument (with a default argument 0—do not change the function). Code such a constructor and discuss the merits of this approach. Would a `setError` function still be required?

None of these error-handling facilities are well integrated into C++. Of course, error handling is one of the most difficult problems in both actual programming and language design. A real error-handling facility is planned for future versions of C++.

Exercise 6.6.2. Exercise 5.3.3 discusses a string class with fixed storage for each string. Add an error handler to the class. Possible errors are overflow during concatenation and access of nonexistent substrings.

Exercise 6.6.3. Find out about error handling in Eiffel (Meyer, 1988). To what extent can the functionality be imitated in C++?

Exercise 6.6.4. Usually the caller of a function is too lazy to check explicitly whether something went wrong in the function call. Languages with built-in exception handling do this automatically, branching to a separate block of code whenever a function call results in an error, but C++ does not. Implement an `ErrorMsg` class that can remember error messages in a static buffer.

```
class ErrorMsg
{       char fname[ 30 ];
        static char buffer[ bufsize ];
        static int bufindex;
public:
        //...
};
```

Error messages are recorded like this:

```
int Stack::push( int n )
{       ErrorMsg e( "Stack::push" );
        if( sptr < STACKSIZE ) return s[sptr++] = n;
        else e.setError( "Overflow" );
}
```

A function that called `push` (maybe indirectly) can query the status of the error message record:

```
void f()
{       ErrorMsg err( "f" );
        // ...
        if( f.isError() ) // at least one error found
        {       // print all error messages found
                char* p;
                while( p = f.getError() )
                        cerr << p;

        }

}
```

The error messages should have the format [*function*] *message*. The calling function can then analyze the source of the error and possibly take corrective action.

6.7. PITFALLS

6.7.1. Using Commas When Accessing Two-Dimensional Arrays

Elements of a two-dimensional array should be accessed with two separate `[]`, for example, `a[i][j]`. But surprisingly, the Pascal-style `a[i,j]` is not a syntax error. The comma in `i,j` is a comma operator, evaluating and discarding its first argument i and then resulting in the value of the second operator j. a[i,j] is therefore identical to a[j], a pointer to the jth row of the array. Usually, this use does lead to a syntax error. If a is a double array of char, then

```
char ch = a[i,j]; // WRONG
```

is illegal—a char* cannot be placed into a char without conversion. But in some contexts, both a char and char* can be acceptable:

```
cout << a[i,j]; // Syntax ok, will print a[j]
```

6.7.2. Forgetting Parentheses When Evaluating a Pointer to a Function

If a function receives a pointer pf to another function, it must be called as (*pf)(), not simply as pf.

```
void exec( void (*pf)() )
{      // ...
    pf; // WRONG
}
```

The statement pf; simply accesses the value of pf (the starting address of some function) and does nothing with it.

C H A P T E R 7

OVERLOADING

7.1. FUNCTION OVERLOADING

Certain function names are meaningful for a wide range of types. It makes sense to compute the length of a string, of a linked list, of a vector, and it is tedious to have to come up with unique names `stringLength`, `listLength`, `vectorLength`. There is the temptation to come up with cryptic abbreviations, `strlen`, `lstlen`, `veclen`. (The standard C library is certainly guilty of that. What do you think `strrchr` does?) And it is all so unnecessary. The compiler could just look inside the (...) and call the appropriate function, depending on whether it finds a string, list, or vector.

C++ does precisely that: The compiler watches the argument(s) of the calls and picks the right functions.

```
int length( char* s )
{    char* t=s;
     while( *t ) t++;
     return t - s;
}

double length( double vec[], int n )
{    for( double r = 0; --n >= 0; r += vec[n]*vec[n] )
         ;
     return sqrt( r );
}

int n = length( "Harry" ); // calls int length( char* )
double l, x[3] = { 1, 0, -2 };
l = length( x, 3 ); // calls double length( double*, int )
```

In old versions of C++, you have to announce your intention to overload a function by declaring

```
overload length;     // C++ Version 1 only
```

before defining either function.

Exercise 7.1.1. Write two functions `pow` that compute a^b. One of them,

```
double pow( double a, int b )
```

should compute $a \cdot a \cdot \ldots \cdot a$ (*b* times) (or $-b$ times the reciprocal if $b < 0$), the other

```
double pow( double a, double b )
```

should compute $e^{b \cdot \log(a)}$ (if a > 0). Write a short program to check that `pow(2,0.5)` and `pow(-2,-2)` get computed correctly.

Type conversions, such as `int` to `double`, are added if necessary to make the values in the call conform to the arguments in the function. The compiler goes through the following steps to find a matching function:

- If an exact match of the argument type is found, use it.
- If there is a unique function that matches after the *promotions* `char`, `unsigned char`, `short` –> `int`, `unsigned short` –> `int` (if `sizeof(short)` < `sizeof(int)`) or `unsigned` (otherwise), `float` –> `double`, use that function.
- If there is a unique function that matches after other standard type conversions, use that function.
- If there is a unique user-defined conversion (Section 7.3) achieving a match, use that function.

0 is an exact match for an `int` and can be converted to a pointer or `double` by a standard conversion. `char` and `short` are not considered exact matches for `int`. Standard conversions that might lead to information loss (such as `int` to `char`, `double` to `int`) are considered. The `unsigned` and `const` attributes are ignored. Argument matching cannot distinguish between `const` and non-`const` objects.

Rules are slightly different for C++ version 1. When looking for matches after standard-type conversions, the compiler picks the first one it finds rather than checking whether it is unique. Small integrals (`char`, `short`) are automatically promoted to `int`, but conversions involving truncation (e.g., `double` to `int`) are not considered at all. Use casts `char(ch)`, `int(x)` if necessary.

If there is more than one argument, then the foregoing matching is applied to all arguments. Only if a unique function can be found achieving a better match in one argument and at least as good a match in all others, will it be taken.

The rules are complex. You should attempt not to create situations in which they do not obviously yield intuitive results.

One can think of member functions as overloaded as well. There can be a `List::length()`, `Queue::length()`, `Vec3::length()`. When compiling `x.length()`, one of them is selected, depending on the class to which `x` belongs. No type conversion is applied. In version 1, no `overload` statement is necessary because the compiler is already prepared to handle structure members (data or functions) with the same name.

Exercise 7.1.2. Write overloaded `print` functions printing an array of integers, an `Employee` record, and an array of `Employee` records.

Exercise 7.1.3. Overload the `min` function to find

- The minimum of two integers.
- The minimum of two `doubles`.
- The minumum of an array of integers.
- The minimum of an array of `doubles`.

7.2. OPERATOR OVERLOADING

By defining special functions, the built-in operators can be defined to act on structured data types. If a function

```
String operator+( const String&, const String& );
```

is defined, returning the result of concatenating the two argument strings, the addition

```
String a;
String b("Harry"), c(" Hacker");

a = b + c; // concatenate strings
```

is translated into a function call a = operator+(b, c). Of course, if you like typing, you can legally code the explicit call as well.

The following operators can be overloaded:

```
+   -  .*   /   %   ^   &   |   ~   !   ,
=   <  >   <<  >>  <=  >=  ==  &&  ||
++  --  +=  -=  *=  /=  %=  ^=  &=  |=
!=  <<=  >>=   ->  []  ()  new  delete
```

The last four are subscript, function call, free store allocation, and recycling. You can only attach `operator` functions to existing operators. You cannot design new operators, tempting as it may be (`:=`, `<>`, `|x|` for absolute values ...). You cannot change the precedence, prefix/postfix application, or the arity: no postfix `!`, binary `~`, or unary `^` are possible. If `++` or `--` are overloaded, it is not possible to distinguish between prefix and postscript application. `operator->` takes no argument and must return a pointer to a structure. In C++ version 1, it is not possible to overload `,` and `->`.

Operator functions must take at least one `struct` (or `class`) argument. Thus, it is not possible to define

```
char* operator+( char*, char* ); // WRONG
```

to concatenate strings given as char*. Operator functions can be either friend or member functions of a class:

```
class Vec3
{      // ...
public:
        double operator*( const Vec3& ) const;
        // ...
};
```

or

```
class Vec3
{      // ...
public:
        friend double operator*( const Vec3&, const Vec3&);
        // ...
};
```

Depending on which is used, the expression v*w is translated to either v.operator*(w) or operator*(v,w). Similarly, a unary minus can be supplied as either a member Vec3 Vec3::operator-() or as a friend Vec3 operator-(Vec3). Depending on the choice, -v is either v.operator-() or operator-(v). The choice usually depends on whether a type conversion should be permitted on the first argument (see Section 7.3). Exceptions are operator=, operator[], operator(), and operator->, which must be member functions.

No special meaning is attached to any of the operators. It is entirely possible to redefine + to denote vector subtraction, an exercise of dubious value. In particular, nothing dictates that an operator= must be assignment or that operator+= makes a += b the same as a = a+b. It is easy to go overboard. Is += really a good choice for stack pushing? Or () for traversing through a linked list? It seems wise to restrict oneself to time-honored mathematical notation, possibly augmented by an occasional cuteness like using || for testing whether lines are parallel.

As you have undoubtedly realized now, the "get from" cin >> x and "put to" cout << x operators are overloaded shifts << and >>. Details are given in Chapter 8.

For the remainder of the section, we will analyze some examples of overloading. We are not quite ready to tackle concatenation in the string class because of the memory management issue (where to put the concatenated string?) and start with complex numbers that use a fixed amount of memory. Complex numbers are sums

$$a + b\mathbf{i}$$

where a,b are real numbers (the real and imaginary parts) and $\mathbf{i}$, the imaginary unit, has the property that $i^2 = -1$. This uniquely defines addition, subtraction, multiplication, and division:

$$(a + b\mathbf{i}) \pm (c + d\mathbf{i}) = a \pm c + (b \pm d)\mathbf{i}$$

$$(a + b\mathbf{i}) \cdot (c + d\mathbf{i}) = ac - bd + (ac \pm bd)\mathbf{i}$$

$$1/(a + b\mathbf{i}) = (a - b\mathbf{i})/(a^2 + b^2) \text{ unless both } a \text{ and } b \text{ are } 0$$

$$(a + b\mathbf{i})/(c + d\mathbf{i}) = (a + b\mathbf{i}) \cdot 1/(c + d\mathbf{i})$$

Here is the `Complex` class:

```
class Complex
{     double re,im;
public:
      Complex( double r = 0, double i = 0 )
                                    { re = r; im = i; }
      double real() const { return re; }
      double imag() const { return im; }
      void inv(); // replace a number by its inverse
      Complex operator-() const
                             { return Complex( -re, im); }
      friend Complex operator+
                         ( const Complex&, const Complex&);
      Complex operator-( const Complex& z ) const
                                  { return *this + (-z); }
      friend Complex operator*( Complex, Complex );
      Complex operator/( Complex ) const;
      Complex operator+=( const Complex& z );
      Complex operator-=( const Complex& z )
                                  { return *this += -z; }
      Complex operator*=( const Complex& z )
                          { return *this = *this * z; }
      Complex operator/=( Complex );
      friend int operator==(const Complex&, const Complex&);
      friend int operator!=(const Complex&, const Complex&);
};


void Complex::inv()
{     double norm;
      if( ( norm = re*re + im*im ) != 0 )
      {     re /= norm;
            im = -im/norm;
      }
}


Complex Complex::operator/( Complex z ) const
{     z.inv(); return *this * z;
}
```

```
Complex Complex::operator/=( Complex z )
{     z.inv();
      return *this *= z;
}


Complex operator+( const Complex& x, const Complex& y)
{     return Complex( x.re + y.re, x.im + y.im );
}

Complex operator*( Complex x, Complex y )
{     return Complex( x.re*y.re - x.im*y.im,
                                x.im*y.re + x.re*y.im );
}


Complex Complex::operator+=( const Complex& z )
{     re += z.re;
      im += z.im;
      return *this;
}
```

We have not opted for maximum consistency or speed in these examples but rather show a variety of possibilities. In practice, all functions would be coded simply by combining the proper re and im rather than calling other functions. This is boring but speedy.

The constructor Complex has default arguments:

```
Complex i(0,1); // 0+1i
Complex a(2);   // 2+0i
Complex z;      // 0+0i
```

It is instructive to see what happens in memory when

```
c = a*b;
```

is executed.

- Copies of a and b are made and placed in the local variables x and y of operator*.
- A temporary variable is created on the stack of operator* and initialized with re = x.re*y.re - x.im*y.im, im = x.im*y.re + x.re*y.im.
- The contents of that temporary variable is copied to another temporary variable on the stack frame of the caller, and the function exits.
- The result is copied from the second temporary variable into c.

The first copying can be avoided by defining

```
Complex operator*( const Complex&, const Complex& )
```

instead. The other copies cannot easily be prevented.

Exercise 7.2.1. Implement the += -= *= /= functions as friends

```
Complex operator+=( Complex&, Complex )
```

Why must the first argument be a reference argument? Why is this actually not desirable? (*Hint:* What is the effect of **x** += **z** if **x** is a **double**?)

Exercise 7.2.2. Why wasn't **operator==** defined as a member function in the foregoing class definition?

Exercise 7.2.3. Consider the string class of Exercise 6.1.6. Define **operator+** (concatenation) and all relational operators (== != < > <= >=). Should these be friends or members? (*Hint:* **if("Harry"** < **s**) ...).

It is worth noting that most operators can be coded as friend functions, receiving either arguments of type **Complex** or **const Complex&**. The latter is more efficient because it only passes the address of the complex number to the function rather than two **doubles**. The += -= *= /= and (if desired) ++ -- must either be member functions, which allow modification of the first argument, or if friends, the first argument must be a non-**const** reference.

For a realistic example involving overloading of function call ( ), consider a **Polynomial** class. To avoid memory issues, we restrict ourselves to polynomials of degree ≤ 10 and store the coefficients $a_0 \ldots a_{10}$ of a polynomial

$$a_0 + a_1 x + a_2 x^2 + \cdots + a_{10} x^{10}$$

in an array **coeff** :

```
class Polynomial
{       double coeff[MAXDEGREE+1];
public:
        Polynomial();
        // ...
        void set( int n, double c ) { coeff[n] = c; }
        double operator()( double ) const;
};

Polynomial::Polynomial()
{       for( int i = 0; i <= MAXDEGREE; i++ ) coeff[i] = 0;
}
```

We want ( ) to denote evaluation, for example

```
Polynomial p;
p.set(0,2); p.set(1,-1); p.set(3,1);    // p = x³ - x + 2
cout << p( 2 );                         // plug in 2 for x:
                                        // 2⁷ - 3 + 2 = 26
```

We use Horner's method:

```
double operator()( double x ) const
{      double r = 0;
       for( int i = MAXDEGREE; i >= 0; i-- )
            r = r * x + coeff[i];
       return r;
}
```

Exercise 7.2.4. Write `operator` functions to add, subtract, and multiply polynomials (truncate degrees > 10).

Exercise 7.2.5. Write a member function `Polynomial::plot` so that `f.plot (a,b)` plots `f` between `a` and `b`. Write a member function `deriv` that computes the derivative.

Exercise 7.2.6. Build a stack-based polynomial calculator. `x` enters the linear polynomial x, a number enters a constant polynomial on the stack. All other polynomials are obtained from them by reverse-polish notation:

```
2 x * 1 - x * 0.5 + x * 4 +
```

creates $2x^3 - x^2 + 0.5x + 4$. `'` computes the derivative, `print` prints, and `plot` plots the result.

Exercise 7.2.7. Overload +, -, * for `Vec3` objects. Define a unary - and use it for the binary - : `a - b` is `a + (-b)`. Be sure to include scalar multiplication `double * Vec3`, `Vec3 * double`, dot product `Vec3 * Vec3`, and cross product `Vec3 % Vec3`. (Unfortunately, you cannot use `x` for cross product.)

Exercise 7.2.8. Overload * for the `Mat3 * Mat3` and `Mat3 * Vec3` (`Vec3`s are column vectors.)

Exercise 7.2.9. Consider the `Point` and `Line` classes of Exercises 5.2.4 and 5.4.4. Implement - to join two points to a line, + to intersect two lines in a point, and `||` to test whether two lines are parallel as well as to compute the line passing through a given point parallel to a given line.

7.3. OVERLOADED `operator[]`

In the `IntArray` class of Section 5.6, we already advertised an overloaded `[]`. Here is the code:

```
class IntArray
{      int value[maxArraySize];
       int lower, upper;
public:
       //...
```

```
        int& operator[]( int );
};

int& IntArray::operator[]( int n )
{    if( n < lower || n > upper )
                              error("Index out of bounds");
     return value[n-lower];
}
```

Because the function return type is `int&`, `a[n]` actually returns a pointer to `a.value[n]` and can be used on the left side of an assignment:

```
a[2] = 5;
```

means

```
* ( pointer to a.value[2-lower]) = 5;
```

Another common application of overloaded `[ ]` is an *associative array*. This is a data structure that associates certain keys, typically strings, with other values. For example,

```
AssocArray a;
a["Harry"] = 5.3;
cout << a["Harry"];
```

A typical implementation consists of an array of strings and a parallel array of `double`. We use a simple hashing scheme for the strings. If a hash collision is found, the next available entry in the string array is used.

```
class AssocArray
{    char* key[ arraySize ];
     double val[ arraySize ];
     char buffer[ bufSize ]; // stores actual strings
     int bufend;

     int locate( const char* ) const; // find hash location
                                       // of a string
public:
     // ...
     double& operator[]( char* );
};

int locate( const char* s ) const
{    int h = hash( s ) % arraySize;
     int i = h;
     do
     {    if( key[ i ] == 0 || strcmp( s, key[ i ] ) == 0 )
                                            return i;

          if( ++i >= arraySize ) i = 0;
     }
```

```
        while( i != h )
        return( -1 );
}


double& operator[]( char* s )
{    int i;
     if( key[ i = locate( s ) ] == 0 ) // new string
     {    key[ i ] = s;
          strcpy( buffer + bufend, s );
          bufend += strlen( s ) + 1;
     }
     return val[ i ];
}
```

Exercise 7.3.1. Add error handling to the `AssocArray` class. The hash table or the string buffer might overflow. (In the former case, it might be a good idea to return a reference to a `zero` location, as in Section 4.4.)

There is no `operator[][]` for double subscripts in C++. As we have seen in Section 6.1, multiple subscripts are really successive applications of single subscripts. With some care, this can be achieved for user-defined types as well. Consider, for example, the `Grid` class of Section 5.3. This class abstracts a terminal display, and we would like to implement `[]` to allow the following operations:

```
Grid d;
d[r][c] = '#';     // modify a value, instead of set(r,c,'#')
if( d[r][c] == ' ' )    // test a value
// ...
```

We must define a `Grid::operator[]` returning a value to which another `[]` can be applied.

```
class Grid
{    char g[GRID_VSIZE][GRID_HSIZE+1];
public:
     // ...
     char* operator[]( int r ) { return g[n]; }
};
```

In the expression `d[r]`, the function returns `d.g[r]`, a `char*` pointing to the rth row of `d.g`. A second `[]` can be applied to that pointer: `d[r][c]` is `*(d[r] + c)` or `d.g[r][c]`. Note that because `d[r]` is a `char*`, `d[r][c]` can appear on the left side of an assignment.

Exercise 7.3.2. Write `operator[]` for the `Vec3` and `Mat3` classes.

7.4. TYPE CONVERSIONS

The use of type conversions is essential for effective operator overloading. If an automatic type conversion `double` → `Complex` were not available, one would either have to write `Complex(2)*z` instead of `2*z` or supply a special `complex operator*( double, Complex )` (and all the other possible operations with `double` as first or second arguments). That would be unbearably dull.

A type conversion from type `X` to type `Y` can be achieved simply by supplying a constructor for `Y` with argument `X` (or `X&`). Typical examples are:

```
Complex( double )
String( char* )
Fraction( int )
```

This device cannot be used to convert back to a built-in type because built-in types are not classes and cannot have constructors. It also cannot always be used to effect a conversion to an existing class—we might not be permitted to add the constructor into the class definition.

To circumvent these restrictions, there is an alternate way of providing a type conversion from type `X` to type `Y`, by supplying a member function `X::operator Y()`.

```
class Fraction
{     int num, den;
public:
      // ...
      operator double();
};

Fraction::operator double()
{     return double(num)/double(den);
}
```

The `istream` class has a conversion `istream::operator void*()` that returns the 0 pointer at end of file or in case of trouble, or a non−0 pointer otherwise. This is invoked in statements such as

```
while( cin >> x )
      // ...
```

which means `while( operator>>( cin, x ).operator void*())` because `cin >> x` returns `cin`, and the `while` loop breaks when the result of converting the structure `cin` into a `void*` yields a 0 pointer.

It should be pointed out that the translator does not do more than one level of user-defined type conversion when trying to match an overloaded function. For example,

```
Fraction f(1,2);     // f = 1/2
```

```
Complex z(2,-1);    // z = 2-i
Complex w = f * z;
```

will not work because the conversion Fraction → double → Complex is too complex. One either has to help the compiler along

```
Complex w = double(f) * z;
```

or supply a type conversion Fraction → Complex, either as a constructor Complex(Fraction) or a Fraction::operator Complex().

Exercise 7.4.1. Add type conversions int → String and String → int to the string class of Exercise 5.3.3. For example, the integer 10 should be converted into the string String("10") and, conversely, a string consisting only of digits (and maybe a leading '+' or '-') should be converted to the corresponding integer. All other strings should be converted to 0.

Exercise 7.4.2. Construct a type conversiondouble → Polynomial, creating a constant polynomial. Define an operator^(Polynomial, int) that computes powers. Test with

```
Polynomial x; x.set( 1, 1 );
Polynomial f = 1 + 3*x - 2*(x^2); // ^ has lower priority
                                  // than *!
```

Exercise 7.4.3. A Point structure contains the x- and y-coordinates of a point. A Rectangle class is defined by two opposing corner points, a Quadrilateral class by its four corner points. Write a type conversion Rectangle → Quadrilateral,

- As a member function of Quadrilateral.
- As a member function of Rectangle.

Write a friend function perimeter of Quadrilateral and test that it can be used to compute the perimeter of a Rectangle. What if perimeter is a member function of Quadrilateral?

Exercise 7.4.4. (Hard) Write a conversion double → Fraction converting a floating-point number into the fraction most closely representing it.

7.5. PITFALLS

7.5.1. Type Conversions and Reference Arguments

Consider a function

```
void swap( double& a, double& b )
{     double temp = a;
      a = b;
```

```
    b = temp;
}
```

to swap two `doubles`. Suppose one of the arguments is a `Fraction`.

```
double x = 3.0;
Fraction f(1,2);

swap( x, f );  // f is not changed
```

A type conversion `Fraction` → `double` is effected, the result is stored in a temporary variable, a reference to that temporary variable is passed to `swap`, and its contents is swapped with **x**. Afterward, the temporary variable is forgotten. **f** is unaffected.

INPUT AND OUTPUT

This is a short chapter collecting information about the C++ stream input and output operations. Both the old stream library and the new iostream library are covered. This is not an exhaustive coverage of the I/O packages. For more details, refer to Stroustrup, 1986, and Lippman, 1989, in the Bibliography at the end of this book.

8.1. THE >> AND << OPERATORS

As you have undoubtedly noticed by now, the "get from" `cin >>` and "put to" `cout <<` operators are simply overloaded `<<` and `>>`, applied to members `cin`, `cout` of some classes. These classes are in fact `istream` and `ostream`, defined in stream.h. If one wants to read from another file, one has to suitably initialize another `istream` object, say `ifile`, and then use `ifile >> ....`

Let us have a closer look at the `<< >>` operators. Why can they chain together, as in

```
cout << "Salary: " << e.salary;
```

According to the operator precedence table, `<<` binds left to right, and the expression is fully parenthesized as

```
( cout << "Salary: " ) << e.salary;
```

Each `<<` has a return value that is identical to its first argument. That is, `cout << "Salary: "` returns `cout`, and the second `<<` is simply `cout << e.salary`. Actually, `ostream`s are fairly sizable objects, and the `operator<<` functions take an `ostream&` and return it. The following are defined inside the `ostream` class:

```
ostream& operator<<( ostream&, char* );
ostream& operator<<( ostream&, int );
```

To define a `<<` function for a user-defined type, an `operator<<` must be declared in the class definition, and it must be a friend because the first argument is an `ostream` and not an object of the user-defined class. Of course, the `ostream` class is not ours to touch, and further `operator<<` member functions cannot be added to it. Here is an output operator for fractions:

```
class Fraction
{   int num, den;
public:
    //...
    friend ostream& operator<<( ostream&, Fraction );
};

ostream& operator<<( ostream& s, const Fraction& f )
{   return s << f.num << "/" << f.den;
}
```

An input operator can be written similarly:

```
istream& operator>>( istream& s, Fraction& f )
{   s >> f.num;
    char ch;
    s >> ch;
    if( ch != '/' ) error( "/ expected" );
    s >> f.den;
    return s;
}
```

The input operator must have a `Fraction&` as second argument because it modifies it. The output operator has a `const Fraction&` for efficiency, passing a reference rather than the actual structure.

Exercise 8.1.1. Supply $<<$ and $>>$ operators to read and write `Employee` records.

Exercise 8.1.2. Supply $<<$ and $>>$ operators to read and write complex numbers. Use a pleasant format, like this:

2.5 + 3.1 i	general
3.1 i	no real part
2.5	no imaginary part
2.5 - 3.1 i	negative imaginary part
1 + i	imaginary coefficient 1

Why was $<<$ $>>$ chosen as input/output operators? Bjarne Stroustrup, 1986 explains that $=$ was considered, but it binds the wrong way (`cout = "Salary" = e.salary` parenthesizes to `cout = ( "Salary" = e.salary )`), and that most people preferred different operators for input and output. $<$ and $>$ were tried, but they were too frequently confused with their original meanings. $<<$ and $>>$ are sufficiently rare in regular C code to stand out.

Exercise 8.1.3. A logical choice might have been <<= >>=. Yes, they bind the wrong way, but one can place the stream argument *to the right*:

```
e.salary >>= cout;
```

That operator would still return `cout` for further chaining. Because the first argument is now a class object, they even can be declared as member functions:

```
ostream& Fraction::operator>>=( ostream& )
```

What is wrong with this idea?

8.2. INPUT AND OUTPUT OF CHARACTERS AND STRINGS

There is an `ostream::put( char )` function that puts a single character to the output stream, such as `cout.put(ch)`. For character-based input, `cin.get(ch)` can be used instead of `cin >> ch`. The difference is that `get` reads a white space character rather than skipping over it. A character can be put back onto the input stream with `cin.putback( ch )`.

Exercise 8.2.1. Write a program that reads in a file from standard input, expands tabs to spaces, and writes the resulting file to standard output. Default tab stops are every 8 columns; other values can be given on the command line (e.g., `tab 3 <test.c >test.out`).

For line-based input, there is a function

```
istream& istream::cin.getline( char* buffer, int bufsize,
    char terminator ='\n');
```

`cin.getline( line, 80 )` reads a line, `cin.getline( word, 20, ' ' )` reads in a word because the termination character has been changed to `' '`. The termination character is left as the next character on the input stream. `getline` is called `get` in the old stream library.

C Note

The C programmer will encounter some familiar concepts. The member functions `get`, `getline`, `put`, and `putback` are the equivalents of `fgetc`, `fgets`, `fputc`, and `ungetc`. C++ can afford prettier names because of function overloading. Calls to the C `f...` functions and the C++ stream functions do not mix because each library includes its own buffering.

In C++ version 1, it is difficult to use << to send individual characters to an output stream because expressions of type `char` are automatically converted to type `int`.

```
cout << '\n';
```

prints 10, the ASCII value of the newline character. Of course, cout << "\n" is okay. But that does not solve the problem if the character is stored in a variable. (In version 2, char is not automatically converted to int, so the problem disappears.) However, the form function can be used:

```
cout << form( "%c", ch );
```

form is an all-purpose formatting function, converting various types to string representations. form takes two (or more!) arguments, a format string, and the item(s) to be formatted. The format string starts with a % and may be followed by

1. An optional - to indicate left justification.
2. An optional integer to indicate field width.
3. For floating-point numbers, an optional . followed by an integer indicating the number of desired digits behind the decimal point.
4. One of the following characters:

d	to print an integer in decimal
o	to print an octal number
x	to print a hexadecimal number
u	to print an unsigned number in decimal
f	to print a floating-point number
e	to print a floating-point number in exponential notation
g	to print a floating-point number in style d, e, or f, whichever is shortest.
c	to print a single character (converts int or char to ASCII)
s	to print a string

   This is not a complete list. Here are some common examples:

   ```
   cout << form( "%10d", n );
   cout << form( "%10.2f", x );
   cout << form( "%-10s", month[i] );
   cout << form( "%c", ch );
   ```

The pointers returned by form point to a circular buffer. Use them soon, or if you need to hold onto the strings, make a copy. The form buffer space gets reused after a while.

To print a %, use %%.

C Note

form is just like =sprintf, except it returns the formatted string as its value. The formatting string can contain arbitrary characters, like "Salary: %10.2f". We have not stressed this to simplify the discussion for the readers unfamiliar with C style formatting.

`form` can also be used for specifying field widths and the number of digits after a decimal point.

```
cout << form( "%-20s", e.name ) << " Salary: " <<
    form( "%10.2f", e.salary) << "\n";
```

It is probably clearer to call `form` just once to format the entire output line:

```
cout << form( "%-20s Salary: %10.2f\n", e.name, e.salary );
```

`form` looks at its first (string) argument and prints all characters in it verbatim, except it interprets substrings starting with a `%` as formatting instructions. There should be exactly as many arguments behind the string argument as formatting codes. The compiler cannot check whether the types match. The prototype for `form` is

```
char* form( char*, ... )
```

and the compiler merely checks whether the first argument is indeed a `char*`. Because `form` is not type-safe, it should be used with caution.

8.3. USING FILES FOR INPUT AND OUTPUT

Linking streams to files is done very differently in the older stream library and the newer iostream package. The newer mechanism is discussed first.

Both the header files iostream.h and fstream.h must be included. To open a stream attached to a file for input, use

```
ifstream is( "input.txt", ios::in );
ofstream os( "output.dat", ios::out );
```

The classes `ifstream` and `ofstream` are derived from `istream` and `ostream` (see Chapter 10). An `ifstream` object is an `istream` object with added capabilities. In particular, all `istream` functions (`get`, `putback`, `>>`) can be used.

Here is an example, a program counting the number of lines in a file. It does that simply by counting the number of `'\n'` characters. The filename is given on the command line.

```
int main( int argc, char* argv[] )
{    filebuf fi;
     int count = 0;
     char ch;

     if( argc == 1 )
                 { cerr << "No filename given."; return 1; }
     ifstream is( argv[1], ios::in );
     if( !is )
     {    cerr << "Can't open input file: " << argv[1];
```

```
            return 2;
        }
        while( is ) // becomes false at end of file
        {    is.get( ch );
             count += ch == '\n';    // add 0 or 1 to count
        }
        cout << count << " lines.\n";
        return 0;
    }
```

Note the use of the standard `cerr` stream that sends output to the screen even if `cout` has been redirected to a file. The return value of `main` is 0 if no error is found, 1 if no file was specified on the command line, and 2 if the input file cannot be opened.

In the old stream library, opening a file for reading and writing is somewhat inconvenient. You must declare a `filebuf` (another class declared in stream.h), call its member function `filebuf::open` with the name of the file you wish to open, and pass the address (!) of the `filebuf` to an `istream` or `ostream` constructor. After that, you can forget the `filebuf` (except, be sure it doesn't go out of scope).

```
    filebuf fo;
    if( fo.open( "output.dat", output ) == 0 )
        error( "Can't open file" );
    ostream os( &fo );
    os << "Hello, File.\n";
```

`filebuf::open` takes two arguments, a string and an open mode, which is one of

```
    enum open_mode { input, output };
```

defined in stream.h.

Here is the same program implemented with the old stream functions.

```
int main( int argc, char* argv[] )
{    filebuf fi;
     int count = 0;

     if( argc == 1 )
                  { cerr << "No filename given."; return 1;}
     if( !fi.open( argv[1], input ) )
     {    cerr << "Can't open input file: " << argv[1];
          return 2;
     }
     istream is( &fi );
     while( is ) // becomes false at end of file
     {    is.get( ch );
          count += ch == '\n';    // add 0 or 1 to count
```

```
        }
        cout << count << " lines.\n";
        return 0;
    }
```

Exercise 8.3.1. Modify the counting program of Section 6.3 to take a source file optionally. A filename can be specified on the command line by either −f*filename* or −f *filename*.

8.4. STREAM STATES

All streams (both input and output) have a *state*, one of

- good
- end of file
- fail
- bad

There is a difference between "bad" and "fail." If the state is "fail," no input/output has been lost, but further operations will not succeed. If the state is "bad," the situation is, well, bad. A stream can easily become not good: Just calling `cin >> n` (n an `int`) when the next string on the input stream is not an integer can make the state "fail" or "bad."

    There are four access functions to report the stream state: `good()`, `eof()`, `bad()`, and `fail()`. `fail()` is true if the stream is in either state "fail" or "bad." `eof()` returns 1 if the end of file is reached *and the stream is not in a bad state*, 0 otherwise.

    In the old stream library, these states are implemented as an enumeration

```
enum stream_state { _good, _eof, _fail, _bad };
```

The states can be tested with the `rdstate` member function

```
if( s.rdstate() >= _fail ) ...
```

and set with the `clear` function.

```
s.clear( _good );
```

In the new iostream library, the state is a bit vector. A stream can be set to be good with

```
s.clear();
```

or set to be bad with

```
s.clear( ios::badbit | s.rdstate() );
```

Clearing the state is necessary if you want to continue reading after the state has been set to "bad" or "fail," for example, by a failed `cin >> n`. In a user-defined `operator>>`, you can set the state to "bad" if you find a wrong object on the input stream and you can't back out, or set to "fail" if you found out right away and can push the character(s) you read back onto the input stream.

Exercise 8.4.1. Enhance the operator>>(istream&, Complex&) function of Exercise 8.1.2. to set the stream to "bad" or "fail" if it could not successfully read a complex number.

An automatic type conversion istream → void* returns 0 if the state is "bad" or "fail," a nonzero pointer otherwise. It is automatically invoked if the return value of >> is used in a condition such as

```
while( cin >> ch )
    // ...
```

This loop reads characters until >> fails, most likely at the end of the file.

Exercise 8.4.2. Write an object-oriented front end to the C f... library. Define

```
class File
{
    int mode; // store whether read/write/both
    int state; // remember whether operations failed
    FILE* fp;
public:
    FILE* handle() { return fp }
        // to allow for fprintf( f.handle(), ... )
    File( const char*, const char* ); // calls fopen
    ~File(); // calls fclose
    File& operator>>( int ); // calls fprintf( "%d", ... );
    // ...
    File& operator<<( int& ); // calls fscanf( "%d", ... );
    // ...
    File& get( char& );
    File& get( char*, int, char );
    File& unget( char );
    File& put( char );
    File& read( void*, unsigned, unsigned );
    File& write( void*, unsigned, unsigned );
    long seek( long );
    long tell();
    int eof();
    operator void*(); // returns this if file ok,
                      // 0 otherwise
};
```

The mode field serves for testing that read/write operations are performed only on files opened with the correct permission. Provide File equivalents for stdin, stdout, and stderr. A usage sample:

```
char word[20];
File f( "input.txt", "r" );
while( !f.eof() )
{    char ch;
     do
     {    f.get( ch );
     } while( ch == ' ' );
     f.unget( ch );
     f.get( word, 20, ' ' );
     cout << word;
}
// f automatically closed by destructor when it leaves
// scope (sec. 9.2)
```

8.5. ATTACHING STREAMS TO STRINGS

Often, input data is line-based, with some variable number of items per input line. Then it is necessary to read in a line (with get/getline) at a time, break it up into fields, and convert each field into a value. The last-named operation can be greatly simplified by tying a stream to the buffer holding the input line.

In the new iostream package, this is achieved as follows:

```
#include <iostream.h>
#include <strstream.h>

const int BUFLEN = 100;
char buf[ BUFLEN ];
istrstream si( buf, sizeof( buf ));
```

In the old stream library, one simply declares

```
#include <stream.h>

istream si( sizeof( buf ), buf );
```

One can now read in and analyze an input line at a time. Suppose, for example, that each input line contains a string field and a floating-point number, followed by a comment of arbitrary length. For example,

```
DE  1944.50  Depreciation for copying machine
```

When using the new iostream library, the following loop can be used to process a file with such records:

```
const int ALEN = 10;
char acct[ ALEN ];
double amt;
```

```
while( cin.getline( buf, sizeof( buf ) )
{    si >> acct >> amt;        //comment field is ignored
     si.seekg( ios::beg );     // reset to start
}
```

In the old stream library, there is no way of resetting the string stream. The remedy is to declare it inside the loop.

```
const int ALEN = 10;
char acct[ ALEN ];
double amt;
while( cin.getline( buf, sizeof( buf ) )
{    istream si( sizeof( buf ), buf );
     si >> acct >> amt;        // comment field is ignored
}
```

Similarly, an output stream can be attached to a string if the output data need to be massaged before actually sending them. In the old stream library, this is very easy:

```
#include <stream.h>

ostream so( sizeof( buf ), buf );
so << acct << amt;
```

Then `buf` contains the character representation of the output and can be manipulated with any string operations.

The new iostream library requires a third argument in the constructor, `ios::out` if output is to start at the beginning of the string, `ios::app` if output is to be appended at the first ' \0 ' in the string. For example,

```
#include <iostream.h>
#include <strstream.h>

ostrstream so( buf, sizeof( buf ), ios::out);
```

The stream can be reset with `so.seekp( ios::beg )`.

8.6. PITFALLS

8.6.1. ?: Has Lower Precedence than << >>

For example,

```
cout << im > 0 ? "+" : "-"; // WRONG
```

does not print what one would expect. It prints the value of `im > 0` (which is 0 or 1) and evaluates to `"+"` if the state of `cin` is not "bad" or "fail," to `"-"` otherwise. That value is discarded. The `?:` expression must be enclosed in parentheses.

```
cout << ( im > 0 ? "+" : "-" ); // OK
```

The relational, logical, Boolean, and assignment operations also have precedence lower than << >>, as has the comma operator.

8.6.2. Declaring a `stream`

C++ has different classes for input and output. Accidentally declaring a

```
stream& operator<<( stream&, X ) // WRONG
```

(instead of ostream&) can lead to strange error messages.

8.6.3. `getline` Leaves the Terminator on the Input Stream.

The following code will lead to an infinite loop:

```
while( cin.getline( buffer, sizeof( buffer ) ) )
                                        // get in version 1
    cout << buffer;
```

because the terminating '\n' stays on the input stream. The first line is read in full, subsequent calls to `cin.getline` report blank lines. Remedy:

```
while( cin.getline( buffer, sizeof( buffer ) ) )
{    char ch;
     cin.get( ch ); // read line terminator
     cout << buffer;
}
```

8.6.4. Improper End-of-File Detection

It can be difficult to locate the end of input when using the stream functions. For example, the following code does not work:

```
int n;

while( !cin.eof() ) // WRONG
{    cin >> n;
     cout << n;
}
```

After the last number is read, the state is not yet _eof and the loop is entered once more. When attempting to read the next number, the end of file is reached, the `cin >> n` read request fails and `cin` falls into state "fail" or "bad," staying in the `while` loop forever. A correct loop is

```
while( cin >> n  )
    cout << n;
```

8.6.5. `filebuf` Out of Scope

In the old stream library, the file-opening procedure is tedious, and one is tempted to package it into a function

```
int open( istream& si, char* name ) // opens a file for input
{    filebuf fi;   // WRONG
    if( !fi.open( name, input ) )
        return 0;
    si = istream( &fi );
    return 1;
}
```

This allocates `fi` on the stack, and it goes out of scope when the `open` function exits. Its storage will soon be overwritten by other function calls. The file buffer can be allocated on the free store (Section 9.1).

```
int open( istream& si, char* name ) // opens a file for input
{    filebuf* pfi = new filebuf;   // BETTER
    if( !pfi->open( name, input ) )
        return 0;
    si = istream( pfi );
    return 1;
}
```

However, this is still not a good solution because the storage space for the `filebuf` cannot be reclaimed when the file is closed.

The only solution is to pass the file buffer into `open` as well:

```
int open( istream& si, filebuf& fi, char* name )
    // opens a file for input
{    if( !fi.open( name, input ) )
        return 0;
    si = istream( &fi );
    return 1;
}
```

C H A P T E R 9

MEMORY MANAGEMENT

9.1. DYNAMIC ALLOCATION

Often it is difficult or impossible to estimate beforehand how many items of a data structure are required in a program run. Then dynamic allocation of storage is required.

There are four areas of storage in every program:

- *Code.* This area contains the machine instructions for all functions. Pointers to functions point here.
- *Static data.* This area contains all global data and all local and member data declared `static`. It is allocated and initialized before `main` starts.
- *Stack.* This area contains all local, non-`static` data, including function arguments. When a block is entered, all variables in it are allocated on the stack; on exit, they are forgotten.
- *Free store or heap.* This area is available on request for data that grows or shrinks as a program executes.

Free store memory is obtained through the `new` operator. `new` is followed by a type name and causes a block of memory, sufficient to hold one instance of the type, to be allocated on the free store. Its value is the address of the allocated block.

```
Date* d;
d = new Date;
```

If the type has a constructor with no argument, `new` calls it. One can supply arguments to a constructor:

```
Complex* pz;
pz = new Complex( 1.5, -2*x );
```

An array can be allocated as well.

```
char* p = new char[ n ];
                        // allocates an array with n characters
```

If an array of a type with constructors is allocated, the constructor without arguments is called on all elements.

```
Complex *az = new Complex[10];
                        // calls Complex() on all az[i].
```

There is no way to pass arguments into the constructor. It is an error to allocate an array of a type with constructors but lacking a constructor without arguments. (Not even default arguments are allowed.)

new is an *operator*, not a function. It causes two function calls: to the free store allocator and to the appropriate constructor.

The delete operator recycles a pointer obtained through new.

```
delete d;
```

The allocated storage is returned to the free store for reuse by a subsequent call to new. If there is a destructor (Section 9.2), it is called. To recycle an array, you can simply recycle its starting address

```
delete pz;
```

if the type has no destructor, or

```
delete[n] pz;
```

if the destructor needs to be called on all array elements. (In that case, you have to remember somewhere how many elements were allocated.) The second form of deallocation is preferred—a destructor might be added later. The array allocation/deallocation syntax is asymmetric. Because its argument is a type, the new operator has the [ ] behind the type name: new char[10]. The argument of delete is an expression, and to delete an array, the [ ] must appear before the pointer variable: delete [10] p1. The command delete p[10] would mean that p is an array of pointers whose tenth element should be deleted. Both new and delete are operators, not functions. They handle free-store management and automatic construction/destruction.

Pascal Note

new and delete are exactly like **new** and **dispose** in Pascal, except that they can allocate arrays of objects and they can perform construction and destruction.

C Note

Do not confuse new and delete with malloc, and free: new X is the equivalent of malloc(sizeof(X)) + constructor calls. delete p is the equivalent of destructor calls + free(p). C++ programs should rarely use malloc and free.

Here is a stack class that allocates the stack on the free store. The class itself contains merely a pointer variable, and a constructor allocates the actual storage by calling `new`. If the stack overflows in a `push` operation, it is moved and copied to a larger location.

```
const int SDEFSIZE = 10;

class Stack
{     int* s;
      int* end;
      int* sp;
public:
      Stack( int =SDEFSIZE );
      ~Stack();
      int push( int );
      int pop();
      int isEmpty() const;
};

Stack::Stack( int size )
{    s = new int[ size ];
     end = s + size;
     sp = s;
}

Stack::~Stack()
{    delete s;
}
const int SGROW = 10;

int Stack::push( int n )
{    if( sp >= end ) // out of space
     {    int* snew = new int[ end - s + SGROW ];
                                     // get larger block

          for( int* p = s; p < end; p++ )
                                     // transfer contents
              snew[ p - s ] = *p;
          end = snew + (end - s) + SGROW;
                                     // set up new pointers
          sp = snew + (sp - s);
          delete s;        // recycle smaller block
          s = snew;
     }
```

```
        return *sp++ = n;
                        // enter value in stack and increment sp
}

int Stack::pop()
{    return *--sp;
}

int Stack::isEmpty() const
{    return s == sp;
}
```

Exercise 9.1.1. Use this stack in the stack-based calculator and verify its dynamic growth capability.

Exercise 9.1.2. Rewrite the pop function to shrink the stack back if it is less than half full. Shrink it to 50% of its size + 10.

A general vector class is another typical example: An instance of type `Vector` contains a pointer variable that is initialized by the constructor to an address on the free store.

```
class Vector
{    double* co; // coordinates
     int dim;
public:
     Vector( int );
     ~Vector() { delete co; }
     double& operator[]( int );
     // ...
};

Vector::Vector( int d )
{    dim = d; co = new double[ d ];
}

double& Vector::operator[]( int n )
{    if( 0 <= n && n < dim )
          return co[n];
}
```

The declaration

```
    Vector v(3);
```

causes the constructor `Vector` to be called and initialize `v.co` with a `new double[3]`. Vectors of completely arbitrary size can be allocated, for example, `Vector w(100)`.

Exercise 9.1.3. Restructure the `Polynomial` class of Section 7.2 to allow for polynomials of arbitrary degree. Supply `operator +` and `operator*` functions.

Exercise 9.1.4. Design an integer array class in which the storage grows on demand:

```
class FlexArray
{     int* mem;
      int lo,hi;
public:
      Array( int, int );
      int lowerBound() const { return lo; }
                        // current lower bound
      int upperBound() const { return hi; }
                        // current upper bound
      int& operator[]; // never fails--increases array
                        // if necessary
};
```

If frequent insertions or deletions occur in the middle of a sequence, then arrays, even dynamically growing ones, are not the appropriate data structure. In this case, one turns to linked lists. A linked list is a sequence of cells, each of which contains an information field and a pointer to the next cell.

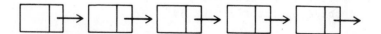

We will distinguish between *cells*, the actual containers of the information, and *lists*, which contain pointers to the first container in a chain and to one currently selected container. The following declaration shows a list of integers:

```
class Cell
{     int info;
      Cell* next;
      friend class List;
};

class List
{     Cell* head;
      Cell* cur; // current position
      Cell* pre; // predecessor of current position
public:
```

```
      List();
      ~List();
      void insert( int n );
                          // insert before current position
      void remove();    // remove current position
      int info() const; // info of current element
      void advance();   // advance current position
      void reset();
      int atEnd() const { return cur == 0; }
};

List::List()
{    head = cur = pre = 0;
}

int List::info() const
{    return cur ? cur->info : 0;
}

void List::advance()
{    if( cur )
     {    pre = cur;
          cur = cur->next;
     }
}

void List::reset()
{    cur = head;
     pre = 0;
}
```

`Cell` has no public access, but all member functions of `List` have been declared friends with the `friend class List` statement. This loop walks through a list 1:

```
for( l.reset(); !l.atEnd(); l.advance() )
do something withl.info();
```

When inserting a new element, new storage space is allocated.

```
void List::insert( int n )
{    Cell* p = new Cell;
     p->info = n;
     p->next = cur;
     if( pre ) pre->next = p; else head = p;
     pre = p;
};
```

When removing a cell, the storage is recycled.

```
void List::remove()
{    if( pre ) pre->next = cur->next; else head = cur->next;
     Cell* p = cur;
     cur = cur->next;
     delete p;
}
```

Exercise 9.1.5. Implement the list package. Write a program that reads numbers from standard input and inserts them in the list. Then print all numbers in the list.

Exercise 9.1.6. Modify the previous exercise to insert all numbers in reverse order. To insert all even numbers before all odd numbers. To insert all numbers and then delete the odd ones.

Exercise 9.1.7. Write a constructor `List::List( int n )` that initializes a list with a single cell containing n.

The destructor removes all cells of a list. The next section explains when it is called.

```
List::~List()
{    Cell* p = head;

     while( p != 0 )
     {    Cell* q = p;
          p = p->next;
          delete q;
     }
}
```

Exercise 9.1.8. Write a `Polynomial` class that implements polynomials as linked lists storing the degree and the coefficient of each term. Supply `operator[]` and `operator+` functions. `p[i]` should be the coefficient of x^i. Can `operator[]` return a `double&`?

9.2. CONSTRUCTION AND DESTRUCTION

Classes can have constructor and destructor members. A *constructor* is a member function with the same name as the class and no return type. (We introduced constructors in Section 5.4.) A *destructor* is a member function with name *~classname*, no arguments, and no return type. A class can have many constructors but at most one destructor. These are not actually functions. You cannot call them. You can only cause them to get called.

Construction deals with initialization of storage that has already been obtained in some way (as static data, on the stack, or on the free store).

Destruction deals with cleanup that should occur before that storage is given up (when the program ends, when a stack-based variable goes out of scope, or just before an object is recycled onto the free store).

Not all classes have constructors. An instance of a class without constructors is initialized with a random value or an exact (memberwise) copy of another object. Many classes, even classes with constructors, do not have destructors. Instances of such classes are just forgotten when they go out of scope, their storage space on the stack later reused. Constructors are very common because they are useful for initialization and type conversion. Destructors are only necessary for classes that need some kind of cleanup, most commonly recycling of data allocated on the free store. Destructor actions are not limited to freeing memory. Other tasks, such as decrementing a reference counter or closing a file, are commonly found in destructors.

A constructor for a class **X** is called in the following circumstances:

- A `static` local or a global variable of class **X** is declared. The constructor is called before `main` starts.
- An automatic variable of class **X** is declared within a block and the location of its declaration is reached.
- A function is called with argument **X**. A function call causes all its argument variables to be allocated and initialized.
- An unnamed temporary variable is created to hold the return value of a function returning **X**.
- An instance is obtained from the free store with `new X`.
- A variable is being initialized that has a member of type **X**.
- A variable is being initialized that is derived from **X** (Section 10.1).

The destructor ~**X** is called:

- After the end of `main` to destroy all `static` local or global instances of **X**.
- At the end of each block containing an automatic variable of type **X**.
- At the end of each function containing an argument of type **X**.
- To destroy any unnamed temporaries of type **X** after their use.
- When an instance of **X** is `deleted`.
- When a variable with a member of type **X** is destroyed.
- When a variable derived from **X** is destroyed.

For example, if a `List` is declared within a block, the destructor ~`List()` is called after the end of the block to recycle all cells contained in the list.

```
{     List l;

    //...

}  // l.~List() called here
```

If `List` had no destructor, `l`, which contains the starting address of the chain of cells on the free store, would be forgotten and the cells would be orphaned on the free store, never to be recycled. Clearly this situation must be avoided or the free store, a finite resource, will eventually be exhausted. All classes with a data member pointing to the free store need destructors or the programmer must actively perform deallocation. The latter is not an option if the class is to be used by a client who may not be aware how the class stores its information.

When initializing an object through a declaration, initializers can be specified in parentheses:

```
Date d(6,16,1959);
```

or

```
Date* pd = new Date(6,16,1959);
```

A class can have many constructors with different argument types. Two constructors are special:

- The constructor with no arguments `X()`
- The *copy-initializer* `X(const X&)`

When an array is initialized, either as `X x[n]` or as `px = new X[n]`, the constructor with no arguments is called on each array element. It is not possible to supply arguments for array initialization, not even default arguments. If a class has constructors, but none of them without arguments, it is an error to allocate an array.

The copy-initializer is called whenever a copy of an object needs to be made. This happens when a function argument is initialized with the value in the call, when a return value is copied out of the function into an unnamed temporary, or when a variable is declared with an initializer:

```
List l = tasklist;
```

This is *not* the same as

```
List l;
l = tasklist;
```

Initialization is not assignment. In the first case, `l` is initialized with `tasklist` through a call to `List(const List&)` (if it exists). In the second case, `l` is initialized with `List()` and `tasklist` is copied into it with `List::operator=` (if that exists). If `X(const X&)` or `X::operator=` do not exist, they default to memberwise copying. We will see in the next section why that is undesirable for classes that keep information on the free store and how suitable copy initializers and assignment operators can be defined.

When a function is called, the function arguments are variables that are allocated on the stack and initialized with a copy of the values in the call. For example, if the function

```
Date add( Date d, int n )
{       Date r;
        // ...
        return r;
}
```

is called with

```
b = add( bday, 10 );
```

two local variables d and n are allocated and initialized, d with a copy of bday and n with 10. The return value is copied from r into an unnamed temporary variable. The sequence of events is:

- Copy r to temp in the scope of the caller (using the copy-initializer if it exists)
- If a destructor exists, destroy r
- Return to caller
- b = temp;
- If a destructor exists, destroy temp

More than one temporary variable may be involved in an expression. For example, if a, b, c, d are complex numbers, the expression

```
cout << a*b + c*d
```

is equivalent to

```
Complex temp1 = a*b;
Complex temp2 = c*d;
Complex temp3 = temp1+temp2;
cout << temp3;
```

Each temporary gets initialized with the return value of an operator function.

When a class with members of another class is constructed, the constructors of the member classes are called. It may be necessary to pass arguments to those constructors. Consider this example. A text-formatting program keeps tables storing the page numbers for each section, each footnote, and each figure. Such tables are arrays of

```
class Item
{       int number;       // sequence number
        char* description;
                // section heading, figure caption, footnote text
        int page;         // page on which item occurs
        friend class Chapter;
};
```

Because the number of such items can vary greatly, the arrays are allocated on the free store:

```
class Table
{     int tablesize;
      Item *table;
      Table() { tablesize = 0; table = 0; }
      Table( int size )
          { table = new Iteminfo[ tablesize = size ]; }
      ~Table() { delete table; }
      friend class Chapter;
};
```

We store information separately for each chapter:

```
class Chapter
{     Table sections;
      Table figures;
      Table footnotes;
      // ...
public:
      Chapter( int secsize =20 );
};
```

The `Chapter` constructor must call the constructor for the three `Table` objects. But the programmer cannot explicitly call a constructor to initialize an existing object. To cause the constructor for the member objects to be called, the following syntax must be used:

```
Chapter::Chapter( int secsize =20 ) : sections( secsize ),
    footnotes( 10 )
{
    // other initializations...
}
```

This causes initialization of `sections` through `Table( secsize )`, `figures` through `Table()` and `footnotes` through `Table( 10 )`. The constructors for the members are called before the code of the object constructor is executed. Member constructors are executed in the order in which they are declared. If a member that is a class object is not specified after the : in the constructor header, it is initialized with a call to the constructor without arguments of that class. This occurs with `figures`, which is initialized to an empty table. It is an error if that class has some constructor but not one without arguments.

When `Chapter` is destroyed, destruction occurs in reverse order: first `~Chapter()` is executed, then `~Table()` is executed for each of the tables. This does not mean that the `Chapter` is actually recycled or forgotten before the `Table`s are destroyed, merely that the code in the `Chapter` destructor is called before the code in the `Table` destructor is executed for each table. Only after the execution of that code is the storage given up.

Because construction and destruction happen so frequently and at times unexpectedly, we will supply one more set of examples to illustrate each case (except for the case of derived classes, which will be introduced in Chapter 11).

STATIC DATA

```
Complex i(0,1);   // a global variable
Fraction a[10];   // a global array
```

i and a are allocated in the static data area. i is initialized through the Complex(double,double) constructor before main starts. a is initialized with 10 calls to Fraction(), and all are initialized to the default value (num=0, den=1). There is no ~Complex or ~Fraction destructor, so no cleanup occurs.

LOCAL VARIABLES

```
int count( List l, int n )
{     List p = l;
      ...
}
```

p is allocated on the stack and initialized with a copy of l, either through a call to List(const List&) if it exists, or as a memberwise copy. At the end of the function, it is destroyed with ~List(), recycling all cells.

FUNCTION ARGUMENTS

```
i = count( tasklist, 0 );
```

When count starts, two local variables l and n are allocated on the stack. l is initialized with a copy of tasklist (either through a call to List(const List&) if it exists, or as a memberwise copy). n is initialized with 0. At the end of the function, the destructor call l.~List() is executed and the contents of the storage locations l and n are forgotten.

UNNAMED TEMPORARIES

```
Fraction z,w;
// ...
cout << z*w;

Fraction operator*( Fraction a, Fraction b )
{     Fraction r;
      // ...
      return r;
}
```

In the call to `operator*(z,w)`, the result is computed in `r`. An unnamed temporary variable, allocated before the call in the scope of the caller, is then initialized with a copy of `r`, either through a call to `List(const List&)` if it exists, or as a memberwise copy. The temporary variable is then given to `operator<<` and subsequently forgotten. If a constructor is called explicitly, it also allocates an unnamed temporary:

```
cout << Fraction( 1,2 )
```

If there was a destructor `~Fraction()`, it would be called before the unnamed temporary is forgotten.

FREE-STORE DATA

```
File* f = new File( "input.dat" );
// ...
delete f;
```

A `File` structure is allocated on the free store, and the `File( char* )` constructor initializes it (by opening the file whose name is given in the constructor). When the `File` storage is recycled, first the destructor `~File()` is called (which closes the file) and then the storage is given back to the free store.

```
List* a = new List[10];
// ...
delete[10] a;
```

An array of 10 lists is allocated on the free store. Each element is initialized to an empty list by a call to `List()`. When the array is deleted, the destructor `~List()` is called 10 times, once on each array element (in reverse order, starting with the last element of the array).

MEMBER DATA

```
struct WordRef
{       char* word;
        List pages; // the pages on which the word occurs
        WordRef( char* w, int firstPage );
        ~WordRef();
}


WordRef::WordRef( char* w, int firstPage )
                                          : pages ( firstPage )
{       word = new char[ strlen( w ) + 1;
        strcpy( word, w );
}
```

```
WordRef::~WordRef()
{    delete word;
}
```

When a `WordRef` object is declared, say `WordRef r("Hello",2)`, then the constructor `WordRef(char*,int)` initializes the storage set aside for `r`. Before its code is executed, the constructor `List(int)` fills the storage area reserved for `r.pages` with a pointer to a list of one cell containing n. Then the body of the `WordRef` constructor initializes `r.word` with a pointer to a new block of memory and fills that block with a copy of the string `w`.

When r goes out of scope, the destructor `~WordRef()` first recycles the string storage space. Then the destructor `~List()` is called, freeing all cells of the list. Then the storage space for r is given up.

The following two situations do *not* involve constructor/destructor calls.

ASSIGNMENT

```
List a,b;
// ...
a = b;
```

The old value of a is replaced with the value b, either through a call to `List::operator=(List)` if it exists, or as a memberwise copy otherwise. The cells in the list that a previously pointed to are not automatically recycled unless the `operator=` has been programmed to take care of that. Assignment is not initialization, and no constructor/destructor activity takes place.

POINTER OR REFERENCE ARGUMENTS

```
int count( const List& l, int n )
{
    ...
}

i = count( tasklist, -1 );
```

The `List&` argument is initialized with the pointer `&tasklist`. As `List&` and `List*` are not classes, no constructors or destructors can be attached to them.

Exercise 9.2.1. To observe constructors and destructors in action, one can simply place debugging messages into the code. Do this in the `Complex` class:

```
Complex::Complex( ... )
{    ...
    cout << "\nConstructing " << long(this)
        << ",re:" << re << ",im:" << im;
}
```

```
Complex::~Complex() { cout << "\nDestructing "
                               << long(this);}
```

Follow through the construction/destruction sequence in the following cases:

- Construction of a local variable (inside `main`).
- Construction of a `static` variable (verify its construction before `main`).
- Passing of a `Complex` to a function.
- Returning a `Complex` from a function.
- Creation of temporary variables in arithmetic expressions.
- Obtaining an array from `new` and recycling it through `delete`.
- Construction of another class with a `Complex` member.

Also verify that assignment and `Complex*`/`Complex&` transfers do not invoke constructors.

9.3. COPYING DYNAMICALLY ALLOCATED OBJECTS

The default copy of one structure to another makes an exact copy of all members. This is desirable when copying complex numbers.

```
z = w;
```

should be the same as

```
z.re = w.re; z.im = w.im;
```

It is usually *not* desirable if one of the members is a pointer to the free store. For example, if a and b are linked lists

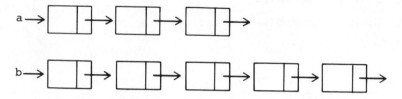

the effect of the assignment

```
a = b
```

is

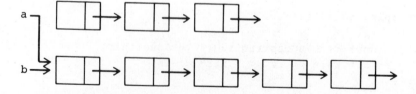

because a.head simply is set to the same address stored in b.head. The old cells of a are not recycled. If b goes out of scope before a does, the destructor b.~List() returns all cells in b (which are now also cells in a!) to the free store, making a.head point to a memory location that it doesn't own.

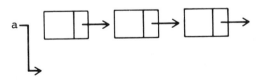

Clearly, memberwise copying is not appropriate in this situation. The intended meaning of the expression a = b is to make a a copy of the entire list pointed to by b, not just of the control structure. Redefining operator= solves that problem. We define two new member functions.

```
void List::free()
{       Cell* p = head;

        while( p != 0 )
        {       Cell* q = p;
                p = p->next;
                delete q;
        }
}

void List::copy( const List& b )
{       head = pre = cur = 0;
        Cell* q = 0;
        for( Cell* p = b.head; p != 0; p = p->next )
        {       Cell* n = new Cell;         // create fresh cell
                n->info = p->info;          // copy info
                if( q != 0 ) q->next = n; else head = n;
                q = n;
                if( p == b.pre ) pre = n;
                if( p == b.cur ) cur = n;
        }
}
```

free is identical to ~List() and recycles all cells in a list. But it is a real function that can be called as a.free(), whereas the destructor cannot be called explicitly by the programmer. copy makes a copy of a list, using fresh cells. The second list is passed as a List& to avoid copying *it* into the function or invoking a destructor on it. Now we can write operator=:

```
List& List::operator=( const List& b )
{    if( this != &b ) // otherwise b = b would lead to
                       // trouble
     {    free();      // i.e. this->free
          copy( b );   // i.e. this->copy(b)
     }
     return *this;
}
```

The function receives references to avoid actual copying or destructor invocation. It returns what it assigns to enable multiple assignments.

```
a = b = c;
```

parenthesizes as

```
a = (b = c);
```

and is translated into the call

```
a.operator=( b.operator=(c) );
```

assigning the return value of the function call `b.operator=(c)` to a. Taking over the assignment operation completely solves the problems of memberwise copying because both old cells are recycled and fresh copies of new cells are made.

However, copying can occur without involving `operator=`. When a new variable is created and initialized with a copy of another one, `operator=` is not called. This can happen in three situations:

- Declaration with initialization `List a = b`.
- Initialization of function arguments.
- Transfer of a function return value to an unnamed temporary.

In these cases, a constructor `List(const List&)` (in general referred to as *copy-initializer* or `X(const X&)`) is invoked. Here is a constructor that simply builds a fresh copy:

```
List::List( const List& b )
{    copy(b); // i.e. this->copy(b)
}
```

For example, in a function call

```
int count( List l, int n )
{
     ...
}
```

```
i = count( tasklist, -1 );
```

the local variable 1 of the function is initialized as `l.List( tasklist )`, which makes a fresh copy of each cell in `tasklist`. When 1 goes out of scope at the end of the function, those fresh cells are deleted with `l.~List()`, and the original cells in `tasklist` are unaffected.

Exercise 9.3.1. Implement these memory management tools. Add a message to the `copy` and `free` functions printing the addresses of new and deleted cells. Verify that passing a list to a function and assigning a list to another makes a fresh copy of each cell.

Making a fresh copy of each cell is clearly inefficient when passing a list to a function that does not modify it. In that case, a reference should be used:

```
int count( const List& l, int n )
```

When called as here, the address of `tasklist` is transferred into a reference variable 1. No construction or destruction takes place.

Exercise 9.3.2. In fact, there still is a problem with that solution. How can `count` look at the list? Only by resetting the list cursor with `l.reset()` and traversing the list. The function therefore has the side effect of modifying the list cursor.

To enable lists to be passed as `const List&` and yet be inspected, design another class `Iterator` that is a friend of `List` and `Cell`. The class provides a constructor resetting a cursor to the beginning of the list and functions `advance, atEnd`, and `info` compatible with the regular list functions. The following code traverses through a list 1.

```
for( Iterator iter(l); !iter.atEnd(); iter.advance() )
    // do something with iter.info()
```

(You will find iterators in Stroustrup, 1986, but he uses `operator()` for the `advance` operation: `iter()` advances the iterator. There is no use arguing about taste, but we would suggest that you consider overloading + + instead if you find `advance` too long.)

Any class `X` that stores data on the free store will need a full set of memory management operators:

`X()` (sets pointer to 0)
`X(const X&)`
`~X()`
`X& X::operator=(const X&)`

Because `operator=` typically deletes the old value of its first argument and then copies its second argument but cannot call the destructor and constructor explicitly, it is very common to have member functions `X::free()` and `X::copy(const X&)` that are shared:

```
X(const X& b) {  copy(b); }
~X() { free(); }
X& operator=(const X& b)
{    if( this != &b ) { free(); copy(b); }
     return *this;
}
```

As another example, we present a simple string class that stores the strings on the free store.

```
class String
{    char* sp; // string pointer--points to string in
                // free store
     void free() { delete sp; }
     void copy( const String& b );
public:
     String() { sp = 0; }
     String( const String& b ) { copy( b ); }
     ~String() { free(); }
     String& operator=( const String& b );

     String( const char* ); // type conversion
                            // "..." -> String
     friend ostream& operator<<( ostream&, const String& );
     friend String operator+( const String&,
                              const String& ); // concatenation
};

String& String::operator=( const String& b )
{    if( this != &b )
     {    free();
          copy(b);
     }
     return *this;
}
```

In the copy function, we must take care to handle the case sp = 0 separately.

```
void String::copy( const String& b )
{    if( b.sp )
     {    sp = new char[ strlen(b.sp)+1 ];
          strcpy( sp, b.sp );
     }
     else sp = 0;
}
```

To make a `String` out of a regular string (zero-terminated `char*`), the string must be copied into the free store.

```
String::String( char* s )
{       strcpy( sp = new char[ strlen(s)+1 ], s );
}
```

Now `String`s can be declared as `String a("Harry")`, and a type conversion `char*` → `String` occurs automatically:

```
cout << a + " Hacker";
```

calls

```
operator+( a, String( " Hacker" ) );
```

To print a string, we supply

```
ostream& operator<<( ostream& s, const String& a )
{       return s << a.sp;
}
```

which calls `operator<<(ostream&,char*)` and returns the same `ostream&`. To concatenate two strings, memory must be allocated to hold the result.

```
String operator+( const String& a, const String& b )
{       String r;

        r.sp = new char[ strlen( a.sp ) + strlen( b.sp ) + 1 ];
        strcpy( r.sp, a.sp );
        strcat( r.sp, b.sp );
        return r;
}
```

Exercise 9.3.3. List *all* constructor, destructor, and `operator=` calls that are executed during the run of the following program:

```
void main()
{       String a("Harry");
        String b("Hacker");
        c = a + " " + b;
        cout << c;
}
```

Verify this by inserting test messages into those functions and running the program.

Exercise 9.3.4. Add the full complement of memory-management operations to the flexible array class of Exercise 9.1.4.

9.4. MEMBERWISE COPYING

As we have seen, structure objects can be copied during initialization (including function call and return) and through assignment. If no special copy semantics is specified through copy initializers (`X(const X&)`) or `operator=`, a default method is used. Care must be taken because some structure members might be objects that *do* have special copy semantics. The following recursive copy rule applies:

- If the object has a copy initializer/`operator=`, it is called.
- If the object is a built-in type or a pointer, a bitwise copy is made.
- Otherwise, memberwise assignment is applied recursively to each sub-object.

In old versions of C++, this rule was not laid down. Instead, the default copy was just a bitwise copy of all members. That can become a problem when one doesn't expect it. Consider, for example, the description of a line in 3-space by a point on it and a direction vector.

```
class Vector // in 3-space
{       double x,y,z;
        // ...
};

class Line
{       Vector point;
        Vector direction;
        // ...
};
```

No copy-initializer or `operator=` is present. Assignment of one line to another is made by bitwise copying. However, suppose that later the `Vector` class is changed to handle vectors of arbitrary dimension

```
class Vector
{       int dim;
        double* co;
public:
        Vector( int ) { dim = d; co = new double[ d ]; }
        Vector( const Vector& );
        Vector& operator=( const Vector& );
        ~Vector() { delete co; }
        // ...
};
```

In C++ version 1, this modification breaks the `Line` code. If one `Line` is initialized with another,

```
Line m = l;
```

the `Vector` fields are still copied memberwise. When either one goes out of scope, the destructor `~Vector` is called, leaving dangling references in the other. The change of the `Vector` code forces a change in the `Line` code. A copy-initializer must be added.

```
Line::Line( const Line& l ) : point( l.point ),
                              direction ( l.direction )
{}
```

This is against the principle that code should continue to work if internals of a class representation have changed. For that reason, C++ version 2 replaced the concept of bitwise copying with that of memberwise assignment.

Frequent copying of objects with free-store components is inefficient. Copying *into* a function can usually be avoided by replacing an argument of type `X` with `const X&`. Then the address of the object (rather than a copy of the object itself) is passed to the function. Implicit arguments of member functions are passed by reference as well. (Their address is copied into `this`.) But it is difficult to avoid the copy of the result *out of* a function. Consider addition in a vector class

```
class Vector
{       int dim;
        double *co; // points to coordinates on the free store
public:
        Vector( int ); // creates a vector and fills it with 0
        Vector operator+( const Vector& );
        // ...
};

Vector::Vector( int d )
{       dim = d;
        co = new double[ d ];
        for( int i = 0; i < d; i++ ) co[i] = 0;
}

Vector Vector::operator+( const Vector& b )
{       if( dim != b.dim ) error( "Dimensions do not match" );
        Vector r( dim );
        for( int i = 0; i < dim; i++ )
             r.co[i] = co[i] + b.co[i];
        return r;
}

Vector a(3), b(3), c(3);
// ...
c = a+b;
```

The `operator+` function receives a pointer (`this`) to a because it is a member function. It receives a pointer to b because we used a reference argument. Copying vectors into the function was avoided. The return value r is computed and returned, that is, copied to an unnamed temporary. Then r is destroyed. The contents of the unnamed temporary is copied into c. The unnamed temporary must receive a distinct copy of the result because the contents of r is destroyed before the result can be copied into c.

The problem could be avoided entirely if the compiler could change the semantics of operator+ to

```
void operator+( const Vector& a, const Vector& b,
                                      Vector& result );
```

and replace calls c = a+b with operator+(a,b,c). But it does not.

Can the copying be avoided by *returning a reference*? A reference to what?

```
Vector& Vector::operator+( const Vector& b )
{       Vector r( dim );
        // ...
        return r; // WRONG
}
```

This returns a pointer to r, a structure containing a dim and a co field located on the stack. When the function exits, that location is no longer reserved and will soon be overwritten. A reference to such a location is clearly worthless. (In addition, r continues to get destroyed.) Or, one could allocate the structure itself (and not just storage for the numbers in the vector) on the free store.

```
Vector& Vector::operator+( const Vector& b )
{       Vector* r = new Vector( dim );
        // ...
        return *r; // OK, but...
}
```

This is fine. The returned reference points to a persistent object on the free store. But how will that object ever get deallocated when it is no longer needed? Destructors cannot be attached to Vector&, and because the return value is stored in an unnamed temporary, it is totally beyond the programmer's control.

The problem is that destructors get called too often (returning Vector) or not often enough (returning Vector&). Should one *not* supply a destructor? One could supply the class user with public free and copy member functions, caution against assigning one Vector to another, recommend passing arguments by reference, and let the user worry about when to copy and when to free. That seems distasteful and error-prone.

Exercise 9.4.1. Jon Shapiro of AT&T suggests the following strategy to overcome the problem of needless copying of structure return values. This trick makes use of the fact that constructors can be overloaded and that they initialize preallocated memory space without copying. Define a dummy class for each operator with no members. They only serve as selectors for constructors.

```
class dummyAdd
            { dummyAdd() {} /* do-nothing constructor */ };
class dummyMul
            { dummyMul() {} /* do-nothing constructor */ };
```

Then define a separate constructor for each operator

```
Complex::Complex( const Complex& x, const Complex& y,
                                            DummyAdd d )
{    re = x.re + y.re;
     im = x.im + y.im;
}
Complex::Complex( const Complex& x, const Complex& y,
                                            DummyMul d )
{    re = x.re*y.re - x.im*y.im;
     im = x.im*y.re + x.re*y.im;
}
```

and translate each operator into the appropriate constructor call.

```
inline Complex operator+( Complex& a, Complex& b )
{    return Complex( a, b, dummyAdd() );
}
inline Complex operator*( Complex& a, Complex& b )
{    return Complex( a, b, dummyMul() );
}
```

Now the statement

```
a = b*c;
```

is translated into

```
Complex temp(b,c,dummyMul()); // initialization, not
                                         function call
a = temp; // still one copy
```

Try this out on your system. Implement subtraction and division as well. If your system has a translator, look at the intermediate C code that is generated by the standard function call method and the constructor call method. If you have a direct compiler, compare code size and run-time of both methods. Although we can see its advantages, we do not like this trick. If this mechanism is so wonderful, why isn't it built into the translator?

A different approach to memory management is used in languages such as Lisp, Smalltalk, and Eiffel. Objects are not actively deallocated, but when memory gets low, a garbage-collection process marks all free-store objects that are no longer pointed to and recycles them. The garbage collector must be tightly integrated into the language because it must be able to recognize when a bit pattern in memory is a pointer to the free store. C++ provides no such capability.

9.5. REFERENCE COUNTING

The technique of *reference counting* is a solution to the problem of slow copies. Rather than constantly allocating and freeing copies of a storage block, a counter is attached to the block that keeps track of how many pointers reference it. When that count drops down to 0, the block is deallocated.

Let us apply that idea to the **Vector** class. We will make a **Vector** a pointer to a class **VecStor** that actually contains the information of a vector and a reference count counting the number of **Vectors** pointing to it.

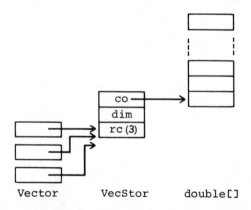

Both the **VecStor** and the actual **doubles** are stored on the free store. Several **Vectors** can point to a single **VecStor**. Once that count is decremented to 0, the **VecStor** and the associated array of **doubles** are recycled.

```
class VecStor
{       friend class Vector; // all Vector members are friends
                             // of VecStor
        int rc;
        int dim;
        double *co; // points to coordinates on the free store
};
```

This class has no public access. Only member functions of **Vector** can access it. It has no constructor or destructor. Instances of **VecStor** are created only in conjunction with **Vectors** and are initialized and destroyed by the **Vector** constructors and destructors.

```
class Vector
{       VecStor* stor;
```

```
          void copy( const Vector& );
          void free();
public:
          Vector( int ); // creates a vector and fills it with 0
          Vector( const Vector& b ) { copy(b); }
          ~Vector() { free(); }
          Vector& operator=( const Vector& b );
          Vector operator+( const Vector& );
          // ...
};

Vector::Vector( int d )
{       stor = new VecStor;
        stor->rc = 1;
        stor->dim = d;
        stor->co = new double[ d ];
        for( int i = 0; i < d; i++ ) stor->co[i] = 0;
}

Vector& Vector::operator=( const Vector& b )
{       if( this != &b )
        {       free();
                copy(b);
        }
        return *this;
}
```

The Vector(const Vector&), ~Vector(), and operator= refer to copy and free functions as in the previous section. copy simply copies the pointer to the VecStor and increments the reference count. free decrements the reference count and, if it becomes 0, deallocates the VecStor.

```
void Vector::copy( const Vector& b )
{       stor = b.stor;
        stor->rc++;
}

void Vector::free()
{       stor->rc--;
        if( stor->rc == 0 )
        {       delete stor->co;
                delete stor;
        }
}
```

The operator+ function is as before.

```
Vector Vector::operator+( const Vector& b )
{    if( stor->dim != b.stor->dim )
                         error( "Dimensions do not match" );
     Vector r( stor->dim );
     for( int i = 0; i < stor->dim; i++ )
         r.stor->co[i] = stor->co[i] + b.stor->co[i];
     return r;
}
```

We need no longer be afraid to copy out the result. r is created with reference count 1. When copying r to the unnamed temporary, the reference count is incremented to 2. When r is destroyed, the reference count drops to 1. If the unnamed temporary is destroyed (e.g., after completion of cout << a + b), the reference count drops to 0 and the storage is recycled.

Exercise 9.5.1. Draw storage diagrams for the following situation:

```
Vector a(4), b(4), c(4);
// a, b, c get filled with values
Vector d(4) = c; // calls Vector(const Vector&)
```

Pay special attention to the reference counts. Then list *all* constructor, destructor, and operator= activity during the execution of

```
d = a + b;
```

Don't forget the unnamed temporary.

Exercise 9.5.2. Recode the String class from the previous section using reference counts. The String class should only have a single pointer stor to a StrObj that contains a reference count 1 and a pointer to the free store. To conserve storage, denote an empty string with stor = 0 pointer (rather than stor = a pointer to a structure with reference count and a pointer to a 0 byte).

Reference counts have one serious problem. If an object whose reference count is > 1 is modified, an *on-the-fly copy* must be performed to avoid changing the meaning of the other references. In our vector class, this can occur with the [] operator. Suppose

```
v = u;
v[0] = -2.5;
```

is executed, we do not want u to change with v. The operator[] code must check for multiple references and make an on-the-fly copy if necessary.

```
double& operator[]( int n )
{    if( n < 0 || n >= stor->dim )
                         error("Index out of bounds");
```

```
    if( stor->rc > 1 )
    {    stor->rc--;
         VecStor* old = stor;
         stor = new VecStor;
         stor->rc = 1;
         stor->dim = old->dim;
         stor->co = new double[ stor->dim ];
         for( int i = 0; i < stor->dim; i++ )
             stor->co[i] = old->co[i];
    }
    return stor->co[n];
}
```

This makes the [] operator far less attractive. Just looking at a cooordinate (cout << v[i]) can force duplication! The operator[] function has no way of testing whether v[i] occurred on the left side of an = or on the right side. Of course, one could provide a separate operator for looking up a coordinate only. It would not need to make a copy.

Exercise 9.5.3. Provide an operator[] for the String class that is "safe": it should make an on-the-fly copy if necessary, and if the index is larger than the string length, it should pad with sufficient spaces. For example,

```
String s("Harry");
s[ 6 ] = 'H';
// now s points to "Harry H"
```

Exercise 9.5.4. Implement a list in which each Cell has a reference count. When the list is copied, the first reference count is incremented. When the list goes out of scope, the first cell's reference count is decremented, deallocating the cell and thereby decrementing the reference count of the second cell, and so forth. *Implementation hints:* You will need another type CellPtr that points to a Cell. Each Cell contains a reference count, a CellPtr to the next cell, and actual information. A List contains a CellPtr to the head. Rather than implementing traversal operations, supply a function int head() with the info of the head and List tail() that returns a list starting at the second cell (whose reference count is then incremented). The code for list traversal becomes

```
for( List t = l; !t.isEmpty(); t = t.tail() )
    // do something with t.head()
```

This is a much more "Lisp-like" list. head/tail are similar to "car/cdr."

Reference counting is not ideal, but in the absence of garbage collection it is just about the only game in town that does automatic deallocation without frequent copying.

Exercise 9.5.5. Reference counts have a major limitation: They fail for circular references. Illustrate this phenomenon by considering the creation of a circular linked list. When the pointer to the circular list is destroyed, the list is not reclaimed because each cell still has a positive reference count. Discuss strategies for circumventing this problem.

9.6. TAKING OVER STORAGE ALLOCATION

There are times when one wants to take storage allocation and deallocation in one's own hands rather than leaving it up to new and delete. This is especially true for dynamic allocation of constant-size objects, such as cells of linked lists or trees.

We will demonstrate a customized storage allocator for Cells of lists. We are not concerned with the structure of the Cell type. Because all cells have the same size (sizeof(Cell)), they can be recycled simply by putting them onto a *free list* and allocated by removing the first cell in the free list and using it to fulfill the request. Here are the functions:

```
union FreeObj
{       Cell   c;
        FreeObj* next;
};

static FreeObj* freelist = 0; // a global variable
const NCELL = 100; // 10 in the picture
```

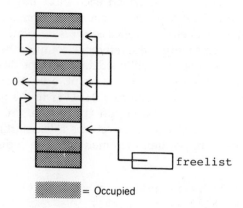

= Occupied

```
void recycle( Cell* f )
{       (FreeObj*)f->next = freelist;
        freelist = (FreeObj*)f;
}
```

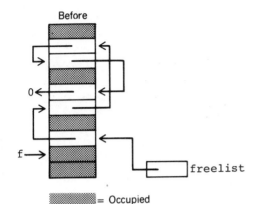

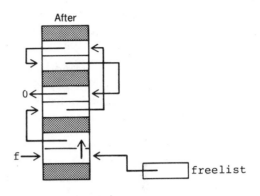

= Occupied

```
Cell* alloc()
{    if( freelist == 0 ) // skip this case at first reading
     {    freelist = new FreeObj[ NCELL ];
               // new cells from free store
          if( freelist == 0 )
               return 0;  // completely out of space
          for( FreeObj* p = freelist; p < freelist+NCELL-1;
                                                        p++ )
               p->next = p+1;
                          // initialize links in free list
          p->next = 0;
     }
     Cell* f = (Cell*)freelist;
     freelist = freelist->next;
     return f;
}
```

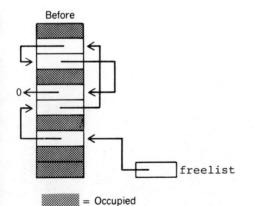

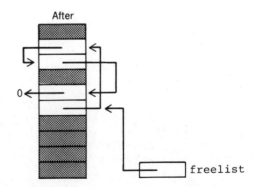

= Occupied

Exercise 9.6.1. Work through the code and draw pictures illustrating the next six calls to alloc (with NCELL = 10).

This allocation is far more efficient than the general purpose new/delete allocator that must pay attention to the sizes of the memory blocks. The allocator can be incorporated into the constructors and destructor for Cell by overloading operator new and operator delete.

```
void* Cell::operator new( size_t bytes )
{    if( bytes != sizeof( Cell ) )
         error("Cannot allocate array of Cells");
     return alloc();
}

void Cell::operator delete( void* p )
{    recycle( p );
}
```

The size_t type is declared in stddef.h to be sufficient to hold sizes of data blocks, that is, typically unsigned or unsigned long.

Note the peculiarities of these operations. operator new receives a byte count of sizeof(Cell) × #elements, rather than simply #elements. [This is necessary if it is used to allocate storage for a *derived class* object (see Chapter 11), which might be bigger.] It returns a void* rather than a Cell*. operator new and operator delete are static member functions. They may not refer to the this pointer or to any class members. For this reason, operator delete requires an explicit (void*) pointer to the object to be deleted.

In the new operator, we are checking whether the #elements is > 1. This could happen in an allocation new Cell[...], and our allocator is not prepared to handle contiguous blocks of cells.

This overloading of new and delete does not work in version 1 of C++. Instead, a *very* obscure mechanism is used, which relies on testing and assigning to the value of this.

```
Cell::Cell( ... )
{    this = alloc();
     // further initialization code
}

Cell::~Cell()
{    recycle( this );
     this = 0;
}

void main()
{    Cell* c = new Cell; // calls alloc
```

```
        // ...
}       // calls recycle when c goes out of scope
```

When assigning to `this` in a constructor, the translator suppresses the regular call to `new`! When assigning 0 to `this` in a destructor, the regular call to `delete` no longer happens. Somehow, the translator watches constructors and destructors very carefully and whenever it finds `this=` somewhere, it will not translate the `new` operator to calls to the default allocator.

It is even possible to test in a constructor whether the object to be constructed is located on the free store or not. If `this` is 0 on entry, the object is to be allocated on the free store, otherwise storage space is already provided on the stack or static data area. If there is a possibility that `Cell`s could be allocated other than via `new Cell`, the constructor should test for it. The destructor gets no information whether it is called through an explicit `delete` or simply because a `Cell` goes out of scope. The constructor must remember the storage class in a data member (called `dyn` in the code that follows).

```
Cell::Cell( ... )
{       if( this == 0 )
        {       this = alloc();
                this->dyn = 1;
        }
        else
                this->dyn = 0;
        // further initialization code
}

Cell::~Cell()
{       if( this->dyn )
        {       recycle( this );
                this = 0;
        }
}
```

If there is no doubt that all `Cell`s are dynamically allocated (as is frequently the case), no special `dyn` field is necessary in the `Cell` structure.

With the better solution offered by C++ version 2, this usage of `this` should quickly fade into the obscurity it so richly deserves.

Exercise 9.6.2. Use the fixed-size allocation technique to manage the cells in the list representation of the `Polynomial` class (Exercises 7.2.7 and 9.1.3). Implement the stack calculator and measure the difference in performance between `new/delete` and custom memory management under some large computations.

Sometimes, storage allocation does not fit the "pointer to free store" model. For example, an area of storage might be identified with a *handle*, some identification number that needs to be converted to a pointer before the storage can be used. The storage might reside on disk (or on an extended memory board in a PC), to be swapped into main memory on demand. Suppose handles are obtained with `Handle getHandle( long )`, recycled with `freeHandle( Handle )` and called into memory with `void* getAddress ( Handle )`. Suppose we want to store objects of a class `Table`. To allocate a table, we cannot simply define

```
void* operator new( size_t n )
{   return getAddress( getHandle( n ) );
}
```

because the handle is nowhere recorded, and it is needed for subsequent operations. C++ version 2 allows us to first allocate the memory and then to call `new` to fill it.

```
Handle th = getHandle( sizeof( Table ) );
Table* t = getAddress( th );
new ( t ) Table( ... );
    // constructor fills preallocated memory
```

In general, the syntax for invoking a constructor on preallocated memory is

```
new ( address ) X( ... ) ;
```

In this situation, it is permissible to call the destructor explicitly:

```
Table* t = getAddress(th);
t->Table::~Table(); // cleans up Table
freeHandle(th);
```

Consistency is not a strong point of this notation. Why not use `t-> Table(...)` for the constructor invocation?

The header file new.h must be included for this to work.

9.7. PITFALLS

9.7.1. Deleting Unallocated Blocks

Passing a pointer to `delete` that was not obtained through `new` is a certain recipe for disaster.

```
char buffer[10];
char *p = buffer;

// ...
if( n >= 10 )
{   p = new char[ 20 ];
    strcpy( p, buffer );
```

```
}
// ...
delete p; // WRONG
```

The free-store manager expects to find information, such as the block size, just below the recycled address. Some implementations are sophisticated, checking whether the returned pointer is within a reasonable range, others are not and simply incorporate the block for later reallocation. It is also an error to delete the same block twice "just to be sure." However, deleting a 0 pointer is safe—it simply does nothing.

9.7.2. Deleting Too Early

When a block is deleted, the free-store manager may overwrite some of the storage. For example,

```
for( p = head; p != 0; p = p->next )
    delete p; // WRONG
```

When the block with address p is deleted, its next field may be overwritten and the p = p->next instruction may fetch a corrupted value. The correct method is

```
for( p = head; p != 0; p = q; )
{   Cell* q = p;
    p = p->next;
    delete q; // OK
}
```

9.7.3. Memberwise Copying of Objects with a Destructor

This error is most common with classes that have a destructor but no copy initializer and operator=. Consider such a class:

```
class File
{   FILE* fp;       // a C-style file pointer
public:
    File() { fp = 0; }
    File( char* name, char* mode ) { fp = fopen( name,
                                                mode ); }
    ~File() { fclose( fp ); }
    fptr() { return fp };
};

Employee read( File f )  // no File(const File&),
                         // f = memberwise copy
{   Employee r;
    fread( r, sizeof( Employee ), 1, f.fptr() );
}                        // f destroyed, fclose called
```

The remedy is to pass a `File&` or `File*` because constructors/destructors are only attached to actual classes, not references or pointers.

9.7.4. Using `operator=` in a Constructor

Constructors, especially copy initializers, are invoked automatically and buggy code in them often gets executed and is hard to trace. A common error is to use data in an object before it is fully built-up. Consider for example a constructor for the `Line` class introduced at the end of Section 9.3. Suppose the data for `Vector` are allocated on the free store, and that there is no constructor `Vector()`.

```
Line::Line( const Line& l )
{    point = l.point;          // WRONG
     direction = l.direction;  // WRONG
}
```

The two assignments use `Vector::operator=`, which first frees the old contents of the left side. But there is no "old" value! The object to be constructed is built from uninitialized memory. Some random value is given to `Vector::free()`, probably with disastrous effect. The remedy is to *construct*, not assign, the members:

```
Line::Line( const Line& l ) : point( l.point ),
                              direction ( l.direction )
{}
```

9.7.5. Defining `operator=` as a Friend

In C++ version 1, it is not illegal to declare `operator=` as a friend. But it is not desirable. Recall that there is only one difference between declaring an operator function as friend or member—whether or not automatic type conversions are permitted on the first argument. For `operator=`, a type conversion on the first member is not desirable. Consider, for example, the following:

```
Complex z;
double x;

x = z;
```

If a member function `Complex::operator=(Complex)` is defined, it is not selected by the foregoing expression because the left side has type `double`. If, however, a `friend operator=(Complex,Complex)` is defined, the first argument is converted into a `Complex` temporary, and that temporary gets assigned `z`.

```
Complex temp( x );
temp = z;
```

The original `x` is unchanged!

INHERITANCE

10.1. DERIVED CLASSES

We will consider some elements of a chart-drawing package. We wish to display cannot draw on a common graphics standard that is available to all readers. To cater to the lowest common denominator in available output devices, we use text-based screen output. Lines are formed with * characters and stored in a double array that is displayed on the screen at appropriate times. A `Grid` class for this purpose was developed in Sections 5.3 and 7.3:

```
class Grid
{    char g[GRID_VSIZE][GRID_HSIZE+1];
public:
     void clear();
     void show() const;
     void line( int rstart, int cstart, int dr, int dc,
                                          int n );
     char* operator[]( int n );
};
```

We start the chart package with a box class (e.g., for a bar chart).

```
class Box
{    int cleft, cright, rtop, rbot;
public:
     Box( int, int, int, int );
     int vsize() const;
     int hsize() const;
     int vcenter() const;
     int hcenter() const;
     void plot( Grid& ) const;
};
```

```
Box::Box( int rl, int cl, int r2, int c2 )
{    cleft = cl, rtop = rl, cright = c2; rbot = r2;
}

int Box::vsize() const
{    return cright - cleft + 1;
}

int Box::hsize() const
{    return rtop - rbot + 1;
}

int Box::vcenter() const
{    return cleft + vsize()/2;
}

int Box::hcenter() const
{    return rtop - hsize()/2;
}

void Box::plot( Grid& g ) const
{    g.line( rtop, cleft, 0, 1, hsize() );
     g.line( rbot, cleft, 0, 1, hsixe() );
     g.line( rbot, cleft, 1, 0, vixe() );
     g.line( rtop, cright, 1, 0, vsize() );
}
```

It can be used like this:

```
Grid g;
Box b( 10,15, 15,20 );
b.plot( g );
g.show();
```

Exercise 10.1.1. Improve the constructor so that it sorts the corner coordinates and achieves cleft < cright, rtop < rbot even if the box was specified by other corners.

The next step is to design a type TextBox, a box filled with text:

This is a box + a char*. Its `plot` function plots the box, then the string inside. Because a `TextBox` *is* a box, and all operations that make sense for a box automatically make sense for a `TextBox`, we will make use of a new language construct: We will *derive* `TextBox` from `Box`.

```
class TextBox : public Box
{    char* text;
public:
     TextBox( int, int, int, int, char* );
     void plot( Grid& g ) const;
};
```

The class definition specifies that a `TextBox` is a `Box` with an additional data item,`text` , and with its own constructor and `plot` function. All other functions (`vsize, vcenter, ...`) are *inherited* from `Box`. The new data elements are placed on top of the `Box` data. A pointer to a `TextBox` is a pointer to a `Box` ! (It just ignores the new data on top.)

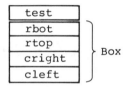

Let us write the `plot` function. To fit the string into the box, it must be broken up into substrings. We will ignore this for now and assume the string fits in one line in which we will center it.

```
void TextBox::plot( Grid& g )
{    Box::plot( g );   // draw the box outline

     int r = hcenter();
     int len = strlen( text );
     int c = vcenter() - len/2;
     for( int i = 0; i < len; i++ )
          g[r][c++] = text[ i ];
}
```

Note the use of the`::` scope resolution operator to call the `plot` function of the base class. The `vcenter` function is a member function of `TextBox` that was inherited from `Box`.

When deriving, one needs to specify only

- The member data added to the base class.
- The member functions added to the base class.
- The member functions replacing base class functions with the same name.

We still need to supply a constructor for `TextBox`:

```
TextBox::TextBox( int r1, int c1, int r2, int c2, char* t )
{    cleft = c1, cright = c2; rtop = r1; rbot = r2; // WRONG
     text = t;
}
```

What should be wrong with that? If `TextBox` is a `Box` , it has a `cleft` field. Why can't it be accessed? `cleft` is a private member of `Box`, and *nobody* can access it without the explicit permission of the `Box` class. `Box` was not asked whether it wanted to be derived from. This may seem paranoid, but it is the only reasonable way of keeping a protection mechanism. If a derived class could access the private members of a base class, anyone could access private members of any class simply by deriving another class from it with the sole intention of peeking inside the base class. Of course, `TextBox` can use the public members `vcenter...` of `Box`.

How then can the `Box` portion of `TextBox` be constructed? Only through the public members. There is a public constructor. But constructors are not functions that the programmer can call at will. The syntax for effecting is similar to invoking a member constructor (Section 9.2). The base class name is used instead of a member name:

```
TextBox::TextBox( int r1, int c1, int r2, int c2, char* t )
    : Box(r1,c1,r2,c2 )
{    text = t;
}
```

However, in C++ version 1, the syntax is slightly different. When passing values to the base class constructor, *no name* is given:

```
TextBox::TextBox( int c1, int r1, int c2, int r2, char* t )
    : (c1,r1,c2,r2 ) // C++ Version 1 -- base class
                     // constructor implied
{    text = t;
}
```

Section 10.3 contains the details about construction and visibility rules.

Exercise 10.1.2. Implement `Box` and `TextBox`. Verify that a `TextBox` *is* a box: All box member functions can be applied to it. If *t* is a `TextBox`, compare the results of `t.plot()` and `t.Box::plot()`. Which `plot` routine does the code `Box* pb = &t; pb->plot();` execute?

Exercise 10.1.3. Improve `TextBox::plot` to break up the character string into multiple lines, each at most `hsize()`-2 characters long. Try to break at white space. If there are more than `vsize()`-2 lines, ignore the remaining ones. For example, `TextBox( 10,10,17,23,"Soybean Production").plot( g );` `g.show();` should result in the foregoing display.

Exercise 10.1.4. Implement a `Point` class storing row and column coordinates of a point. Redefine the `Box` class to store two corner points and rewrite the `Box` and `TextBox` constructors.

After we rushed to embrace this new language concept, let us consider a more traditional alternative. `TextBox` could have made `Box` a member rather than deriving from it.

```
class TBox
{    Box b;
     char* text;
// ...
} ;
```

The memory layout looks just the same.

The members of b cannot be accessed directly, but neither could the base-class members. There are indeed only two differences.

- A pointer to a `TBox` is not automatically a `Box*`.
- A public member function of `Box` cannot be applied to a `TBox`.

If t is `TBox` then `t.vcenter()` is not correct. The function only applies to a box. If `t.vcenter()` is desired, it must be coded to call `t.b.vcenter()` . Here is a complete `TBox` type. Note in particular the member constructor call and the need to redefine the box measurement functions.

```
class TBox
{    Box b;
     char* text;
public:
     TBox( int rl, int cl, int r2, int c2, char* t )
     : b(rl,cl,r2,c2 ) { text = t; }
     void plot( Grid& g ) const;
     int vsize() const { return b.vsize(); }
     int hsize() const { return b.hsize(); }
     int vcenter() const { return b.vcenter(); }
     int hcenter() const { return b.hcenter(); }
} ;
```

```
void TBox::plot( Grid& g )
{    b.plot( g ); // draw the box outline

     int r = hcenter(); // same as above
     int len = strlen( text );
     int c = vcenter() - len/2;
     for( int i = 0; i < len; i++ )
          g[r][c++] = text[ i ];
}
```

Although eminently workable, this solution lacks the elegance of simply inheriting the box measurement functions. There is also a second disadvantage that will become clear in the next section: Class member data items do not support "virtual functions."

This section introduced the first use of inheritance: Inheritance can be a *convenience feature.* You can take an existing, working class, add a few new data or function members, and replace only the functions that need to be modified. However, inheritance is a multifaceted concept, and other applications of it are described in subsequent sections.

Exercise 10.1.5. Consider the `Vector` class developed in Section 9.5. *Derive* a safe array of `double` class from it. Add as data a lower bound `lo` and modify `operator[]` to return `Vector::operator[]( i - lo )` or print an error message if `i` is out of range. Pay special attention to the constructor.

Exercise 10.1.6. As in the previous exercise, start with the `Vector` class and derive a flexible array class in which the array grows automatically when a new index is requested.

10.2. VIRTUAL FUNCTIONS

In the last section we noted that a pointer to a derived class automatically points to the base class. One can put `Box` pointers in an array or linked list, some of which are pointers to plain boxes and others to `TextBoxes`. Of course, one cannot put the actual plain or `Text` boxes into an array or linked list because they differ in size, whereas all pointers have the same size. Here is a box list type:

```
class BoxList
{    // ...
public:
     BoxList();
     ~BoxList();
     void insert( Box* n );
     void reset();
     void advance();
     Box* info() const;
```

```
        int atEnd() const;
};
```

Now we can insert both plain and text boxes:

```
BoxList bl;

bl.insert( new Box( 0,5,10,15 ) );
bl.insert( new TextBox( 10,13,20,23,"Soybean Production") );
```

The value of `new TextBox(...)` is a `TextBox*`, which is in particular a `Box*`, and it can be inserted in the list without type conversion. But what is the use? When walking through the list and retrieving `Box*` pointers,

```
for( l.reset(); !l.atEnd(); l.advance() )
        // do something with p = l.info();
```

there is no way of telling whether a particular pointer p points to a plain box or a text box.

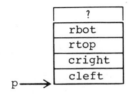

When calling `p->plot()`, it will merely call `Box::plot()`. One could add a *type field* into the box that has different values for plain boxes, text boxes, boxes with drop shadows, pie chart segments, and whatever other items we might come up with in the chart program. By inspecting `p->type` one could switch to the correct `plot` function:

```
switch( p->type )
{       case 0:
                p->plot(); break;
        case 1:
                ((TextBox*)p)->plot(); // cast operator is weaker
                                       // than ->
                break;
}
```

This is certainly a time-honored programming strategy, and there is nothing wrong with it for a program that never changes. However, we want to keep our program flexible for further enhancement. It would be desirable to free future generations of coders from the error-prone task of searching through the entire body of existing code for all occurrences of ->type (in `switch ( t->type )` or a function pointer table(`*fp[ t->type ]()`) whenever a new plottable item is introduced.

A truly marvelous concept, a *virtual function*, solves that problem. Making the `plot` function `virtual` in the base class

```
class Box
{     // ...
      virtual void plot( Grid& g ) const;
};
```

alerts the compiler automatically to make a type field that distinguishes a plain `Box` and all its derived classes and to translate each call

```
p->plot(); // p a Box*
```

into a run-time selection of the correct plot. Think of `plot` as *run-time overloaded*. Each item is plotted according to its type.

```
BoxList bl;

bl.insert( new Box( 0,5, 10, 15 ) );
bl.insert( new TextBox( 10,13,20,23,"Soybean Production") );

for( l.reset(); !l.atEnd(); l.advance() )
     l.info()->plot(); // uses Box::plot or TextBox::plot
```

To enable this feature, each function to be run-time selectable must be declared `virtual` in the base class. Only member functions can be virtual.

Exercise 10.2.1. Write a program that can read in plain and text boxes and test the run-time selection of the virtual `plot` function. A fancy solution is to provide a `operator>>( istream&, Box*& )`. Where does the decision whether to get a `new Box` or a `new TextBox` take place?

To add an `info` function that lists specific box information for debUgging purposes, the base and derived classes must be enhanced as follows:

```
class Box
{     // ...
      virtual void info() const;
};

void Box::info() const
{     cout << "[" << rtop << " " << cleft << "|"
           << rbot << " " << cright << "]";
}

class TextBox : public Box
{     // ...
      void info() const;
}
```

```
void TextBox::info() const;
{      Box::info();
       cout << " " << text;
}
```

The following code lists the box-specific information for each box in a list.

```
for( l.reset(); !l.atEnd(); l.advance() )
        l.info()->info(); // uses Box::info or TextBox::info
```

The selection of the correct function occurs at run-time.

Exercise 10.2.2. Add the `info` function and test it.

How does this programming method differ from the `switch` solution? Adding another plottable item is localized. For example, to add a box with shading

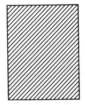

one provides

```
class ShadedBox : public Box
{      char shade; // the character used inside the box
public:
       // ...
       void plot( Grid& g ) const;
       void info() const;
};
```

and code for the `plot` and `info` functions. *No existing code needs to be modified.*

Exercise 10.2.3. Add a `ShadedBox` to your code. Verify that the list traversal code did not change.

The implementation of the virtual function feature is left to the discretion of the compiler, and some authors feel that such details should be of no concern to the reader. I provide an explanation of the mechanism used by the standard C++ → C translator to show that virtual functions can be implemented with a surprisingly low space and time overhead.

A class that has at least one `virtual` member function allocates an additional data member, a pointer to a function table. You can think of this data member as a type field. An instance of a derived class is built on the base class structure, so it automatically inherits the pointer field. But it contains a different value, a pointer to a table with different function entries.

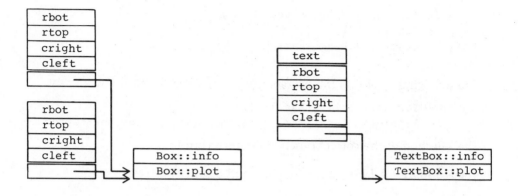

Recall that the function name **Box::plot** without the **()** refers to the *starting address* of the function. A pointer to an unknown object can still execute a virtual function as long as it knows the position of the function in the table.

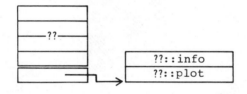

Think of the table of function pointers as an instruction manual. Each object comes with its own instruction manual, and all object manufacturers agree that the instructions for **plot** are on page 0, for **info** are on page 1, and so on. All one has to do when asked to perform a task with an object of unknown type is to get the instruction manual from the glove compartment, open it on the agreed page, and execute the instructions. The call

    p->info()

is translated into a call to

    *(p-> *function table + offset of* **info**)

The operations are:

- Taking the table address from the structure.
- Looking up the function address at a constant offset in that table.
- Calling that function.

The space overhead is equally modest. For each class, a small table is allocated with the starting addresses of virtual functions. Each *instance* of a class (base or derived) has a single additional pointer field. This is a problem only if there are a great many instances of the same class and a pointer cannot be tolerated in each of them.

Who enters the table pointer and when? The compiler generates code *function table= table address* in the constructors that get executed when a new object is allocated, either statically (`Box b`) or dynamically (`p = new TextBox`).

Clearly this mechanism is very efficient, much more efficient than a typical hand-coded `switch` statement.

Exercise 10.2.4. If you have a C++ → C translator, look at the C output of a virtual function call and of the virtual table construction.

There is no agreement among computer scientists as to what makes a language object-oriented. Some people call Ada or Modula-2 object-oriented; others say a language without garbage collection is not truly object-oriented. I believe that virtual functions are the touchstone of object-orientation. If an object can decide at run-time how to behave and one can place a number of objects into a list and tell each one of them "do your thing," the responsibility of program flow truly lies with the objects.

In my opinion, a language such as Ada is not object-oriented. This is not a value judgment. Ada has some features (generic types, error handling) that C++ lacks, and it may well be a good language for its intended purpose (embedded systems), but it has no language support for overloading functions at run-time. Of course it is possible to hand-code this and do object-oriented programming in a non object-oriented language, just as it is possible to write structured programs in Fortran.

Exercise 10.2.5. This exercise gives an indication of the implementation of a multiple "undo" command in a word processor. For simplicity, we will just implement a (useless) line processor, editing a single line of text. Commands are:

(any character key)	Enter the character at the cursor location
[Ctrl-L]	Move cursor left
[Ctrl-R]	Move cursor right
[Ctrl-B]	Move cursor to the beginning of the line
[Ctrl-E]	Move cursor to the end of the line
[Del]	Delete character under the cursor
[Bksp]	Delete character before the cursor
[Ctrl-U]	Undo the previous command
[Ctrl-D]	Redo the previous command
[Ctrl-Q]	Quit

Any number of "Undo" commands should be supported, back to the starting state of a completely blank line.

Design a base class `Command` . Derive from it commands to move the cursor, to insert a character, to delete a character. Keep an array of pairs of `Command*` . Every time a new command is entered (except undo/redo), enter both the command and its inverse onto that array. Undo goes backward in the array, executing the inverses, and redo goes forward, reexecuting the previously entered commands.

Find out how you can get unbuffered input on your system and how you can move the cursor and insert/delete characters in a line. Encapsulate those system-dependent details.

Exercise 10.2.6. Add commands to the program of the previous exercise:

[Ctrl-I]   Toggles the "insert mode" from insert to overtype
[Ctrl-A]   Deletes all characters after the cursor

10.3. VISIBILITY AND CONSTRUCTION

Which members of a base class are visible to a derived class? To the outside world when contained in a derived class? We saw in the last section that private members of a base class cannot be accessed in a derived class. Public members of the base class are accessible to member functions of the derived class. But to make them *public* members of the derived class, the keyword `public` must be inserted after the`:` derivation symbol. This sounds confusing, and it is. Consider the example from the last section, with the word `public` removed from the derivation.

```
class Box
{    int cleft, cright, rtop, rbot;
public:
        Box( int rl, int cl, int r2, int c2 );
        int vsize() const;
        int hsize() const;
        int vcenter() const;
        int hcenter() const;
        virtual void plot( Grid& g ) const;
};

class TextBox : Box
{    char* text;
public:
        TextBox( int, int, int, int, char* );
        void plot( Grid& g ) const;
};
```

Ift is a`TextBox` , then

- `t.cleft` is an error. Private members of the base class cannot be accessed from the derived class.
- `t.vsize()` is okay inside a member function of `TextBox` but not inside any other function. Public members of a non-`public` base class become private members of the derived class.

- A cast `(Box*)t` is not legal outside a member function because it could be used to circumvent the previous restriction.

All this is usually undesirable. Why shouldn't other functions be able to measure `t.hsize()` ? Why indeed? To make public members of the base class public in the derived class, the base class must be declared `public`.

```
class TextBox : public Box
{    // ...
};
```

Public base classes are far more common than their more secretive cousins, and it is too bad that their declaration is longer. However, it is understandable from the close analogy between a base class and a class member. If `Box` would have been a class member

```
class TBox
{    Box b;
     // ...
}
```

it would have been impossible as well to refer to `t.hsize()` .

Consider a base class like `Box`. Some members such as `hsize()` should be public members of any of its derived classes. For efficiency, it would be desirable to make `cleft` and so forth accessible to derived classes, but only as private members. The mechanism discussed so far does not offer this choice. Either all public members of a base class are public members of the derived class (`class TextBox : public Box`) or none are (`class TextBox : Box`). For this reason, there is another level, called `protected`. (This feature was introduced in C++ version 1.1.) A `protected` member of the base class is visible to all member functions of all classes derived from it, but not to any other functions. The following setup is common.

```
class Box
{
protected:
    int cleft, cright, rtop, rbot;
public:
    int vsize() const;
    // ...
};

class TextBox : public Box
{    char* text;
public:
    // ...
};
```

- `t.cleft` is okay inside a member function of `TextBox` but not inside any other function. Protected members of the base class become protected members of the derived class.

- `t.vsize()` is okay everywhere. Public members of a public base class stay public in the derived class.

When designing a class that you expect others to use as a base for derivations, follow these rules:

- Place items that *nobody* needs to know about in the private section.

- Place items that might be useful for members of derived classes in the `protected` section.

- Place items that the derived class might want to make public into the `public` section. It still is up to the derived class whether to go ahead and make these items public (`Derived : public Base`) or not (`Derived : Base`).

A constructor for a derived class usually needs to initialize the base class members. Because it rarely has access to all of them, the base class constructor needs to perform this task. Because constructors are not functions, the derived class constructor cannot simply call the base class constructor. To cause the constructor to be called, its arguments are placed before the body of the derived class constructor.

```
TextBox::TextBox( int rl, int cl, int r2, int c2, char* t )
    : Box(rl,cl,r2,c2 )
{    text = t;
}
```

This syntax is very similar to a member constructor call:

```
TBox( int rl, int cl, int r2, int c2, char* t )
    : b(rl,cl,r2,c2 )
{    text = t;
}
```

In fact, both kinds of constructor invocations may be present if a derived class also has class members.

```
class StringBox : public Box
{    String s;
public:
    StringBox( int, int, int, int, String );
    // ...
};

StringBox::StringBox( int rl, int cl, int r2, int c2,
                                            String str )
    : Box(rl,cl,r2,c2 ), s(str)
{}
```

The constructor itself has no more work to do. We mention again that in C++ version 1 the name of the base class is omitted from the constructor specification.

```
StringBox::StringBox( int c1, int r1, int c2, int r2,
                                            String str )
    : (c1,r1,c2,r2 ), s(str) // Version 1
{}
```

Note the difference between base class constructor invocation (with the type name) and member constructor invocation (with the member name). It is instructive to visualize the entire sequence of events. Keep in mind that constructors never actually obtain storage, they just serve to fill preallocated memory.

- First storage for the object is allocated (on the static data area, stack, or heap).
- Then the base class constructor initializes the base area.
- Then the member class constructor(s) are launched on their areas.
- Then the body of the constructor is executed.

Destructors run in the opposite order. The destructor does not actually destroy the object in question. It contains code that must run before the object is forgotten or recycled.

Here is the sequence of destructor events:

- First the class destructor code is executed.
- Then the destructor of each member is executed.
- Then the destructor for the base class is executed.
- Then the object is forgotten or recycled.

Exercise 10.3.1. Write a set of functions that recursively evaluate nested arithmetic expressions. Allowable expressions are:

number	any `int`
sum	sum(e_1, e_2,... en)
product	prod(e_1, e_2,... en)
difference	diff(e_1, e_2)
quotient	quot(e_1, e_2)

For example:

```
sum( 2, prod( 3, 4, -2 ), diff( 3, quot( 8, 2 ) ), 10 )
```

Design a base class `Expr` with virtual functions `eval` and `print`. Design a list type `ExprList`. Derive classes `Number` (containing an int), `Sum`, and `Product` (containing an `ExprList`), `Difference`, and `Quotient` (containing two `Expr`). Your program should read in an expression from standard input, print it back out, and print its value.

Exercise 10.3.2. Change the `print` functions in Example 10.3.1 to print expressions in standard algebraic notation, such as

```
2 + 3*4*(-2) + (3-8/2) + 10
```

The challenge is not to print unnecessary `()` .

Exercise 10.3.3. Change the `print` function once more to print quotients as fractions!

$$1 + \frac{10 - 2}{3} \over 2 * 12$$

Hint: Buffer the output in a 2-dimensional array. Implement a virtual function `size` returning a structure containing the number of rows/columns needed for an expression. (For example, vertical size of a fraction = vertical size of numerator + 1 (for the fraction bar) + vertical size of denominator. Vertical size   of sum = max of vertical sizes of the summands.)

Exercise 10.3.4. Add a square root operator and display it as in

$$\frac{a + \backslash\,|\,\overline{b}}{2 * c}$$

If you have an IBM PC or another system with special math characters, display

$$\frac{a + \sqrt{b}}{2 \cdot c}$$

instead.

10.4. INHERITANCE HIERARCHIES AND MULTIPLE INHERITANCE

It is quite common to have an entire hierarchy of derivation with some classes twice or more removed from a base class. In our chart package, we may well have plottable objects that are not boxlike, such as pie-chart segments.

The `plot` function should therefore be based in a type `PlotObj` from which both `Box` and `PieSegment` are derived.

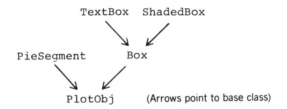

(Arrows point to base class)

```
class PlotObj
{
public:
     virtual void plot( Grid& ) const;
};

void PlotObj::plot( Grid& ) const
{    error( "This can't happen." );

}

class Box : public PlotObj
{
protected:
// ...
public:
     void plot( Grid& ) const;
};

class TextBox : public Box
{    // ...
};
```

The PlotObj class has no data items. It merely holds the other classes together by providing a common virtual plot function. No actual instance of a plain PlotObj will ever be created because it has no conceivable use. Such a class is called an *abstract base class*. If an instance is created accidentally and plotted, the default version of plot() generates an error. (A virtual function must always have a default, even if it is never intended to be used. {} is okay as is generation of an error message.)

In C++ version 2, a virtual function can be explicitly declared as abstract, for example,

```
class PlotObj
{
public:
     virtual void plot( Grid& ) const =0;
};
```

A class with at least one abstract virtual function becomes an abstract class, and the compiler will not permit creation of any instances of the class itself. Of course, pointers to the class, pointing to (nonabstract) derived class instances, are permitted.

Exercise 10.4.1. Discuss the memory layout of a `TextBox` in this hierarchy. Where is the pointer to the virtual function table located?

Exercise 10.4.2. Restructure the inheritance tree by basing it on a `PlotObj` and including a `PieSegment` class. You can find algorithms for drawing slanted lines and circles in any textbook on computer graphics, for example, Pokorny and Gerard, Chapters 2 and 3. Or, if you are lazy, implement a `Diamond` class instead.

In Version 1 of C++, the inheritance graph is always a tree because a derived class can only have a single base class. That is not always desirable. Suppose that we wish to make use of an existing class

```
class TextObj
{
protected:
     char* font; // e.g. "Helvetica"
     int ptsize; // e.g. 10 point
public:
     virtual void print( char*, Grid&, int x, int y ) const;
};
```

that can display text strings in various fonts on a grid object. In this scenario, a grid object is not likely to be an 80 × 25 array—one can't very well show a lot of different type styles on it. It could be a much higher resolution screen bitmap, or a linked list of PostScript commands. (PostScript is a graphics description language. There are laser printers and phototypesetters that can translate PostScript commands into text and graphical shapes.) Now a text box

Soybean
production

could make good use of the services provided by both the `Box` and the `TextObj` class.

```
class TextBox : public Box, public TextObj // Version 2.0
{    char* text;
public:
```

```
        // ...
        void plot( Grid& g ) const;
};

void TextBox::plot( Grid& g ) const
{    plot( g ); // plot from Box
     print( text, g, vcenter(), hcenter() ); // print from
                                             // TextObj

}
```

The inheritance graph now looks like

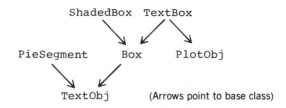

(Arrows point to base class)

It is no longer a tree because **TextBox** has two base classes. If one thinks of the edges as having a direction (arrows pointing from the base class to the derived class), the inheritance graph is a *directed acyclic graph* (DAG). There can be no cycles because no class can be its own direct or indirect derived class.

Couldn't one just define a **TextBox** as

```
class TextBox : public Box // using single inheritance
{    char* text;
     TextObj t;
public:
     // ...
     void plot( Grid& g ) const;
};

void TextBox::plot( Grid& g ) const
{    plot( g ); // plot from Box
     t.print( text, g, vcenter(), hcenter() );
}
```

This looks almost the same as the foregoing code. But now a **TextBox** is no longer a **TextObj**. It cannot be placed onto a list of **TextObj**. The benefit of inheritance is not merely access to data. Class members are adequate for that. More important is the ability to select the correct member function at run-time when the object is grouped together with other objects sharing a common base class.

The syntax for multiple inheritance is a straightforward extension. The attribute `public` must be separately listed for each base class:

```
class TextBox : public Box, public TextObj
```

Any number of base classes can be specified. A constructor that calls base class constructors must explicitly name the base classes:

```
TextBox::TextBox( Box b, char* t, char *fontName,
                                        int pointSize =10 )
    : Box( b ) , TextObj( fontName, pointSize )
{    text = t;
}
```

(The old syntax in which the base class name was omitted is no longer acceptable when more than one base class is present.) All public members from any of the base classes can be accessed. If two of them happen to have the same name, the scope resolution operator must be used, for example, `Box::info()` and `TextObj::info()` can distinguish between two inherited `info()` functions.

Multiple inheritance poses several technical problems, which explains its omission in early versions of the C++ language. The most obvious is: A pointer to a derived class no longer automatically points to the base class. Consider the `TextBox` derived from two base classes:

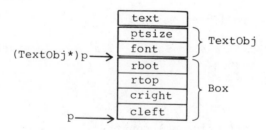

If the memory layout is as shown here (and there is no guarantee for that), a pointer `TextBox* p` points automatically to the `Box` portion but not the `TextObj` portion. Yet often we want it to point there. For example, `p->print(...)` should receive the starting address of the `TextObj` portion as `this`.

The translator handles this automatically. When a pointer to a derived class is converted to a pointer to one of the base classes (either by an explicit cast or by a base member function call), the appropriate offset is added. The programmer must be more careful than ever about explicit type conversion.

Casually placing a `TextBox*` into a `void*` and subsequently casting it as a `TextObj*` will not work at all.

Exercise 10.4.3. Design a `TextObj` class. If you are ambitious and have access to a graphics display or printer, recode the `Grid` class and support different fonts and sizes, as your local hardware permits. If not, settle for styles that can be displayed with standard characters only:

```
Regular ALL-CAPS  W i d e  Underlined
```

Then design the `TextBox` class and test it. (Of course, you can't do this exercise if you only have version 1 of C++.)

Multiple inheritance is particularly useful if a class can be combined from several preexisting classes. For example, one might want to have a `ShadedTextBox`:

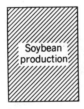

The most natural solution is to make a `ShadedTextBox` an object that is both a `ShadedBox` and a `TextBox`:

```
class ShadedTextBox : public ShadedBox, public TextBox
{     // ...

};
```

Here is the inheritance graph:

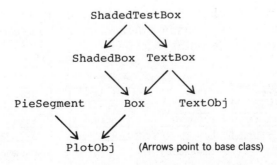

This is much better than defining a `ShadedTextBox` as a `TextBox` with ashade data member. The shading function can be inherited, and a `ShadedTextBox` is *both* a `TextBox` and a `ShadedBox` .

However, there is a serious problem. Both parent classes derive from `Box`, and there are two different boxes in each instance of `ShadedTextBox`.

shade
rbot
rtop
cright
cleft
text
rbot
rtop
cright
cleft

If s is a `ShadedTextBox`, what is `s.vcenter()`? It is ambiguous and must be made explicit through scope resolution: `s.ShadedBox::vcenter()` or `s.TextBox::vcenter()` . After all, there *might* be different boxes stored in both parts, even though that is not our intention in this example. Wasting the space for both boxes is undesirable, as is the worry to keep the information in both of them identical. *Virtual base classes* are designed to overcome this problem.

If `TextBox` and `ShadedBox` both declare `Box` to be virtual,

```
class TextBox : virtual public Box { ... };
class ShadedBox : public virtual Box { ... };
    // keyword order not significant
```

then a class inheriting from both gets only a single instance of `Box`. The declaration of `ShadedTextBox` is unchanged,

```
class ShadedTextBox : public TextBox, public ShadedBox
{ ... };
```

and the common virtual classes are coalesced to a single copy. No matter how often a virtual base class occurs in a derivation, only one common instance is created. The memory layout is as follows:

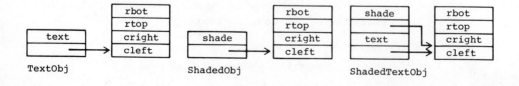

The virtual base class is stored separately from the derived classes. The doubly derived class has two copies of the pointer to the common virtual base class. This is necessary to have a pointer to a `ShadedTextObj` convertible to a pointer to `TextObj` or `ShadedObj`.

Because a single copy of the virtual base class is shared, there is a restriction on virtual base class construction: A virtual base class may be initialized only from the *most* derived class or with a constructor requiring no arguments.

Why is this necessary? If both `TextObj` and `ShadedObj` initialize `Box` with explicit arguments, which of the two should initialize the `Box` portion of a `ShadedTextObj` ? The only safe strategy is to deny it to both. But `Shaded-TextBox` is more derived than either and can initialize `Box`:

```
ShadedTextBox(...) : Box(...), ShadedObj(...), TextObj(...)
{};
```

This initializes the shared instance of `Box`. If such a constructor is present, it is not possible to derive again from `ShadedTextBox` and another class with a `virtual Box` base.

The order of construction is:

- Virtual base classes (through constructor without arguments).
- Base classes, in order of declaration.
- Member classes, in order of declaration.
- Derived class.

Destruction proceeds in reverse order.

Exercise 10.4.4. Implement the `ShadedTextBox` with virtual base classes. If you are using a character-based display, first shade and then let the text overwrite over the `/`.

10.5. PITFALLS

10.5.1. Using the Base Class Instead of a Pointer

Base classes usually carry no or very little information. Most actual data sit on top of them, in a derived class. It therefore usually makes no sense to pass an actual instance of a base class in or out of a function. For example,

```
void rotate( PlotObj p, double angle ); // WRONG
```

This function cannot possibly work. A `PlotObj` carries *no* information except a virtual function table pointer. If an object is passed into the procedure, only the base portion of it is copied. However,

```
void rotate( PlotObj* p, double angle ); // OK
```

can work, presumably by virtual function calls through `p` .

10.5.2. Casting to a Private Base Class

Private base classes are rarely useful. A private base class is as well hidden to the outside world as a private data member. Not even its existence is acknowledged. In particular, it is not possible to cast from a derived class to a private base class. Whenever virtual functions are used, the base class must be made public:

```
class PlotList // a list of PlotObj
{     // ,...
public:
    void insert( PlotObj* );
    // ...
};

class Box : PlotObj // not public
{    // ...
public:
    void plot() const;
}

Box* b = new Box( 10,15,15,20 );
PlotList l;
l.insert( b ); // ERROR--can't convert Box* -> PlotObj*
```

The remedy is to make `PlotObj` a `public` base class.

10.5.3. Forgetting Defaults for Virtual Functions

Each instance of a virtual function must have a definition, even if it lies in an abstract base class and will never be called. The compiler wants to insert something into the corresponding slot of the virtual function table. Reasonable solutions are:

```
class PlotObj
{    // no data
public:
    virtual void plot() const {} // do nothing
    virtual void rotate( double )
                        { cerr << "This can't happen." }
    virtual int vcenter() { return 0; } // {} would give
                                        // error message
    // ...
};
```

In C++ version 2, *pure virtual functions* can be declared:

```
class PlotObj
{
public:
    virtual void plot() const =0;
    // ...
};
```

The compiler then enforces that PlotObj is an abstract class, and any attempt to declare an actual PlotObj will be flagged as an error.

CHAPTER 11

MODULES

11.1. FILES AS MODULES

C++ programs are usually broken up into a number of source files, each containing groups of related functions and data. Only one of the files contains `main`. These source files are compiled separately into object files. Commonly used object files are packed together into a library file. The program is produced by linking object files with modules from custom and standard libraries. The linker takes only the modules that the program needs from the libraries, fixes up data and function addresses, and produces an executable file. The details depend on the operating system.

If one file changes, then that file must be recompiled and the program must be relinked. The majority of files are unaffected. This feature is called *separate compilation*. Contrast this with standard Pascal: All functions are nested inside a single **program** statement, all in one file. Any change requires recompilation of the entire code. Of course, many implementations of (nonstandard) Pascal added schemes to support modularity.

Each program module is a collection of global data items and functions. The programmer can control which data and functions are visible to the outside. This is quite similar to the data-hiding capability of classes, although the syntax is rather different. Here are some guidelines for efficient module design:

- *Don't share unless you have to.* Once you share something, other people just might start using it. Then you can't change it without their consent.

- *Keep the interface simple.* If each programmer must learn many details to understand other modules, they don't have time to get their own work done.

- *Don't share storage.* In C++, you can't give selective access to global data. *Everyone* can inspect and change global data once you permit access to anyone. Use functions for inspection and controlled modification.

You will note that the same guidelines are applicable for the design of classes.

Let us now consider the details of information hiding in modules. For historical reasons, the syntax has little in common with the syntax for classes. Regrettably, the default is to share all global data and functions in a module. (However, `const` and `inline` objects are private by default.) When prefixed by the word `static` (!), the item is kept private.

```
static int counter;
static void clearall();
static int lookup( char* word, char* table[], int tsize )
{
    //...
}
```

The choice of `static` is traditional but unfortunate. The keyword `static` already has another use, to declare a local variable static (retaining its value after it is out of scope), as in

```
int random( int s =0 )
{    static int seed; // static has no connection with
                       // data hiding

     if( s != 0 )
     {    int oldseed = seed;
          seed = s;
          return oldseed;
     }
     // compute next random number ...
}
```

Of course, `seed`, being local, is also hidden from other modules (as well as other functions in the same module). There can never be an ambiguity between the two uses of `static`. When applied to a local or class member variable, it means "make it persistent." When applied to a global variable or function, it means "make it private."

The designers of C++ could have offered `private` as an alternative, letting the C-style use of `static` sink into obscurity, but they didn't.

You should, as a matter of habit, declare all items `static` unless they were explicitly promised to the public when the module was designed. Each module makes certain data and functions available to other modules, namely the ones not declared `static`.

On the other hand, constants default to being private:

```
const Complex j(0,1);
```

is not accessible in other modules. If you want to share a constant, you have to give it "external linkage":

```
extern const Complex j(0,1);
```

If another module needs to access a public variable or function, it must tell the compiler. To use data from another module, give its declaration (but omit any initializer) and prefix it with the keyword `extern`.

```
extern int linenumber;
extern double scheduleTimes[ NPROCESS ];
extern const Complex j; // no initializer
```

To call a function from another file, the compiler needs to know its name, the types of all of its arguments, argument defaults (if any), and the type of the return value. This information is stated in a *prototype*

```
int getword( char*, char );
double sqrt( double );
int rand( int = 0 );
```

Variable names and `extern` are optional.

```
extern int getword( char* buffer, int buflen );
```

It is a good idea to include variable names because they can remind you of their meanings. Of course, the compiler only cares about type checking and ignores the variable names. It does need argument defaults, in case a function call has less than the maximum number of variables and defaults must be supplied.

For function declarations, the `extern` keyword is optional because the compiler can tell the difference between a function prototype and a definition. If the (`...`) are followed by a `;`, it is a prototype, if they are followed by { `...` }, it is a definition.

Commonly, these prototypes are placed in a header file. See Sections 11.3 and 11.4 for details.

Prototypes can be used to advertise a function that comes later in the same module. In fact, some programmers prefer to first list the prototypes of all functions in a module and then write the function definitions. Others sort functions to have the definition precede their first use. With that style, `main` comes last in its module. But that arrangement is not always possible. Sometimes there is a circular chain of function calls. For example, in a recursive descent expression parser, `expression()` calls `term()`, `term()` calls `factor()`, and `factor()` calls `expression()`. In that case, use a prototype as a forward declaration for one of the functions to break the deadlock.

When using external data and functions, the compiler checks for type consistency. Of course, this demands truth in advertising. The compiler only sees the module it is compiling and has no way of comparing the actual definition of a variable with its advertisement in an `extern` declaration. If a module claims

```
extern double eventDuration( Event );
```

but the defining module actually implements

```
int eventDuration( Event e ) {...};
```

you are in big trouble. The compiler will generate code that interprets the bit pattern returned by the function as a `double`. Because floating-point numbers are formatted rather differently from integers, this is a sure recipe for disaster.

Programs change constantly. What was an `int` yesterday may well be a `double` today, and it is easy to have `extern` declarations that reflect yesterday's realities. We will see in Sections 11.3 and 11.4 how that can be avoided by placing them into a header file, to be maintained by the designer of the module containing the declarations.

Note that a public variable must be defined in exactly one module, with either a definition (and an optional initializer)

```
int cursor;
```

or an `extern` declaration with an explicit initializer

```
extern int cursor = 0; // must be definition because
                       // of initializer
```

and declared in all modules that use it:

```
extern int cursor; // no initializer
```

Some compilers are wishy-washy about this requirement, allowing multiple definitions (as long as one has at most one initializer) or none at all (i.e., declarations only). Public constants also must have exactly one definition (with `extern` to override the private default)

```
extern const Complex j(0,1);
```

and declarations

```
extern const Complex j; // no initializer
```

in all modules using it.

The `extern` command can take an optional string command to link with non-C++ functions. For example,

```
extern "Pascal" HAB winInitialize( USHORT );
extern "C"
{    int strlen( char* );
     char* strcpy( char*, char* );
}
extern "C"
{
#include <string.h>
}
```

Such directives tell the translator to use the system-dependent rules for calling functions written in other languages. The compiler may need to generate different code for function calls (e.g., pushing the arguments in another order) or different linker instructions may need to be generated. (This extension of the **extern** command is not supported in C++ version 1.)

C Note

Some C compilers introduce special keywords such as **pascal** or **cdecl** for mixed-language programming. This is similar to **extern "..."**, except using a string is smarter. It does not introduce new keywords for these machine-dependent constructions.

If a module uses a **struct**, **class**, or **typedef** defined in another module, the entire declaration must be replicated, as must everything it depends on. For example, to use a stack class defined elsewhere:

```
const int STACKSIZE = 20;

class Stack
{      int s[ STACKSIZE ];
       int sptr;
public:
       Stack() { sptr = 0; }
       int push( int );
       int pop();
       int isEmpty() const { return sptr == 0 };
};

Stack numStack;

// ...

if( !numStack.isEmpty() )
    cout << numStack.pop();
```

It may come as a surprise that the *client* module gets so much information about the stack class. It gets to see the stack class definition, including the private portion. Why isn't the private part secret? What stops the client programmer from peeking into it? The second question is easy to answer. Nothing stops the programmer, but of what use is the information? It is impossible to actually access numStack.sptr—the compiler flags it as an error. This entirely conforms to the wish of the stack designer who might later change from an array to a linked list. But why isn't the private part simply omitted, just as the bodies of external functions are omitted? The client module may declare instances of the stack class, and the compiler needs to know how much storage space to allocate for the structure. And the compiler needs to replace inline functions that may contain member accesses. If all classes were represented as pointers to a structure and if inline functions were not supported, the private part could indeed be omitted. Some languages, such as Modula 2, take this route, at the cost of additional pointer indirection and greater function call overhead for trivial functions.

There is no required order for the various declarations in a C++ file. However, professional programming teams usually standardize on some layout. A typical structuring convention is:

- Header comment, including copyright notice and author's name(s)
- Revision list comment
- #include statements
- const declarations
- Class and type definitions
- Global data
- Forward declarations (i.e., function prototypes)
- Functions

Such conventions are usually described in a *style guide* document to which each team member is expected to conform. Such style guides can be very detailed, spelling out module layout, comment layout, conventions for naming variables, functions and types, usage of uppercase and lowercase characters, and even the number of spaces per tab stop.

Exercise 11.1.1. Write a small program that is distributed over two source files, one (hello) only containing main:

```
void main() { hello(); }
```

and the other (message) containing

```
char message[] = "Hello, world\n";
void hello() { cout << message; }
```

Supply static and extern as appropriate. Find out how to compile and link these files on your system. Typical commands are

```
CC hello.c message.c
```

or

```
ccxx hello.cxx message.cxx
```

Now change the message string to "Hello, modular world\n" and find out how to rebuild the executable file without recompiling the hello module. Typical commands are

```
CC hello.o message.c
```

or

```
ccxx hello.obj message.cxx
```

Exercise 11.1.2. Split up the stack-based calculator program of Section 1.3 into two files, hiding all details of the stack implementation.

Exercise 11.1.3. The previous exercise used a stack *module*, implementing a single stack. Instead, redo the exercise with a stack *class* that potentially can be used to declare several stacks. The stack class should be implemented in a separate source file. The **class Stack** declaration needs to be present in both files.

Exercise 11.1.4. Implement a module that performs *full justification* of text.

A flush-right margin should be achieved by fitting as many words as possible onto a line and adding additional spaces between words. Your module should have the following public functions:

```
void setMargin( int );
 // set the right margin and start a new paragraph
void addWords( char* );
 // add more words to the current paragraph
void flush();
 // finish the current paragraph. The last line should be
 // left-justified only.
```

No data and no other functions should be public. Completed lines should be sent to standard output. Use the following code for testing:

```
extern void setMargin( int );
extern void addWords( char* );
extern void flush();
int main()
{    char buffer[ 200 ];
     setMargin( argc > 1 ? atoi( argv[1] ) : 66 );
     while( cin.getline( buffer, sizeof( buffer ) )
     {    if( strlen( buffer) == 0 ) // blank line
               flush();
          else
               addWords( buffer );
          char lf; cin.get( lf ); // eat '\n'
     }
     flush();
}
```

11.2. THE PREPROCESSOR

We are digressing in this section to introduce the preprocessor tool. The C++ language has no effective built-in mechanism to organize modules, but the preprocessor can be used for that purpose.

Compilation of a C++ program involves several steps. The first step is invariably the *preprocessor*. This is a special program that prepares the source file for the compiler. All lines starting with a # are preprocessor directives.

The #include < *filename*> or #include " *filename*" command directs the preprocessor to open the file and include all of its lines for inspection by the compiler. If the filename is enclosed in <>, only the "standard places" for header files are searched. If the filename is enclosed in "", the preprocessor first looks in the current directory and then in the standard places. The files to be included can contain anything. The preprocessor doesn't understand C++ and just includes the lines for the compiler. Usually they contain class definitions, extern declarations, and function prototypes. Many programmers have a personal header file with their favorite constructs such as

```
enum Bool { FALSE, TRUE };
inline int max( int x, int y ) { return x > y ? x : y; }
typedef char* String;
```

They include it at the top of each of their source files.

The #define directive instructs the compiler to perform a "search and replace" on the input text. For example,

```
#define  PRIVATE  static
```

replaces all occurrences of PRIVATE with static, as in

```
PRIVATE void clearall();
```

#undef removes a macro definition.

The preprocessor is heavily used in C programs to define constants and inline functions

```
#define  BUFLEN  20
#define  MAX( x, y ) ((x) > (y) ? (x) : (y))
```

but the C++ const, enum, and inline facilities do a better job. The MAX macro shows two remarkable features: Macros can do argument substitution, for example,

```
x = MAX( a, 2 );
```

becomes

```
x = ((a) > (2) ? (a) : (2));
```

and macros know nothing about the language:

```
x = MAX( a[i++], 2 );
```

becomes

```
x = ((a[i++]) > (2) ? (a[i++]) : (2));
```

which increments i twice and delivers the wrong result if a[i] is larger than 2. C++ inline functions do not suffer from that problem.

Use of macros frequently points to a deficiency in the language. C programmers use them for constants and inline functions because C does not have the appropriate language constructs. For the same reason, they are used in C++ to implement generic types (Section 12.2). And many programmers define their own keywords, such as **PRIVATE**, to replace the ugly static. It is even possible to define

```
#define BEGIN {
#define END }
#define IF if(
#define THEN )
#define WHILE while(
#define DO )
#define REPEAT do {
#define UNTIL( x ) } while(!(x))
```

and pascalize the language to an amazing degree. Don't do this when working in a team—your fellow C++ programmers will not be happy about having to play preprocessor to be able to read your code.

Code can be conditionally passed to the compiler with the #if directive. The #if line evaluates whether a constant-integer expression (which may not contain any sizeof, enum constants or casts) is nonzero.

```
#define PROCESSOR 386

...

#if PROCESSOR == 386
...
#elif PROCESSOR == 68000
...
#else
...
#endif
```

The expression defined(*name*) is 1 if *name* has been #defined, 0 if not.

```
#if defined( GERMAN ) || defined( FRENCH )
#undef ENGLISH
#endif
```

#ifdef *name* is a shortcut for #if defined(*name*) and #ifndef *name* stands for #if !defined(*name*).

```
#ifdef( GERMAN )
    cout << "Datei " << filename << " nicht gefunden.\n";
#endif
```

To select the German language version, a line

```
#define GERMAN
```

can be placed in the code. GERMAN is then defined to be the empty string, but all that matters for #ifdef is whether or not it is defined. It is also usually possible to pass definitions to the compiler on the command line:

```
ccxx  -DGERMAN  wp.cxx
```

Check your compiler manual for details.

Exercise 11.2.1. Take the stack calculator of Section 1.3 and insert debugging code that prints the stack after each push or pop. That code should only be compiled when debugging is in progress: Bracket it with

```
#ifdef DEBUG
...
#endif
```

and compile with DEBUG defined as the empty string. Check whether you can define DEBUG in the compiler command line.

More sophisticated debugging can be achieved by setting a debug level (#if DEBUG > 3 ...).

Exercise 11.2.2. Many source-level debuggers cannot show inline functions. Design and test a scheme where a keyword INLINE resolves to inline when DEBUG is not defined, to the empty string otherwise.

11.3. HEADER FILE MANAGEMENT

Each module makes certain data and functions available to the public, namely, all non-static functions and global variables. Other modules may import them. It would be inconvenient and error-prone if module users had to enter all extern declarations manually. Instead, it is customary that the designer of the module create a special header file, with the same name as the exporting module but extension .h. (Some systems use .hxx or .hpp.) The importing module includes it with a #include directive. You have done this many times, for example, #include <stream.h>.

This section deals with the design of header files, a boring and unpleasant issue because C++ offers no language support for it. You may safely skip this section until you feel the need for a header file maintenance strategy.

Header files can contain the following items:

- Prototypes of functions, including default arguments
- Complete definitions of inline functions
- Declarations of variables (without initialization)
- Declarations of numeric constants
- Declaration of const storage (without initialization)
- Class declarations, including the private portion and the inline member functions

Of course, whenever one of these items changes in the defining module, the header file must be updated to reflect the change! For this reason, maintenance of the header file is the responsibility of the module designer. Outdated header files are a major source of trouble. There are several strategies to avoid them. None of them is perfect, but it is important to settle on one of them. Otherwise it is just a matter of time before the source and header files are at odds with each other.

One common strategy is to #include the header file into the defining module as well as the client modules. To a certain extent, C++ cooperates very well. The compiler doesn't mind seeing multiple prototypes of the same function. When it encounters the definition of a function whose prototype it already saw, it will check whether the advertising coincides with the actual definition and issue an error message if not.

For example, suppose we wish to export a function

```
int getRecord( Employee& e ) { ...}
```

A prototype is placed into the header file:

```
int getRecord( Employee& );
```

Because the header file is #included at the top of the source file, the compiler encounters the prototype first and will check the actual function definition against it. If the function definition has been changed to

```
void getRecord( Employee& e ) { ...}
```

but the header file has not yet changed, an error message will be issued. The same protection applies to variables and constants. If a variable

```
extern double scheduleTimes[ 5 ];
```

is advertised in the header file, and the actual definition is

```
int scheduleTimes[ 5 ] = {  1, 1, 2, 3, 5 };
```

the mismatch will be detected. Note that the initializer is only supplied for the actual definition of the variable.

The sharing of struct, class, and typedef is more complicated because the compiler does *not* like to see them more than once. Rather than checking for consistency, it mindlessly complains about the redefinition. That is unfortunate. The class definitions must then reside in the header file, separate from the code for the member functions.

The situation is even more confusing for constants, because some const are simply inline replaced by their numeric values by the compiler, such as

```
const int BUFLEN = 30;
```

Others actually occupy storage:

```
extern const char* version = "Version 3.10";
extern const Date bday( 6, 16, 1959 );
```

Inline replaced constants must be placed in the header file as

```
const int BUFLEN = 30;
```

and *not* duplicated in the source file. The compiler will complain if it sees two declarations of the same inline constant

```
const int BUFLEN = 30;
...
const int BUFLEN = 30; // ERROR
```

rather than quietly checking for consistency. Constants occupying storage should be declared in the header file without the initializer

```
extern const char* version;
extern const Date bday;
```

and defined in the source file, just as variables.

Public inline functions face the same problem as inline constants. The compiler needs to see the definition and not just the declaration whenever compiling a client module. The definition must therefore reside in the header file. The compiler will not tolerate seeing it twice and it cannot be replicated in the source file.

Here is a table summarizing the foregoing discussion. All items are global items to be shared with other modules.

Item to Be Shared	In .c File	In .h File
Uninitialized data	`Employee staff[100];`	`extern Employee staff[];`
Initialized data	`int reportwidth = 80;`	`extern int reportwidth;`
Inline constants		`const int NSTAFF = 100;`
Stored constants	`extern const` `Complex j(0,1);`	`extern const Complex j;`
Functions	`Complex log(Complex z)` `{ ... }`	`Complex log(Complex);`
Inline functions		`inline int min(int x,int y)` `{ return( x<y ? x : y ); }`

Classes,
structures,
unions
	`Date Date::add(int n)`
	`{ ... }`
		`class Date`
		`{ int d,m,y;`
		`public:`
		    `int day() { return d;}`
		    `Date add(int);`
		    `...`
		`};`

typedef, enum		`typedef void (*FunPtr) ();`

Exercise 11.3.1. Describe the header files for the modules of the programs in Exercises 11.1.2 through 11.1.4.

Sometimes one header file must include another, and it can then happen that the same header file is encountered more than once. Because the compiler cannot tolerate multiple definitions of the same `struct`, `class` or `typedef`, this can lead to compiler errors. The preprocessor can be used to work around this language deficiency. Surround the declarations with

```
#ifndef symbol
#define symbol
```

declarations that should only be read once

```
#endif
```

If this block is encountered for the second time, the *symbol* is defined and the block is skipped. The traditional choice for the symbol is the name of the include file with the period removed, such as **INPUTH**.

It should be emphasized that C++ does not enforce or support any of the rules that we have laid down here. The responsibility for module management lies with the programmer.

11.4. AUTOMATIC EXTRACTION OF HEADER FILES

This section presents a technique for automatic extraction of header files from source files. It has been my experience that this method is far less error-prone than the manual method described in the previous section. ("The best header files are the ones that are untouched by human hands.") An AWK script is presented that automatically generates the .h files. It can be run whenever the source file changes (see AKW, 1988 for a description of AWK). This section can be safely skipped if you are not interested in automatic header file generation.

The header file maintenance method described in the previous section relies on including each header file in its own source file. This is definitely desirable to check against mismatches between function and variable declarations and definitions. But it has the unpleasant effect of separating logically related items into two files: class declarations and inlines into the header file, other data and functions into the source file, function and variable declarations in both. This section presents a different strategy. The header file is built automatically from the source file but not included into its own source. Conformance between declarations and definitions is guaranteed as long as the header file is rebuilt whenever the source file changes. I have found an AWK script to be reasonably efficient in this regard.

To make it easy on the extraction script, we require that all constructs to be included in the header file are prefixed with the keyword **EXPORT**. This keyword should be defined in a project header file as the empty string:

```
#define EXPORT
```

Every function or global variable should be preceded by either **EXPORT** or **static**. Consider an input module input.c with the following data and functions:

```
#include "project.h"

EXPORT int lineCount = 0;
static int isWhite( char ch )
{ ... }
static char skipWhite()
{ ... }
EXPORT int getline( char* buffer, int buflen )
{ ... }
EXPORT int getword( char* word, int wordlen )
{ ... }
```

The input.h file derived from input.c contains the lines

```
extern int lineCount;
extern int getline( char* buffer, int buflen );
extern int getword( char* word, int wordlen );
```

To include class definitions and inline functions in the header file, precede them by **EXPORT** as well. Consider the defining module stack.c:

```
#include "project.h"

EXPORT const int STACKSIZE = 20;

EXPORT class Stack
{     int s[ STACKSIZE ];
      int sptr;
public:
      Stack() { sptr = 0; }
      int push( int );
      int pop();
      int isEmpty() const;
};

int Stack::push( int n ) { ...}

int Stack::pop() { ... }

EXPORT inline int Stack::isEmpty() const
                                    { return sptr == 0; }
```

The extracted header file stack.h is:

```
#ifndef STACKH
#define STACKH
```

```
const int STACKSIZE = 20;

class Stack
{     int s[ STACKSIZE ];
      int sptr;
public:
      Stack() { sptr = 0; }
      int push( int );
      int pop();
      int isEmpty() const;
};

inline int Stack::isEmpty() const { return sptr == 0; }

#endif
```

The tool has several limitations, imposed by the complicated C++ declaration syntax. All declarations beginning with **EXTERN** const are assumed to be inline constants:

```
EXPORT const int MAXSIZE = 200;
```

This is, of course, the most common case. But other uses of const will confuse the script:

```
EXPORT const char* f( int );
```

must be rewritten to the equivalent

```
EXPORT char const* f( int );
```

(but *not* as **EXPORT** char* const f(int);! As long as the const comes before the *, it declares the string to be constant.) It is important that stored constants are correctly declared as **EXPORT extern const**. Otherwise the script will confuse them with inline constants or, if they have constructor arguments (**EXPORT** const Complex z(x,y);), with a function declaration! These problems could be overcome by a more sophisticated tool.

Here is the AWK script.

```
# C++ module header file generator

function bracecount( s, left, right ) {
  return( split(s,lsplit,left)-split(s,rsplit,right))
}

function strupper( s )
{  for( i = 1; i <= 26; i++ )
     gsub( substr( "abcdefghijklmnopqrstuvwxyz", i, 1 ),
        substr( "ABCDEFGHIJKLMNOPQRSTUVWXYZ", i, 1 ), s )
```

```
      return s
}

BEGIN {

   outfile = ARGV[1]
   sub( /\.[cC](xx|pp)?/, ".h", outfile )
   print "[mdgen.awk]  Copyright (C) Cay Horstmann."
   print ARGV[1] " -> " outfile

   if( match( ARGV[1], /[^\\\/]*\./ ) ) {
      hname = strupper( substr( ARGV[1], RSTART,
                                           RLENGTH-1 ) ) "H"
      print "#ifndef " hname >outfile
      print "#define " hname >outfile
      print "" >outfile
   }
   getline                                 # copy header comment
   oldStyle = substr( $0, 1, 2 ) == "/*"
   while( oldStyle || index( $0, "//" ) ) {
      sub( /\.[cC](xx|pp)?/, ".h" )
                                  # change filename to filename.h
      print >outfile
      if( index( $0, "*/" ) ) oldStyle = 0
      getline
   }

   keyword[ "typedef" ] = 1;
   keyword[ "enum" ] = 1;
   keyword[ "class" ] = 1;
   keyword[ "struct" ] = 1;
   keyword[ "union" ] = 1;
   keyword[ "inline" ] = 1;
   keyword[ "const" ] = 1;

}

$1 == "EXPORT" {
                                  # tag for items to be included
   print "" >outfile
                                  # separate items by blank line

   if( keyword[ $2 ] ) {
                             # if one of the standard keywords
      $1 = ""                                # delete EXPORT
```

```
        endIndicator = $2=="inline" ? "}" : ";"
        b = bracecount( $0, "{", "}" ); # skip past matching {}
        while( b || !index( $0, endIndicator ) ) {
            print >outfile
            getline
            b += bracecount( $0, "{", "}" )
        }
        print >outfile
}


else if( $2 == "/*" || $2 == "// " || $2 == "" ) {
    getline
                                # test for preprocessor command
    if( substr( $1, 1, 1 ) == "#" )      # on the next line
    {   print >outfile
                                    # could be # define, include
        while( substr( $0, length( $0 ) ) == "\\" ) {
            getline
                                # could be multiline define
            print >outfile
        }
    }
}


else if( $2 == "extern" && $3 == "const" )
{   $1 = ""                                  # delete EXPORT
    if( split( $0, out, "=" ) == 1)
                                    # split off initialization
        split( $0, out, "(" );
    print out[1] ";"  >outfile
}


else {
                            # function/variable declaration
    $1 = "extern"
                                # replace EXPORT with extern
    b = bracecount( $0, "(", ")" );
                                    # skip past matching ()
    while( b ) {
        print >outfile
        getline
        b += bracecount( $0, "(", ")" )
    }
    split( $0, out, "=" )
                                # split off initialization
```

```
          if( bracecount( out[1], "(", ")" ) )
              print $0 ";" >outfile
                                      # oops--"=" was for default arg
          else {
              split( out[1], out, ";" )
                                  # split off semicolon (if exists)
              print out[1] ";"  >outfile
          }
      }
  }

  END {                                    # print #endif
      if( ARGC > 1 ) {
          print "" >outfile
          print "#endif" >outfile
      }
  }
```

The BEGIN portion sets the keyword array, produces the #ifndef FILEH/ #define FILEH lines, and copies the first comment of the source file (presumed to contain a copyright notice, etc.) into the header file. Any file extension .c, .cxx, or .cpp in the comment is translated into a .h extension.

The main portion checks for the tag EXPORT. If it is present and followed by one of the strings in the keyword array, lines are copied until a matching brace count returns to 0 and (except for inline) a semicolon is found.

If EXPORT is followed by a comment or is alone in the line, the next line is checked for a preprocessor statement (#define or #include). That line is then copied, together with any continuation lines (e.g., for a multiline #define of a generic type).

If EXPORT is followed by extern const, the initializer of the constant (which starts either with an = or a () is split off.

Otherwise the EXPORT is assumed to introduce a function or variable. It is changed to print out as extern. This time, input lines are gathered until a matching parenthesis count returns to 0. An "=" initializer, if present, is stripped off.

If the script is stored in a file extracth.awk, header files can be produced simply by running

```
awk  -f  extracth.awk  input.C
```

Naturally, this AWK script is not bulletproof. But it should be easy to adapt it to any reasonable coding style. This flexibility was a major reason for choosing AWK to build the extraction tool.

Exercise 11.4.1. Add EXPORT statements to the modules of the programs in Exercises 11.1.2 through 11.2.4 and test the extraction tool.

11.5. PITFALLS

11.5.1. #define and Comments

Never place a // style comment behind a #define. It will become part of the substitution text.

```
#define PRIVATE static      // to declare a private
                           // function--WRONG

PRIVATE int count(Widget* w)
```

will be replaced by

```
static      // to declare a private function--WRONG int
            // count (Widget *w)
```

and the function header becomes part of the comment! This obviously confuses the compiler to no end and leads to bizarre error messages.

11.5.2. Mismatches Between Declarations and Definitions

If header files are maintained manually, it can be very easy to change a definition in the .c file while forgetting to update the .h file. Such errors are typically hard to find. Consider the following examples:

In .c File	In .h File (Forgot to Update)
`class Employee`	`class Employee`
`{ int id;`	`{ int id;`
`char name[20];`	`char name[20];`
`int age;`	`double salary;`
`double salary;`	`// ...`
`// ...`	`} ;`
`} ;`	
`double hoursWorked`	
`( Employee& );`	`int hoursWorked( Employee& );`

A module including the outdated header file will no longer work. When declaring an employee,

```
Employee* e = new Employee;
```

insufficient storage will be set aside. When calling the changed hoursWorked function,

```
nh = hoursWorked( *e );
```

the return value will be meaningless.

This kind of error is bound to happen unless a *strategy* for header file management is in place. Sections 11.3 and 11.4 discuss two such strategies.

C H A P T E R 12

GENERIC CLASSES

12.1. CONTAINER CLASSES

Suppose we wish to build a reusable stack class. What kind of objects should be stacked? Pointers are a good choice for a generic stack, as one can always stack the addresses of the objects. (Of course, one must come up with some storage space elsewhere for the actual objects.) But pointers to what? C++ makes available the type `void*`, a pointer to some unspecified item. It is nothing more than a memory address. It tells us where an item starts in memory, but one cannot tell how many bytes it occupies. For that reason, it is not possible to take the `*` of a `void*`(how many bytes should be fetched?) or add a number to it (how many bytes is `p+1` away from `p`?). The compiler flags any such attempts as errors. Any pointer can be placed into a `void*` variable without a type mismatch warning. For the opposite conversion, from `void*`, to any `X*`, a cast is always necessary. There are only three things one can do with `void*` pointers. Copy them, compare them, or cast them.

The interface of a generic stack class is

```
class Stack
{    //...
public:
    Stack();
    void* push( void* );
    void* pop();
    void* top() const;
    int isEmpty() const;
};
```

What can one do with a stack of `void*`? Suppose one actually wants to stack `Employees`. Put their addresses on the stack.

```
Employee staff[100];
Stack estack;
// ...
```

```
estack.push( &staff[n] );
// ...
Employee e = * (Employee*) estack.pop();
  // the cast is necessary--can't take the * of a void*
```

We are only storing the addresses of the employee structures. If the contents of an address changes or the structure is no longer in scope, the pointer on the stack may no longer be valid. It is usually better to make a copy of the information before pushing:

```
Employee* p = new Employee; // get storage space from the
                            // free store
*p = staff[n];
estack.push( p );
// ...
p = (Employee*) estack.pop();
Employee e = *p;
delete p; // recycle storage space
```

Exercise 12.1.1. Fill in the details of the "stack of pointers" class. Using the function of Exercise 5.1.2, read in employee records, allocate storage space with new, and push them onto a stack. Then pop them off and print them.

Our next example is a queue. Data can be inserted at one end and removed at the other. The queue contains void* because the size of the objects to be queued can vary. Natural implementations for queues are linked lists and circular arrays.

```
class Queue
{   // ...
public:
    Queue();
    void add( void* );        // add to queue
    void* inspect() const;    // look at next member
                              // to be dequeued
    void* remove();           // remove from queue
    int length() const;       // number of currently
                              // enqueued objects
};
```

Simulation programs typically contain several queues, one for the cars in front of each traffic light or customers in line at each teller window.

Exercise 12.1.2. Implement the Queue class, using a circular array:

```
class Queue
{     void* q[ MAXENTRIES ];
      int in; // index of next position for insertion
```

```
        int out; // index of next position for removal
    public:
        // ...
    };
```

Exercise 12.1.3. Implement a simple simulation: bank customers arrive and enter a queue. An array of tellers serves them. We need a few statistics: The time between two arrivals is well described by the *exponential distribution*. To generate a sequence e_n of random numbers that are exponentially distributed with mean μ, take a sequence of random numbers u_n that are uniformly distributed in the interval [0, 1] and compute

$$e_n = -\mu \cdot \log(u_n)$$

Uniformly distributed random numbers are obtained by a call to rand(), which returns a random integer between 0 and **MAX_RAND**. (rand and **MAX_RAND** are declared in stdlib.h, log is declared in math.h.) The time for the next arrival is

```
nextArrival = prevArrival - mu *
                            log( rand()/double ( MAX_RAND ) );
```

Similarly, assume processing time to be exponentially distrubuted (with a different mean λ). The purpose of the simulation is to measure the average time each customer spends in the queue, depending on:

- The number of tellers.
- Arrival rate (average of μ seconds between successive arriving customers).
- Processing rate (average of λ seconds per customer).

Implementation hints: Design a class **Customer** that stores the arrival time in the queue and a class **Teller** that stores whether the teller is currently busy and, if so, until when. A loop for(sec = 0; sec < maxsec; sec++) ticks away at the seconds, continually checking whether a teller becomes free or whether a new customer is coming. Use **new** and **delete** for obtaining and recycling storage space for customers, as described previously. Try out four tellers, an average of one customer every 30 seconds, and an average transaction length of 200 seconds.

12.2. USING THE PREPROCESSOR

Unfortunately, C++ does not currently offer a language construct for parametrized classes. One can have stacks of integers, strings, or pointers, but each must be declared separately. As done so often, one can use the preprocessor to fake it.

We wish to implement stacks of any type (**int**, **double**, **Employee**). We first show what the class user has to do.

```
#include <generic.h>

declare(Stack,int);
Stack(int) numStack;
// ...
declare(Stack,double);
Stack(double) lvalStack;
// ...
Stack(double) rvalStack;
```

With other words, before creating a `Stack(X)` for the first time, a `declare(Stack,X)` must be issued. From the user's side, this seems tolerable.

The `declare` macro is defined in generic.h. `declare(x,y)` glues the word `declare` after the first argument and supplies the second argument to the resulting macro:

```
#define declare(x,y) name2(x,declare)(y)
```

`name2(a,b)` is another macro that glues two tokens together. In an ANSI conforming compiler, the token pasting operator ## concatenates its arguments, and `name2(a,b)` is defined as `a##b`. Older C compilers don't have the token pasting operator but use other schemes (such as `a/**/b` in Unix System V). For example, `declare(Stack,int)` results in the macro call `Stackdeclare(int)`.

It is the class designer's role to define two macros: `Stackdeclare(X)` and `Stack(X)`. The second one is simply

```
// The following macro must be supplied by the stack
// designer
#define Stack(X) name2(X,Stack)
```

so that

```
Stack(int) numStack;
```

becomes

```
intStack numStack;
```

The first macro, `stackDeclare( ... )`, causes the declaration of a class ...stack.

```
// The following macro must be supplied by the stack
// designer
#define Stackdeclare(X)                          \
class Stack(X)                                   \
{    X s[ STACKSIZE ];                           \
     X sptr;                                     \
public:                                          \
     Stack(X)() { sptr = 0; }                    \
     X push( X n ) { return s[sptr++] = n; }     \
```

```
X pop() { return s[--sptr]; }              \
X top() const { return s[sptr-1]; }        \
int isEmpty() const { return sptr == 0 }   \
}
```

The \ must come immediately before the newline, with no intervening white space. They extend the lines to form a single preprocessor source line. This blows away many preprocessors that were not designed for such massive macro expansion. To keep the length down, all functions are inline and error-handling is not included.

Exercise 12.2.1. Implement this generic stack class and create two stacks of int and another stack of **double**. Your compiler should have an option to stop processing after the preprocessor. Find out how to do that and look at the preprocessor output, that is, the file that the compiler sees.

Exercise 12.2.2. Design a generic "safe array" type:

```
class Array(X)
{    ...

public:
     Array(X) ( int lo, int hi );
     X& operator[]( int );
};
```

that can be used in the following fashion:

```
declare( Array, char );
Array( char ) a(1,10);
a[ 10 ] = '*';
char ch = a[ 11 ]; // should generate error
```

The class should contain a pointer X* mem to a block of memory that is obtained from the free store: mem = new X[hi-lo+1].

12.3. USING INHERITANCE

Inheritance can be used to provide a type-safe interface to stored void* pointers.

Consider a stack stacking void*.

```
class Stack
{    // ...
public:
     Stack();
     void* push( void* );
     void* pop();
     void* top() const;
```

```
        int isEmpty() const;
};
```

Suppose we wish to stack matrices, or rather pointers to them because our stack class can only store pointers. We derive a `MatrixStack`:

```
class MatrixStack : public Stack
{    // no new data
public:
    MatrixStack() {}; // to force calling the base class
                      // constructor
    Matrix* push( Matrix* p )
                        { return (Matrix*) Stack::push( p ); }
    Matrix* pop() { return (Matrix*) Stack::pop(); }
    Matrix* top() const { return (Matrix*) Stack::top(); }
};
```

No new data have been introduced. Actually, no new functions have been introduced either. The inline functions merely provide a type-safe interface.

```
MatrixStack s;
Matrix* m;
Vector* v;

s.push( m ); // inline replacement: s.Stack::push( m );
v = s.pop(); // WRONG--v cannot receive a
             // (Matrix*) s.Stack::pop()
```

Note that `isEmpty()` is inherited from `Stack` without change.

In the last chapter we saw examples of an abstract base class, a class that had no data members but merely existed to hold together a number of other classes through its virtual functions. The technique introduced in this section is on the other end of the spectrum, where all the work is done in the base class and the derivation merely does type conversion.

The same technique can be used to declare an `EmployeeStack` holding `Employee*` pointers. Because the derivation is fairly short, the preprocessor trick of Section 12.2 can be applied to create a generic type.

```
#include <generic.h>
#define Stack(X) name2(X,Stack)
#define Stackdeclare(X)                              \
class Stack(X) : public Stack                        \
{                                                    \
public:                                              \
    Stack(X)() {}                                    \
    X* push( X* p ) { return (X*) Stack::push(p); }  \
    X* pop() { return (X*) Stack::pop(); }           \
    X* top() const { return (X*) Stack::top(); }     \
}
```

Stacks of `Employee*` can be obtained as

```
declare(Stack,Employee);
Stack(Employee) es;
```

Recall that the `declare` macro defined in the file generic.h calls the macro `Stackdeclare( Employee )` and that `Stack( Employee )` glues together as `EmployeeStack`. The `declare` macro should only execute once to produce the `class EmployeeStack` declaration. After that, any number of `Stack ( Employee )` can be declared.

It is indeed unfortunate that one has to resort to this technique to achieve type parametrization. Like all preprocessor hacks, its mere existence points to a glaring omission in the language. Efforts are under way to develop a facility for parametrized types (see Stroustrup, 1988).

Exercise 12.3.1. Make a generic list macro for a list type derived from a list of `void*` and then declare and test a `List(Date )`.

To store small items, such as integers or `doubles`, it just isn't worth allocating additional storage and memory, making the foregoing method unattractive. The next exercise shows how to use derivation to produce generic linked lists that store items directly, without using pointers.

Exercise 12.3.2. Starting with a `List`/`Cell` pair that stores *no information,*

```
class Cell
{    Cell* next;
     friend class List;
};

class List
{    Cell* head;
     Cell* cur; // current position
     Cell* pre; // predecessor of current position
public:
     List();
     ~ List();
     void remove(); // remove current position
     void advance();
     void reset();
     int atEnd() const;
};
```

derive an `IntList`/`IntCell` type

```
class IntCell : Cell
{    int info; // add info field
     friend class IntList;
};
```

```
class IntList : List
{    // no additional data
     int info() const; // info at cursor
     void insert( int n ); // insert integer before cursor
};
```

The `int` field is simply placed above the `next` pointer in each `IntCell`, and no additional pointers are used.

Exercise 12.3.3. Make a generic list class using the foregoing technique that enters actual members of class `X` rather than `X*` into the cells.

Exercise 12.3.4. Make a hash-table class that contains an array (of a size specifiable in the constructor, with default size some prime number about 100) of linked lists of `void*`. Entries with the same hash value are to be entered in the list. Implement `insert` and `find` member functions. Who supplies the hash function, the class, or the user?

12.4. GENERIC REFERENCE COUNTING

Because reference counting is a fairly mechanical operation, one can use inheritance to supply its behavior to other classes. We have two base classes:

```
class Object
{
protected:
     Storage* stor;

     void copy( const Object& );
     void free();

     Object( Storage* s =0 );
     Object( const Object& b ) { copy(b); }
     ~Object() { free(); }
     void assign( const Object& );
          // for use in derived operator=
public:
     int null() const { return stor==0; }
          // test whether pointer is 0
};

Object::Object( Storage* s )
{    if( stor = s )
          s->rc++;
}

void Object::copy( const Object& b )
```

```
{     if( stor = b.stor )
          stor->rc++;
}

void Object::free()
{     if( stor && !--stor->rc )
          delete stor;
}

void Object::assign( const Object& b );
{     if( this != &b ) { free(); copy(b); }
}

class Storage
{
protected:
      int rc; // reference count
      Storage() { rc = 0; }
      virtual ~Storage() {}
      friend class Object;
}
```

The *virtual destructor* can be replaced by a real destructor in a derived class to perform the necessary cleanup, usually to recycle a block to the free store.

This can be used to attach memory management by reference count to any data type. We illustrate the technique first with a `Vector` class. We separate `Vector` (a pointer) from `VecStor` (a structure containing the reference count, a dimension field, and a pointer to an array of doubles). All public access happens through `Vector`.

```
class Vector : public Object
{     // no additional member data
      operator Object() { return *(Object*) this; }
public:
      Vector( int d ) : ( new VecStor( d ) ) {}
      Vector( const Vector& v ) : (v) {}
      ~Vector() {}
      Vector& operator=( const Vector& b )
                              { assign( b ); return *this; }
      // all actual vector operations go here...
};

class VecStor : public Storage
{     int dim;
      double* co;
      VecStor( int d );
      // sets co to new double[d] and clears it
```

```
~VecStor() { delete co; }
// replaces virtual base destructor
friend class Vector;
};
```

The operator Object is necessary in operator= to convert b from a Vector to an Object. Although a Vector* is automatically an Object*, a Vector or Vector& is not cast into the base type without a type conversion.

Exercise 12.4.1. Sometimes the virtual destructor may be undesirable because it adds a pointer to each instance of Storage. Rewrite the Vector class without a virtual destructor by manually performing the deletion of the co-ordinates in ~Vector. Only delete when the reference count is about to go to 0.

The big problem with this technique is the fact that a Vector does not contain a VecStor*. Although not an issue for the class user who simply applies the member functions, it is troublesome for the class designer who has to write them. Consider writing a Vector::length function returning the length ($\sum x_i^2$) of a vector. The stor field points to Storage, not VecStor and must be cast to access the dim and co fields:

```
double Vector::length() const
{    double r = 0;
     for( int i = 0; i < ((VecStor*)stor)->dim; i++ )
     {    double xi = ((VecStor*)stor)->co[i];
          r += xi*xi;
     }
     return sqrt( r );
}
```

This soon gets tiresome. The solution is to provide two private access functions dim() and co().

```
class Vector : public Object
{    // no additional member data
     int dim() { return ((VecStor*)stor)->dim; }
     double* co() { return ((VecStor*)stor)->co; }
public:
     double length() const;
     // ...
};
```

The length function becomes

```
double Vector::length() const
{    double r = 0;
```

```
for( int i = 0; i < dim(); i++ )
{    double xi = co()[i];
     r += xi*xi;
}
return sqrt( x );
}
```

which is quite readable and as efficient as the first solution because the access functions are inline.

Exercise 12.4.2. Derive a `String` class from `Object` to add memory management to strings.

Exercise 12.4.3. Add reference counting to a `List` (of integers) class by preceding the entire list with a reference count.

Exercise 12.4.4. Apply the reference count strategy to the `List` class of Exercise 9.5.4 with a reference count for each cell. That is, `Cell` is derived from `Storage`.

Exercise 12.4.5. Make a generic list type storing `Objects` (pointing to storage with reference counts). As in the preceding exercise, each cell should have its own reference counts. Use this to implement a list of strings.

Exercise 12.4.6. Use the generic list type of the preceding exercise to implement a heterogeneous list, containing some strings, some integers, some lists thereof. Read in lists such as

```
( Joe 12 ( Harry ( 1 2 3 ) Carl ) -3 )
```

and print them with a virtual `print` function of `Object`.

12.5. THE IMPLEMENTATION OF A GENERIC CLASS HIERARCHY

One of the promises of object-oriented programming is code reusability. Programmers should not have to recode linked lists, hash tables, binary trees, and other basic data structures. Standard libraries should provide these building blocks. This section discusses some considerations involved in library building.

We will consider an object hierarchy that is rooted in a base class `Object`. All other classes are derived from it. Container classes, like arrays and sets, contain `Objects` and *are* `Objects`. It is then easy to combine them into complex structures. For example, a hash table can be an array of sets of objects with the same hash value. A real-world example of such a library is the NIH class library (see Gorlen, 1987).

Exercise 12.5.1. A user of a `String` data type wants to declare and use `String`s without much concern for what they are. In particular, the user would not care whether `String` is a class or a `typedef` for a pointer to a class:

```
typedef StringObj* String;
```

(Depending on the choice, member function would be written as `s.length()` or `s->length()`, either of which would be acceptable.)

Pointers have a big advantage: A pointer to a string class derived from the root object class is automatically converted to a pointer to the root object class. Explain this by considering a function call passing a `String` to a function expecting an `Object`, where both `String` and `Object` are pointers.

Discuss the disadvantages of this approach as well. Consider the implementation of `operator` functions and activation of constructors and destructors.

We need to consider what items to place in containers such as lists, arrays, or trees. The straightforward solution is to place `Object*` pointers into them. That does lead to a large number of pointer indirections. Consider a binary tree node holding a pointer to a `String`:

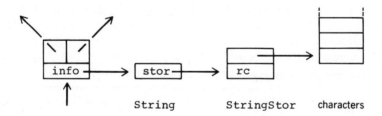

A storage improvement is possible if *all* objects are of the same form as `String`, containing only a single pointer. Then those objects (containing a single pointer) have uniform size and can be placed directly into containers.

This is an attractive idea for another reason: it allows unified storage management. Consider the foregoing tree node. In addition to the string pointer, it contains two pointers to child tree nodes. Our aim is to replace the string pointer with a string object and the two child pointers with tree *objects*.

```
class BinTree : Object;

class BinTreeStor : Storage
{    Object info;
     BinTree left;
     BinTree right;
// ...
} ;
```

Each object contains a pointer to a block of memory with a reference count.

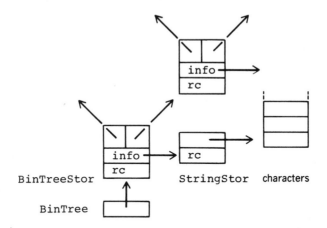

The objects are classes containing pointers, and not just pointers; therefore, one can attach constructors, destructors, and `operator=` to them that manage the reference counts. If the tree gets deleted, the destructor for the root automatically calls the destructors for the class members, recursively deleting all tree nodes and stored objects (unless they are referenced elsewhere, as evidenced by a reference count > 1). No memory management needs to be programmed explicitly.

To implement this approach, two parallel inheritance hierarchies are required. The library user sees the root `Object` and classes derived from it, such as `String` and `BinTree`. Each instance of these classes contains a single pointer. The library implementor designs classes derived from `Storage` to hold the actual information. The two base classes and the process for adding derived classes were described in the previous section.

Let us consider the implementation of a generic binary search tree class. A binary search tree is constructed such that the object stored in each node is larger than all objects in its left subtree and smaller than the one in its right subtree. This requires that the objects in the tree can be compared with each other. They should belong to a class `OrderedObject`, a class derived from `Object` with a function to compare two objects.

```
class OrderedObject : public Object
{
public:
    int comp( OrderedObject o ) const
    { return stor->comp( (OrderedObjectStor*) o.stor ); }
};

class OrderedObjectStor : Storage
{       friend class OrderedObject;
```

```
        virtual int comp( const OrderedObjectStor* o ) const;
            // returns a negative number if *this < *o,
            // 0 if they  are the same,
            // a positive number otherwise
};
```

Exercise 12.5.2. Why is `comp` declared `virtual` in `OrderedObjectStor`, not in `OrderedObject`? Hint: Derive `String` from `OrderedObject`. What function is selected in a call `s.comp( t )`?

A binary search tree contains ordered objects and a member function to insert them:

```
class BinTree : public Object
{
public:
    OrderedObject info() const { return stor->info; }
    BinTree left() const { return stor->left; }
    BinTree right() const { return stor->right; }
    void insert( OrderedObject );
    // ...
};

class BinTreeStor : Storage
{   OrderedObject info;
    BinTree left;
    BinTree right;
    BinTreeStor( OrderedObject o ) : info( o ) {}
    friend class BinTree;
    //  ...
}

void BinTree::insert( OrderedObject o )
{    if( stor == 0 )
        stor = new BinTreeStor( o );
    else
    {   int c = info().comp( o );
        if( c < 0 )
            left().insert( o );
        else if( c > 0 )
            right().insert( o );
    }
}
```

This is simple enough. How do we use it? Suppose our problem calls for building a tree of employee records, sorted by employee ID. We must fit the **Employee** class into our framework by deriving it from `OrderedObject`:

```
class Employee : public OrderedObject
{
public:
    const char* name() const;
    int id() const;
    double salary() const;
    // ...
};

class EmployeeStor : OrderedObjectStor
{   char name[ 30 ];
    int id;
    double salary;
    // ...
    int comp( const OrderedObjectStor* ) const;
};
```

The `EmployeeStor` version of `comp` *must* have the prototype

```
int EmployeeStor::comp( const OrderedObjectStor* s ) const
```

because it cannot differ from the prototype of the virtual function it replaces. It must assume that the second `OrderedObjectStor` really points to an `Employee` and make an explicit type conversion:

```
int EmployeeStor::comp( const OrderedObjectStor* s ) const
{    return( id - (EmployeeStor*)s->id );
}
```

Unfortunately, there is no C++ construct to specify that an explicit argument of a virtual function should be of the same type as the implicit argument.

To insert `Employees` into a `BinTree`, they must be converted into `OrderedObjects`. This is the conversion that C++ is reluctant to admit because `Employee` and `OrderedObject` are not pointers but classes containing pointers. Because the designer of `Employee` may not touch the definition `OrderedObject`, a conversion function

```
Employee::operator OrderedObject() { return
                                *(OrderedObject*) this; }
```

should be added to the `Employee` class.

Exercise 12.5.3. Write a program reading employee records from a file, inserting them into a binary tree and printing the tree in order to produce a list of employees sorted by ID number. `print()` should be a virtual function of `Storage`.

Exercise 12.5.4. The `BinTree::insert` code will fail if the binary tree contains not only `Employee` records but also other `OrderedObjects`. Use the technique of Section 12.2 to derive an `EmployeeTree` with a type-safe `insert` function.

Exercise 12.5.5. Build a type hierarchy, based on a root `Object`, containing the following classes:

- Numbers (`int`).
- Linked lists of `Objects`.
- Sets, with operations union and intersection, and no duplicate members.

Derive `Set` from `List`. You will need a virtual `operator==` to test whether two objects are identical. Because lists can contain other lists or sets, `operator==` must be called recursively. Two lists are equal if they have equal members at the same position. Two sets are equal when they have the same members in some order.

Exercise 12.5.6. Add a class `OrderedObject` to the previous exercise. Add a class `OrderedList` containing only `OrderedObjects` with a member function `sort`. Multiple inheritance is necessary for a properly modeled hierarchy: Sets are ordered (by inclusion $\subseteq$), even if their elements are not. `Set` must therefore be derived from both `List` and `OrderedObject`.

C H A P T E R   13

EXAMPLES OF OBJECT-ORIENTED DESIGN

13.1. SIMULATION

One of the origins of C++ is the Simula simulation language, and indeed C++ is well suited to event-simulation programs. In a simulation, objects such as cars or customers are moved around an environment. Typically objects have varying characteristics (speed, fuel level, number of items to purchase) and varying behavior under certain situations (will not enter a queue if it is longer than 10 people, will accelerate if the traffic light turns yellow and is less than 100 meters away).

A base class is prepared for each kind of object that holds the values describing state, properties, and default behaviors. Alternative behaviors are modeled with virtual functions. An event queue contains events and time stamps that are executed by a scheduler.

13.1.1. The Factory Layout

Consider the example of a factory automation simulation. Certain machines produce objects that are to be picked up by mobile robots and brought to other machines consuming them. Here is a typical layout:

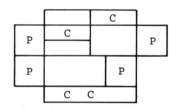

P   Producer

C   Consumer

———   tracks for the robots

The robot vehicles move on the tracks and perform the following actions:

- A moving robot moves one unit ahead in its current direction every 15 seconds.
- An empty robot passing a widget piled up by a producer stops and picks up the widget. This takes 45 seconds.
- A full robot passing an empty consumer stops, unloads the widget, and passes it to the consumer. This takes 45 seconds.

The producers produce goods at a certain rate (whose maximum the simulation is supposed to determine) and pile them around them into the first free position, clockwise starting from the right. The consumers consume the goods and need 90 seconds to digest each one.

The layout of the factory is read in from a text file containing the corridors marked with blank spaces and the robots with 1 2 3 4... The . around the producers are storage pads for the widgets.

```
XXXXXXXXXXXXXXXXXXXXXXXX
XXXXX                XXXXX
XXXXX XXXXX XXCXX XXXXX
X                        X
X ... XXCXX XXXXX ... X
X .P.           XXXXX .P. X
X ... XXXXX XXXXX ... X
X                        X
X ... XXXXXXX ... XXXXX
X .P. XXXXXXX .P. XXXXX
X ... XXXXXXX ... XXXXX
X                    XXXXX
XXXXX XXCXXCXXXXX XXXXX
XXXXX                XXXXX
XXXXXXXXXXXXXXXXXXXXXXXX
```

To describe the geometry of the situation, we introduce data types `Coord` and `Direction`:

```
enum Direction { NORTH, NE, EAST, SE, SOUTH, SW, WEST, NW };

struct Coord
{    int r,c;

     Coord() {}
     Coord( int row, int col ) { r = row; c = col; }
     Coord operator+( Direction );
     int operator==( Coord );
};
```

`Coord` is implemented as a `struct`. No data-hiding is intended, we merely seek the convenience of overloading the + and== operators.

```
Coord Coord::operator+( Direction d )
{    static int rDir[] = { -1, -1, 0, 1, 1, 1, 0, -1 };
     static int cDir[] = { 0, 1, 1, 1, 0, -1, -1, -1 };

     return Coord( r + rDir[ d ], c + cDir[ d ] );
}


int Coord::operator==( Coord b )
{    return r == b.r && c == b.c;
}
```

The following function computes the rotated directions:

```
Direction turn( Direction d, int deg )
{    while( deg < 0 ) deg+=360;
     return ( d + deg/45 ) % 8;
}
```

Recall that the values in an `enum` are assigned to the integers 0, 1, 2, . . . unless explicitly set otherwise.

To further move around in our factory world, we will define a `Layout` class that holds the factory layout (simply by storing the character pattern in a terminal display `Grid`, as defined in Sections 6.1 and 7.2). We derive from the `Grid` class to inherit the `show` and `operator[]` functions.

```
class Layout : public Grid
{    int rows; // the actual number of rows
public:
     void read();
     char& operator[]( Coord );
     void advance( Coord& ); // iterator
     int atEnd( Coord ); // for iterator
};
```

The following function reads a pattern from standard input:

```
void Layout::read()
{    rows = 0;
     char buffer[ GRID_HSIZE ];
     char nl;

     while( cin.good() && rows < GRID_VSIZE )
     {    cin.get( buffer, sizeof( buffer ) );
          cin.get( nl ); // get newline
          strcpy( Grid::operator[](rows++), buffer );
```

```
    }
}
```

We define another `operator[]` taking a `Coord` argument:

```
char& Layout::operator[]( Coord co )
{    return Grid::operator[](co.r)[co.c];
}
```

For example,

```
Layout l;
Coord c(2,3);
if( l[c] == ' ' ) l[c+NW] = '@';
```

Finally, we supply a way of walking a `Coord` variable through the layout, advancing it to the right until the end and then wrapping to first position of the next line.

```
void Layout::advance( Coord& co )
{    if( Layout::operator[](co) != '\0' ) co.c++;
     else if( co.r != rows-1 ) { co.c = 0; co.r++; }
}


int Layout::atEnd( Coord co )
{    return co.r == rows-1 && Layout::operator[](co) == '\0';
}
```

These functions implement an iterator mechanism:

```
for( Coord c(0,0); !l.atEnd( c ); l.advance( c ) )
     // do something with l[c]
```

13.1.2. Event Scheduling

Let us define the basic objects of the simulation: robots, producers, and consumers.

```
class Robot
{    Coord pos;
     Direction dir;
     int full;      // 1 if carrying a widget, 0 if not
     char id;       // '1', '2', ...
     void step();
public:
     Robot( Coord, char );
     void pickup( Coord );
     void feed( Coord );
     void move();
};
```

```
class Producer
{    int rate; // widget production rate
     Coord pos;
public:
     Producer( Coord, int );
     void produce();
};

class Consumer
{    Coord pos;
     int full; // 1 if currently eating, 0 otherwise
public:
     Consumer( Coord );
     void consume();
     void done() { full = 0; }
friend void Robot::feed( Coord );
};
```

The main activity throughout the simulation is the transaction of *events*. For example, when a consumer receives a widget, it tells the scheduler, "Remind me in 90 seconds that consumption is completed." All events are held in an event queue that is continually traversed by the scheduler. When the simulated system time has reached the time stamp of an event, it is removed from the queue and executed. This is a perfect setup for derived classes and virtual functions. A base class `Event` holds the time stamp and a virtual `signal` function. Derived `DoneEating`, `Move`, and `Produce` events supply actual `signal` functions and store a pointer to the specific piece of equipment that needs to be signaled.

```
class Event
{    protected:
     long time;
     Event( long t ) { time = t; }
public:
     virtual void signal() {};
friend class EventQueue;
};

EXPORT class Move : public Event
{    Robot* r;
public:
     Move( Robot *rp, long t ) : (t) { r = rp; }
     void signal() { r->move(); }
};

EXPORT class DoneEating : public Event
{    Consumer* c;
```

```
public:
    DoneEating( Consumer* cp, long t ) : (t) { c = cp; }
    void signal() { c->done(); }
};

EXPORT class Produce : public Event
{   Producer* p;
public:
    Produce( Producer* pp, long t ) : (t) { p = pp; }
    void signal() { p->produce(); }
};
```

The events are kept on a queue that is implemented as a linked list. The list type is implemented as the usual collection of cells containing void*.

```
class Cell
{   void* info;
    Cell* next;
friend class List;
};

class List
{   Cell* head;
    Cell* cur; // current position
    Cell* pre; // predecessor of current position
public:
    List();
    ~List();
    void insert( void* n ); // insert before current
                            // position
    void* remove();         // remove current position
    void* info();           // info of current element
    void advance();         // advance current position
    void reset();
    int atEnd();
};
```

All member functions are like the ones in Section 9.1, except for List::remove, which returns the info of the cell that is removed.

```
void* List::remove()
{   if( !cur ) return 0;
    if( pre ) pre->next = cur->next;
                                        else head = cur->next;
    Cell* p = cur;
    void* r = cur->info;
    cur = cur->next;
    delete p;
```

```
        return r;
}
```

We derive an `EventQueue` from the list type. Note that `List` is a private base class and its public functions (such as `insert`, `remove`) are not available to clients of `EventQueue`. This is desirable because a queue is not intended to support arbitrary insertion and removal. The list is kept sorted by increasing time stamps. Event processing simply consists of removing events from the head of the list as long as their time stamp is no later than the system time and executing their `signal` functions.

```
class EventQueue : List
{     public:
      EventQueue() {}
      void enqueue( Event* e );
      int dequeue( int t );
};

void EventQueue::enqueue( Event* e )
{     for( reset(); !atEnd() && ((Event*)info())->time <
                                        e->time; advance() ) ;
      insert( e );
}

int EventQueue::dequeue( int t )
// removes head of queue if its time stamp is < t and
// signals event
// returns 1 if event with time stamp < t found, 0
// otherwise
{     reset();
      if( atEnd() || ((Event*)info())->time > t ) return 0;
      Event* e = (Event*)remove();
      e->signal();
      delete e;
      return 1;
}
```

It is assumed that all events are placed on the queue with a call like `enqueue( new Move(...) )`, with storage for the event data allocated on the free store. The `dequeue` function hands the event storage to the deallocator after execution.

13.1.3. The Main Program

Here is the main program. It supports three command line options:

    -R*n* : Production rate. Produce a widget every *n* seconds.
    -T*n* : Total simulation time. Run simulation for *n* minutes.
    -S*n* : Show intervals. Display status every *n* seconds.

The program processes the command line options, reads in the layout, and scans it for the locations of robots, consumers, and producers. Those are inserted into linked lists. Then the robot and producer lists are traversed, and for each element a "move" or "produce" event is scheduled. The main loop removes events from the queue, checks whether the new status should be displayed, and advances the simulated clock.

We will use a very primitive method of manipulating the screen, with terminal escape sequences. Under DOS, you must install ANSI.SYS to enable interpretation of the escape sequences. If you have a non-ANSI terminal, you may substitute the appropriate commands for clearing the screen and moving the cursor, or you can just remove the print statements for a sequential display.

```
void clearScreen()
{    cout << "\x1B[2J"; // clear screen
}


void cursorHome()
{    cout << "\x1B[H";   // move cursor to home position
}

long time = 0;
List consList, robotList, prodList;
Layout factory;
EventQueue schedule;

void main( int argc, char *argv[] )
{    int prodRate = 360;
     int totalTime = 180;
     int showTime = 180;
     int nextShowTime = 0;

     for( int i = 1; i < argc; i++ )
         if( argv[i][0] == '-' )
             switch( toupper( argv[i][1] ) )
             {    case 'R':
                       prodRate = atoi( argv[i]+2 );
                       break;
                  case 'T':
                  totalTime = atoi( argv[i]+2 )*60;
                       break;
                  case 'S':
                  showTime = atoi( argv[i]+2 );
                       break;
             }
     factory.read();
     char ch;
```

```
for( Coord p(0,0); !factory.atEnd( p );
                            factory.advance( p ) )
    switch( ch = factory[ p ] )
    {     case 'P':
              prodList.insert(
                      new Producer( p, prodRate ) );
          break;
          case 'C':
              consList.insert(
                              new Consumer( p ) );
          break;
          default:
              if( '0' <= ch && ch <= '9' )
                  robotList.insert(
                              new Robot ( p, ch ) );
          break;
    }

for( robotList.reset(); !robotList.atEnd();
                            robotList.advance() )
    schedule.enqueue(
        new Move( (Robot*) (robotList.info()), 15L ) );

long n = 0; // to start production at time 15, 30, ...

for( prodList.reset(); !prodList.atEnd();
                            prodList.advance() )
{    Producer* pp = (Producer*)(prodList.info());
     schedule.enqueue( new Produce( pp, n+=15 ) );
}

clearScreen();
while( time <= totalTime )
{    while( schedule.dequeue( time ) )
         ;
     if( time >= nextShowTime )
     {    cursorHome();
          cout << time << "\n\n";
          factory.show();
          nextShowTime += showTime;
     }
     time+=15;
}
}
```

We use terminal escape sequences to clear the screen and to move the cursor to the home position before each display. This causes the display to continually overwrite itself, creating a visual sensation of robots moving through the corridors.

13.1.4. The Behavior of the Objects

Finally, we must specify how our simulated objects behave. Consumers are easiest. They just need a constructor and they need to signal a 90-second delay when starting to eat a widget:

```
Consumer::Consumer( Coord p )
{     pos = p;
      full = 0;
}


void Consumer::consume()
{     full = 1;
      schedule.enqueue( new DoneEating( this, time + 90 ) );
}
```

Producers pile up widgets in the area surrounding them, until it becomes full. Then they enter the next production event, with a delay depending on their production rate.

```
Producer::Producer( Coord c, int r )
{     pos = c;
      rate = r;
}


void Producer::produce()
{     int found = 0;
      Direction d = EAST;

      do
      {     if( factory[ pos + d ] == '.' )
            {     factory[ pos + d ] = '@';
                  found = 1;
            }
            else
            d = (d+1)%8;
      }
      while( !found && d != EAST );
      schedule.enqueue( new Produce( this, time+rate ) );
}
```

Robots are necessarily more sophisticated. They must be able to pick up a widget and feed it to a consumer. After a move, they must look around if there is a widget available for pickup or a consumer to feed. The **move** function is very simpleminded. When the robot encounters a barrier, it merely rotates 90 degrees and tries again next time.

```
Robot::Robot( Coord c, char ch )
{    pos = c;
     dir = EAST;
     full = 0;
     id = ch;
}

void Robot::pickup( Coord pos )
{    factory[ pos ] = '.';
     full = 1;
     schedule.enqueue( new Move( this, time + 45 ) );
}

void Robot::feed( Coord p )
{    Consumer* c;

     for( consList.reset();
          !( ( c = (Consumer*)(consList.info())))->pos == p );
          consList.advance() )
          ; // find the consumer with those
            // coords in the list
     if( !c->full )
     {    c->consume();
          full = 0;
     }
     schedule.enqueue( new Move( this, time + 45 ) );
}

void Robot::step()
{    if( factory[ pos + dir ] == ' ' )
     {    Coord p;

          factory[ pos ] = ' ';
          pos = pos + dir; // += not defined
          factory[ pos ] = id;
              // look around and see whether there is
              // anything interesting on the wayside
          for( int i = 0; i < 4; i++ )
              switch( factory[ p = pos + turn( dir,
                                            i * 90 ) ] )
              {    case '@':
                       if( !full )
                                { pickup( p ); return; }
                       break;
                   case 'C':
                       if( full ) { feed( p ); return; }
                       break;
```

```
                     }
            }
            schedule.enqueue( new Move( this, time + 15 ) );
    }


    void Robot::move()
    {    if( factory[ pos + dir ] != ' ' )
             dir = turn( dir, 90 );
         step();
    }
```

Exercise 13.1.1. Put all pieces together and compile the program into an executable file with name sim. To start the program, the layout must be populated with robots

```
xxxxxxxxxxxxxxxxxxxxxxx
xxxxx   1              xxxxx
xxxxx xxxxx xxCxx xxxxx
x                 2        x
x ... xxCxx xxxxx ... x
x .P.         xxxxx .P. x
x ... xxxxx xxxxx ... x
x                         x
x ... xxxxxxx ... xxxxx
x .P. xxxxxxx .P. xxxxx
x ... xxxxxxx ... xxxxx
x       3            xxxxx
xxxxx xxCxxCxxxxx xxxxx
xxxxx               xxxxx
xxxxxxxxxxxxxxxxxxxxxxx
```

Place these lines in a file named layout and start the program with

```
sim < layout -S15 -T30
```

This displays the state of the factory every 15 seconds, for a total of 30 minutes. Experiment to get a better traffic flow. Place more robots to achieve full production, with empty space on each producer's launch pad. You can erect or knock down some factory walls as well. To get a view of the long-term behavior, try running sim < layout -S3600 -T1440 (one day with outputs every hour).

Exercise 13.1.2. When running the simulation, a flaw of the Robot::move function becomes apparent: When two robots collide, both change direction. Design a "Mark II" model that has a more reasonable behavior. Derive a class Mark2 from Robot and make move a virtual function. Make all even-numbered robots Mark IIs. Note that the change is very straightforward, illustrating the C++ promise of easy code maintenance.

Exercise 13.1.3. Improve the bank teller simulation of Exercise 12.1.3. by adding an event queue. Events are new customer arrival and teller work completion.

Exercise 13.1.4. Design a traffic-light simulation: Model an intersection of four roads with a traffic light. Cars enter all four ends with a certain arrival rate (see Exercise 12.1.3). Let the cars enter with average speed v_0 and no acceleration. When a car gets faster than v_0, comes too close to the one in front of it or a red traffic light, it decelerates. When a car is slower than v_0 and there is no other car or red light too close, it accelerates. A typical compact car accelerates from 0 to 30 miles/hour in about 4 seconds, from 0 to 60 miles/hour in about 13 seconds. To come to a complete stop from 60 miles/hour takes about 150 feet. Make your life easier by using the metric system: distance in meter, speed in meter/second, and acceleration in meter/second^2. Then determine reasonable values for acceleration and deceleration.

Each second, adjust speed and position of the car: Remember from calculus or physics that $\Delta v = a \cdot \Delta t$ and $\Delta s = v \cdot \Delta t + \frac{1}{2}a \cdot \Delta t$. Make each stretch of road 500 meters long. Choose reasonable values for initial speed and traffic-light phases. Measure the number of cars waiting at a red light as a function of the arrival rate.

13.2. A HOME ACCOUNTING SYSTEM

In this section, we will build a rudimentary accounting system for balancing checking accounts and gathering information for income tax filing.

13.2.1. Basic Accounting Concepts

We have a collection of *accounts*, including actual checking and savings accounts as well as accounts for rent, food, medical expenses, and charitable contributions. Each account has a parent account. For example, the accounts RENT, FOOD, MEDICAL have the parent account EXPENSES. The account SALARY has the parent account INCOME. If you receive salary from more than one source, each source may be arranged as a child account of SALARY. We make the account graph into a tree with the node TOP. TOP has four children: ASSETS, LIABILITIES, INCOME, and EXPENSES. Checking and savings accounts as well as cash are assets; bank loans are liabilities. The accounting system processes *transactions* such as:

Pay $700 rent out of my checking account on February 5th.

This transaction reduces the CHECKING account balance by $700 and increases the RENT account balance by the same amount. We will enter this transaction as

```
T CHECKING RENT 700 5
```

ignoring the month. The plan is to enter a batch consisting of all transactions in a given month and reconcile them with the checking account statement.

We need the day to compute the checking account interest, which depends on the daily balance.

In general, a transaction

T *a b amount date*

is processed by telling account *a* to reduce itself by the given amount and posting a corresponding increase to account *b*. When an amount is posted to an account, it recomputes its balance and passes the posted amount on to its parent account. Because both *a* and *b* are updated simultaneously, this is double-entry bookkeeping in its most basic form. The accounts balance if

$$\text{ASSETS} - \text{LIABILITIES} = \text{INCOME} - \text{EXPENSES}$$

For example, the foregoing transaction reduces ASSETS by $700 and increases EXPENSES by the same amount. If the equation held before the transaction, it continues to hold afterward.

Some transactions are different. For example, when you deposit your paycheck on the second of the month,

```
T   SALARY  CHECKING  2435.10  2
```

it appears that both SALARY and CHECKING should go up. If you pay back an installment of a loan,

```
T   CHECKING  BANKLOAN  500  30
```

the surpluses of both CHECKING and BANKLOAN should be reduced. This seeming anomaly can be explained by looking at the balance equation

$$\text{ASSETS} - \text{LIABILITIES} - \text{INCOME} + \text{EXPENSES} = 0$$

Surpluses in accounts with ancestor **LIABILITIES** and **INCOME** (with minus signs in the equation) should be kept as negative values, in **ASSETS** and **EXPENSES** (with plus signs in the equation) as positive values. Accountants call the first kind of accounts *debit accounts*, the second kind *credit accounts*. (These names are unrelated to the terms "crediting" and "debiting" of an account.) When printing the balance of a debit account, the sign should be reversed. The **TOP** account should always have balance 0.

Undoubtedly, any certified public accountant will shudder when confronted with this exposition of double-entry bookkeeping, but it will serve well enough for our purpose.

13.2.2. The Account Classes

We could build a class hierarchy with a base class for the **TOP** account and a derived class for each actual account. The class hierarchy would then parallel the account tree. But this would be very inflexible. To add another account (say BRIBES), another class would have to be designed and the program would have to be recompiled. Marketing such a program can hardly be expected to do wonders to our ROYALTIES account.

Instead, we will classify accounts by their behavior. We already saw that credit accounts act differently from debit accounts—the latter reverse the sign when reporting their balance. CHECKING is an example of an interest-bearing account. Interest is computed on the daily balance and compounded monthly. Finally, we will implement an account type for recurring payments. For example, the amount for the rent stays constant at $700 every month. To pay rent, the RENT account can be estabished as an "autopay" account with a payment amount of $700. A transaction

```
P RENT   5
```

pays out rent on the fifth of the month.

We have discovered four classes of accounts: debit, credit, interest-bearing, and autopay. We will model them with the following inheritance hierarchy:

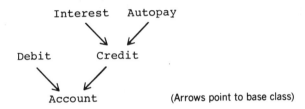

(Arrows point to base class)

Here are the class definitions.

```
const int CODELEN = 10;

class Account
{
protected:
     char code[ CODELEN ];
     int level;
     double bal;
     Account* parent;
public:
     Account( char*, Account* =0 );
     char* name() { return code; }
     virtual double balance() { return 0; }
     virtual void post( double, int );
     virtual void print( ostream& );
     virtual void pay( int ) {};
};

class Debit : public Account
{
```

```
public:
    Debit( char*, Account* =0 );
    double balance() { return -bal; }
};

class Credit : public Account
{
public:
    Credit( char*, Account* =0 );
    double balance() { return bal; }
};

class Interest : public Credit
{   double rate;
    int lastday;
    double accumInt;
public:
    Interest( char*, double, Account* =0 );
    void pay( int );
    void post( double, int );
};

class Autopay : public Credit
{   double amount;
public:
    Autopay( char*, double );
    void pay( int );
};
```

The level field in Account indicates the level, that is, the distance from the root TOP. It is used when printing the account. The post virtual function posts a balance change to the account. For an Interest account, it also compounds the interest accumulated between the day of the last transaction and the day of the current transaction. These data are stored in the lastday and accumInt fields. The pay virtual function generates an autopay action when applied to an Autopay account, and it pays out the interest on an Interest account. (It should then be called with the last day of the month as argument.)

Here are the class constructors:

```
Account::Account( char* c, Account* p )
{   strcpy( code, c );
    parent = p;
    level = parent ? parent->level + 1 : 0;
    bal = 0;
}
```

```
Debit::Debit( char* c, Account* p ) : (c,p) {}

Credit::Credit( char* c, Account* p ) : (c,p) {}

Autopay::Autopay( char* c, double a, Account* p ) : (c,p)
{    amount = a;
}

Interest::Interest( char* c, double r, Account* p ) : (c,p)
{    rate = r;
     accumInt = 0;
     lastday = 1;
}
```

We will read the accounts from standard input in the format

A *type code parent* [*amt*]

where *type* is **C**, **D**, **A**, or **I** for a credit, debit, autopay, or interest-bearing account. The last two also carry an *amt* field, for the autopay amount or the interest rate. Sample inputs are

```
A   I   CHECKING   ASSETS   5.5
A   D   INCOME   TOP
```

The accounts are kept in an array:

```
const int NACCOUNT = 100;
int na = 1;
Account* accts[ NACCOUNT ];
```

The following function locates an account, given its code:

```
Account* find( char* n )
{    for( int i = 0; i < na; i++ )
          if( strcmp( n, accts[i]->name() ) ) == 0 )
               return accts[i];
     return 0;
}
```

An account is read in with the `readAccount` function, which is called after the initial **A** has been read from the input stream.

```
Account* readAccount( istream& si )
{    char cmd;
     double a;
     char acode[ CODELEN ], pcode[ CODELEN ];

     si >> cmd;
     si >> acode >> pcode;
```

```
Account* p = find( pcode );
if( p == 0 ) return 0;

switch( cmd )
{   case 'C': return new Credit( acode, p );
    case 'D': return new Debit( acode, p );
    case 'I': si >> a; return
                           new Interest( acode, a, p );
    case 'A': si >> a; return
                           new Autopay( acode, a, p );
}
}
```

13.2.3. Putting It Together

The main function reads in all **A**, **T**, and **P** commands from standard input, creates all accounts defined with **A** commands, posts all transactions from the **T** commands, and handles all pays from the **P** commands. At the end of the input file, all accounts are printed.

```
int main( void )
{   Account* a;
    Account* b;
    char cmd;
    char acode[ CODELEN ], bcode[ CODELEN ];
    int day;
    double amt;

    accts[ 0 ] = new Credit( "TOP" );
    while( cin >> cmd )
    {   switch( cmd )
        {   case 'A':
                a = readAccount( cin );
                if( a && na < NACCOUNT )
                    accts[ na++ ] = a;
                break;
            case 'T':
                cin >> acode >> bcode >> amt >> day;
                a = find( acode );
                b = find( bcode );
                if( a && b )
                {   a->post( -amt, day );
                    b->post( amt, day );
                }
                break;
            case 'P':
```

```
                    cin >> acode >> day;
                    a = find( acode );
                    if( a ) a->pay( day );
                    break;
            }
        }
    for( int i = 0; i < na; i++ )
            accts[ i ] -> print( cout );
    }
```

An account is printed with the `print` member function. `print` calls `balance` to get the correct value for a debit account.

```
void Account::print( ostream& so )
{    for( int i = 0; i < 4*level; i++ ) so << " ";
     so << code;
     for( i = 4*level+strlen( code ); i < 40; i++ )
            so << ".";
     so << form( "%10.2f\n", balance() );
}
```

The basic `post` message simply updates the balance and posts the amount to the parent. The date is ignored.

```
void Account::post( double amt, int day )
{    bal += amt;
     if( parent )
         parent->post( amt, day );
}
```

When an amount is posted to an interest-bearing account, the interest accumulated since the last posting is computed. (It is assumed that postings occur in chronological order.) Then the amount is posted.

```
void Interest::post( double amt, int day )
{    if( day > lastday )
     {    accumInt += (day - lastday)*bal*rate/100/365;
          lastday = day;
     }
     Account::post( amt, day );
}
```

The `pay` action for an autopay account involves posting a transaction to the checking account, making the payment and the current account, recording the payment.

```
void Autopay::pay( int day )
{    Account* chk = find( "CHECKING" );
     if( chk )
     {    chk->post( -amount, day );
```

```
            this->post( amount, day );
    }
}
```

The `pay` action for an interest-bearing account receives as `day` argument the last day of the month, computes the remaining interest, and pays it out of the INTEREST account.

```
void Interest::pay( int day )
{   Account* intr = find( "INTEREST" );
    if( intr )
    {   this->post( 0, day+1 );
        intr->post( -accumInt, day );
        this->post( accumInt, day );
        accumInt = 0;
        lastday = 1;
    }
}
```

Here is a typical input. We first list all accounts and then the transactions, in chronological order. The starting balances for the checking and savings accounts are obtained by transferring them out of the liability account ADJUST. This is a "generally accepted accounting practice," which keeps the accounts balanced from the outset. The last two transactions force the computation of the interest.

```
A  C  ASSETS      TOP
A  I  CHECK       ASSETS       4.0
A  I  SAVING      ASSETS       5.25
A  D  LIABILIT    TOP
A  D  ADJUST      LIABILIT
A  D  INCOME      TOP
A  D  SALARY      INCOME
A  D  INTEREST    INCOME
A  C  EXPENSES    TOP
A  A  RENT        EXPENSES     700
A  C  FOOD        EXPENSES
A  C  MEDICAL     EXPENSES
A  C  UTILITIES   EXPENSES
A  C  ELECTRIC    UTILITIES
A  C  PHONE       UTILITIES
A  C  MISC        EXPENSES
T     ADJUST      CHECKING     814.43     1
T     ADJUST      SAVING       4312.50    1
P     RENT                                1
T     SALARY      CHECKING     2415.12    2
T     CHECKING    SAVING       1000.00    5
T     CHECKING    ELECTRIC     23.37      8
```

```
T    CHECKING    FOOD         14.05    12
T    CHECKING    PHONE       104.93    14
T    CHECKING    FOOD         39.12    18
T    CHECKING    MISC        100.00    20
T    CHECKING    FOOD         84.50    25
P    CHECKING                          31
```

The program output is the following account chart.

```
   TOP . . . . .          0.00
          ASSETS .     6504.01
             CHECKING  1168.39
             SAVING    5335.61
          LIABILIT     5126.93
             ADJUST    5126.93
          INCOME .     2443.05
             SALARY    2415.12
            'INTEREST    27.93
          EXPENSES     1065.97
          RENT . .      700.00
          FOOD . .      137.67
          MEDICAL         0.00
          UTILITIES     128.30
             ELECTRIC    23.37
             PHONE      104.93
          MISC . .      100.00
```

The TOP account is 0, as it should be. The CHECKING, SAVING, and IN-TEREST fields can be checked against the bank statement.

Exercise 13.2.1. Find out how your bank account accumulates interest. (This can be surprisingly difficult. Some banks apparently believe that these details should be of no concern to mere mortals. If you tell your bank that you want to check the calculations by computer, they may really clam up. In that case, be persistent.) If necessary, modify the `Interest` class to reflect your bank's method. Run 1 month's worth of actual transactions. Check whether the account chart agrees with your bank statement.

Exercise 13.2.2. Change the day field to a `Date` field to accommodate bank statements that start in the middle of the month.

Exercise 13.2.3. Make the system more user-friendly. The accounts should be kept in a file separate from the transactions. That file should list the initial balances of all accounts. The new transactions should be read in from another file. After entering all transactions, show the account chart. Accountants call this a *trial balance*. Ask the user whether it is okay or not. If so, save the accounts with the new balances. Append the transactions to a file of old transactions. If not, the user must fix the mistakes in the file with the new transactions and try again.

13.3. A MATRIX CALCULATOR

We will end this book the way we began: with a calculator. However, our new calculator will be quite sophisticated. It handles vectors and matrices in addition to regular numbers.

13.3.1. Overview of the Design

Vectors will be entered as

```
(1 0 -2)
```

and matrices as sequences of row-vectors. For example,

```
[(1 0 -2) (0 2 4) (0 0 1)]
```

stands for

$$\begin{pmatrix} 1 & 0 & -2 \\ 0 & 2 & 4 \\ 0 & 0 & 1 \end{pmatrix}.$$

For simplicity, we restrict ourselves to integer 3-vectors and 3×3 matrices. Operations are again stack-based:

```
(1 1 1) (1 0 -2) *
```

computes the scalar product (-1) and

```
(1 1 1) [(1 0 -2) (0 2 4) (0 0 1)] *
```

the product "vector · matrix," resulting in the vector (1 2 3). We will support + - * but no division. We want the main program to be substantially like the one in Section 1.2. Let us review a number of design constraints:

- Numbers, vectors, and matrices should be derived from a common class. For example, printing the result should be achieved simply by `cout <<` `pop()`, with an overloaded printing function.
- Numbers, vectors, and matrices have different sizes and cannot be stacked. The stack must therefore contain pointers.
- Because the object information is not stored on the stack, storage space must be obtained through `new`.
- The type and size of the result of an arithmetic function depends on the arguments supplied at run-time. For example, vector · vector = number, vector · number = vector.

- Storage space for return value information must be obtained through `new` as well, and the function must return a pointer, because at compile-time it cannot be determined how much information to copy.
- The space obtained from the free store should be automatically deallocated.

The following design achieves these goals: A class `MathObj` contains a pointer to a class `MathBase` from which `Number`, `Vector`, and `Matrix` are derived. `MathObj` has the usual complement of storage management functions (constructor, destructor, copy-initializer, and `operator=`). `MathBase` has virtual print and arithmetic functions.

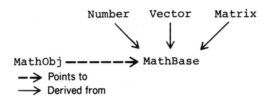

13.3.2. The Main Program

The code for the main program is almost identical to the code in Section 1.2, with all `int` replaced by `MathObj`. Division has been removed and multiplication made order-dependent. (Matrix multiplication is not commutative!)

```
const int STACKSIZE = 20;

MathObj stack[ STACKSIZE ];
int stackPointer = 0; // points to the next free stack entry

void push( MathObj n )
{    if( stackPointer <= STACKSIZE - 1 )
     {    stack[ stackPointer ] = n;
          stackPointer++;
     }
}

MathObj pop()
{    if( stackPointer > 0 )
          stackPointer--;
     return stack[ stackPointer ];
}

int main()
{    char ch;
     MathObj num, second;
```

```
    cin >> ch;
    while( ch != '=' )
    {
        if( '0' <= ch && ch <= '9' ||
                                    ch == '(' || ch == '[' )
        {   cin.putback( ch );
            cin >> num;
            push( num );
        }
        else
            switch( ch )
            {   case '+':
                    push( pop() + pop() ); break;
                case '*':
                    second = pop();
                        push( pop() * second ); break;
                case '-':
                    second = pop();
                        push( pop() - second ); break;
                default:
                    cout << "Input error."; return 1;
            }
        cin >> ch;
    }
    cout << pop() << "\n";
    return 0;
}
```

This is ideal for the class user. The objects can be used naturally, without any further knowledge of implementation details. As we will see, the implementation of this comfort poses considerable problems.

13.3.3. Mathematical Objects

Let us begin with the requirements for the `MathObj` class:

```
class MathObj
{   MathBase *stor; // actually points to number, vector
                    // or matrix
public:
    MathObj(); // initialize to number 0
    MathObj( MathBase* );
    MathObj( const MathObj& );
    ~MathObj();
    MathObj& operator=( const MathObj& );
    friend MathObj operator+( MathObj, MathObj );
```

```
        friend MathObj operator-( MathObj, MathObj );
        friend MathObj operator*( MathObj, MathObj );
        friend istream& operator>>( istream&, MathObj& );
        friend ostream& operator<<( ostream&, MathObj );
};
```

The output is straightforward:

```
ostream& operator<<( ostream& s, MathObj o )
{       o.stor->print( s );
        return s;
}
```

where `print` is a virtual member function of `MathBase`, which is replaced by actual print functions in each derived class `Number`, `Vector`, and `Matrix`.

```
class MathBase
{       // ...
public:
        virtual void print( ostream& );
};

class Number : MathBase
{       int val;
public:
        void print( ostream& s ) { s << val; }
        // ...
};

class Vector : MathBase
{       int val[3];
public:
        Vector( int, int, int );
        void print( ostream& s )
        { s << "(" << val[0] << " " << val[1] << " "
                                << val[2] << ")"; }
        // ...
};
```

We would like to make use of the operations on vectors when defining matrix operations. We could declare a matrix as an array of three vectors (its row vectors)

```
class Matrix : MathBase
{       Vector val[3]; // not efficient
public:
        // ...
};
```

However, this forces duplication of the data fields in **MathBase**, namely the pointer to the virtual function table and a reference count that will eventually be added to **MathBase**. Instead, we will supply functions **row** and **col** that compute row and column vectors, and a constructor that builds a matrix from its row vectors.

```
class Matrix : MathBase ·
{    int val[3][3];
public:
     Matrix( Vector, Vector, Vector );
     Vector row( int i )
     { return Vector( val[i][0], val[i][1], val[i][2] ); }
     Vector col( int j )
     { return Vector( val[0][j], val[1][j], val[2][j] ); }
     void print( ostream& s );
     // ...
};
```

```
void Matrix::print( ostream& s )
{    s << "[";
     row(0).print( s ); s << "\n";
     row(1).print( s ); s << "\n";
     row(2).print( s );
     s << "]";
}
```

For input, we must allocate storage for the new result.

```
istream& operator>>( istream& s, MathObj& o )
{    char ch;
     MathBase* p;

     cin >> ch;
     switch( ch )
     {    case '(':
               p = new Vector; break;
          case '[':
               p = new Matrix; break;
          default:
               p = new Number; break;
     }
     s.putback( ch );
     p->read( s );
     o = MathObj( p );
     return s;
}
```

read is a virtual function of **MathBase**, and actual versions are

```
void Number::read( istream& s )
{    s >> val;
}

void Vector::read( istream& s )
{    char ch;

     s >> ch;
     if( ch != '(' ) error( "( expected" );
     s >> val[0] >> val[1] >> val[2] >> ch;
     if( ch != ')' ) error( ") expected" );
}

void Matrix::read( istream& s )
{    char ch;

     s >> ch; if( ch != '[' ) error( "[ expected" );
     for( int i = 0; i < 3; i++ )
     {    Vector v;
          v.read( s );
          for( int j = 0; j < 3; j++ )
               val[i][j] = v.val[j];
     }
     s >> ch; if( ch != ']' ) error( "] expected" );
}
```

13.3.4. Vector and Matrix Operations

Next, we need to overload the arithmetic operations. Let us start with the multiplication operator. The following combinations occur:

```
Number * Number : Number
Number * Vector : Vector
Number * Matrix : Matrix
Vector * Number : Vector
Vector * Vector : Number (scalar product)
Vector * Matrix : Vector
Matrix * Number : Matrix
Matrix * Vector : error (vectors are row vectors)
Matrix * Matrix : Matrix
```

We want to define a multiplication function **mul** that selects the correct multiplication at run-time. It must be a virtual function of **MathBase**. Its return value must be a **MathBase*** because its actual realizations can return various objects of different sizes. For the same reason, its second argument must be a `MathBase*`. The first argument is implicit: virtual functions must be member functions. The prototype therefore is:

```
virtual MathBase* MathBase::mul( MathBase* )
```

This forces the prototypes of the three actual `mul` functions in the derived classes, as instantiations of virtual functions *must* agree with the virtual prototype:

```
MathBase* Number::mul( MathBase* )
MathBase* Vector::mul( MathBase* )
MathBase* Matrix::mul( MathBase* )
```

The class user is interested in `MathObj`s, and `mul` is really a service function for

```
MathObj operator*( MathObj a, MathObj b )
{    return MathObj( a.stor->mul( b.stor ) );
}
```

Consider `Number::mul`. We know that the first (implicit) argument is a `Number`. The second argument still could be a pointer to any type. A second run-time selection is necessary. To that end, we define a virtual function

```
virtual MathBase* MathBase::mulNum( Number* )
```

`mulNum` is a multiplication with an argument known to be a number. Each derived class has its own definition of `mulNum`:

```
MathBase* Number::mulNum( Number* p )
{    return new Number( val * p->val );
}
```

```
MathBase* Vector::mulNum( Number* p )
{    return new Vector( val[0]*p->val, val[1]*p->val,
                                       val[2]*p->val );
}
```

```
MathBase* Matrix::mulNum( Number* p )
{    return new Matrix(
         row(0).mulNum(p), row(1).mulNum(p),
         row(2).mulNum(p) );
}
```

The return value must still be a `MathBase*`, although we know its precise return types in each of the three cases. However it must agree with the declaration of the virtual function in the base class.

`Number::mul` simply makes a virtual function call on its second argument:

```
MathBase* Number::mul( MathBase* q )
{    return q->mulNum( this );
}
```

Similarly, there are virtual functions `mulVec` and `mulMat`. A total of nine functions

$$
\left.\begin{matrix} \texttt{Number} \\ \texttt{Vector} \\ \texttt{Matrix} \end{matrix}\right\} \texttt{::mul} \left\{\begin{matrix} \texttt{NUM} \\ \texttt{VEC} \\ \texttt{MAT} \end{matrix}\right. \texttt{(MathBase* q)}
$$

implement the nine combinations from the table. Note that because of the argument flip, these functions must return the product of `*q` and `*this`. For example,

```
MathBase* Matrix::mulVec( Vector* a )
{    return new Vector(
            col(1).mulVec(a), col(2).mulVec(a),
                                        col(3).mulVec(a) );

}
```

Exercise 13.3.1. Write the five remaining multiplication functions. Whenever possible, reduce the matrix functions to operations on row or column vectors.

If `p` and `q` are `MathObj*`, the call

`p->mul( q )`

first causes selection of the appropriate version of `mul`, depending on the actual type of the object to which `p` points. That `mul` function is simply of the form

$$
\texttt{return q->mul} \left\{\begin{matrix} \texttt{Num} \\ \texttt{Vec} \\ \texttt{Mat} \end{matrix}\right. \texttt{(this);}
$$

and the type of `q` selects the correct function. This double virtual function call is necessary because we need run-time overloading of both arguments of the multiplication.

The `operator+` must similarly be resolved through functions `add`, `addNum`, `addVec`, `addMat`. Because adding is only permitted for objects of the same type, six of the nine `...::add...` functions simply exit with an error message. For subtraction, it is easiest to define a unary minus function and code

```
MathObj operator-( MathObj a, MathObj b )
{    return a + (-b);
}
```

Exercise 13.3.2. Program the addition and subtraction functions.

13.3.5. Memory Management

As always, there is the issue of memory management. All values obtained from the read routines and all results of arithmetic operations are allocated on the free store. They should be recycled at the proper moment. Because the program user merely handles `MathObjs` that point to `MathBase`, a reference count can be placed in `MathBase`. The reference count keeps track of the number of `MathObj` pointing to it. When a `MathBase` is created, it starts with 0. The constructor `MathObj( MathBase* )` increments it:

```
MathObj::MathObj( MathBase* p )
{      stor = p;
       p->rc++;
}
```

The copy-initializer `MathObj( const MathObj& )`, the destructor `~MathObj`, and `operator=` manipulate the reference count in the usual way.

Exercise 13.3.3. Trace the reference counts of all objects (the two inputs and the result) during the processing of the input

```
(1 -3 2) (1 1 2) * =
```

Pay attention to unnamed temporaries and function arguments. Verify that all reference counts drop to zero at the end of the program.

Exercise 13.3.4. Complete the matrix calculator and test it.

Exercise 13.3.5. Change the calculator to handle vectors and matrices with `Complex` entries.

Exercise 13.3.6. Implement matrices as arrays of row vectors.

Exercise 13.3.7. Change the calculator to handle vectors and matrices of arbitrary size.

Exercise 13.3.8. Add operations to compute the determinant, matrix inverse, and solution space of a system of linear equations $A \cdot x = b$.

Exercise 13.3.9. Add polynomials (of arbitrary degree) to the calculator. Implement the operation of inserting a matrix into a polynomial (e.g., if $p(x) = 1 + 2x + x^3$ and A is a square matrix, then $p(A) = 1 + 2A + A \cdot A \cdot A$). Extend matrix operations to matrices with polynomial entries and compute the *characteristic polynomial* $\det(A - x \cdot I)$ of a matrix. Check with a few examples that inserting a matrix into its characteristic polynomial results in the 0 matrix (the Cayley-Hamilton theorem).

BIBLIOGRAPHY

[AKW] Alfred Aho, Brian Kernighan, and Peter Weinberger. *The AWK Programming Language,* Addison-Wesley, 1988.
Describes the AWK programming languages. We use AWK for a header file extraction tool (Section 11.4).

[Gorlen] Keith Gorlen. "An Object-Oriented Class Library for C++ Programs," Proceedings of the Usenix C++ Workshop in Santa Fe, 1987.
Describes the OOPS (now NIH) class library, an object-oriented class library for C++.

[Hansen] Tony L. Hansen. *The C++ Answer Book.* Addison-Wesley, 1989.
Advertised as providing solutions to all exercises in Stroustrup (1986), this book delivers much more. It contains many annotated examples of excellent C++ code.

[Koenig] Andrew Koenig. *C Traps and Pitfalls,* Addison-Wesley, 1988.
A delightful book, full of advice for the C programmer. Much of it is of interest to the C++ programmer as well.

[Lippman] Stan Lippman. *C++ Primer,* Addison-Wesley, 1989.
A thorough reference for all the murky details of C++ version 2.0.

[Meyer] Bertrand Meyer. *Object-Oriented Software Construction,* Prentice-Hall, 1988.
This book lucidly explains techniques of object-oriented programming. Contains an introduction into Eiffel, a language designed by B. Meyer. Several chapters are devoted to explaining why no other language quite measures up. This is a great book, even if you don't care about Eiffel.

[Pokorny & Gerard] C. Pokorny and C. Gerard. *Computer Graphics: The Principles Behind the Art and Science.* Franklin, Beedle, 1989.
A very usable reference for computer graphics. Contains the usual 2D and 3D lines and curve algorithms, color models, and a nice introduction to fractals.

[Stroustrup 1] B. Stroustrup. *The C++ Programming Language,* Addison-Wesley, 1986.
A terse but complete description of C++ version 1.1, by the designer of the language.

[Stroustrup 2] B. Stroustrup. "Parametrized Types for C++," Proceedings of the Usenix C++ Conference in Denver, 1988.
Describes a design for parametrized types that may be implemented in a future version of C++.

INDEX